**50% OFF!**

PTCB Online Test Prep Course

We consider it an honor and a privilege that you chose our PTCB Study Guide. As a way of showing our appreciation and to help us better serve you, we have partnered with Mometrix Test Preparation to offer you 50% off their online PTCB Prep Course.

Mometrix has structured their online course to perfectly complement your printed study guide. Many PTCB courses are needlessly expensive and don't deliver enough value. With their course, you get access to the best PTCB prep material, and you only pay half price.

WHAT'S IN THE PTCB TEST PREP COURSE?

- ✓ **PTCB Study Guide**: Get access to content that complements your study guide.

- ✓ **Progress Tracker**: Their customized course allows you to check off content you have studied or feel confident with.

- ✓ **1050+ Practice Questions**: With 1050+ practice questions and lesson reviews, you can test yourself again and again to build confidence.

- ✓ **PTCB Flashcards**: Their course includes a flashcard mode consisting of over 325 content cards to help you study.

TO RECEIVE THIS DISCOUNT, VISIT THE WEBSITE AT

link.mometrix.com/ptcb

USE THE DISCOUNT CODE:
STARTSTUDYING

IF YOU HAVE ANY QUESTIONS OR CONCERNS, PLEASE CONTACT MOMETRIX AT SUPPORT@MOMETRIX.COM

FREE DVD  FREE DVD

From Stress to Success DVD from Trivium Test Prep

Dear Customer,

Thank you for purchasing from Trivium Test Prep! Whether you're looking to join the military, get into college, or advance your career, we're honored to be a part of your journey. To show our appreciation (and to help you relieve a little of that test-prep stress), we're offering a **FREE *PTCB Essential Test Tips DVD*** by Trivium Test Prep. Our DVD includes 35 test preparation strategies that will help keep you calm and collected before and during your big exam. All we ask is that you email us your feedback and describe your experience with our product. Amazing, awful, or just so-so: we want to hear what you have to say!

To receive your **FREE *PTCB Essential Test Tips DVD***, please email us at 5star@triviumtestprep.com. Include "Free 5 Star" in the subject line and the following information in your email:

1. The title of the product you purchased.
2. Your rating from 1 – 5 (with 5 being the best).
3. Your feedback about the product, including how our materials helped you meet your goals and ways in which we can improve our products.
4. Your full name and shipping address so we can send your **FREE *PTCB Essential Test Tips DVD.***

If you have any questions or concerns please feel free to contact us directly at 5star@triviumtestprep.com.

Thank you, and good luck with your studies!

* Please note that the free DVD is <u>not included</u> with this book. To receive the free DVD, please follow the instructions above.

PTCB Exam Study Guide 2024-2025:

4 Full-Length Practice Tests and Pharmacy Technician Certification (PTCE) Prep [8th Edition]

Jeremy Downs

Copyright © 2024 by Ascencia Test Prep

ISBN-13: 9781637989425

ALL RIGHTS RESERVED. By purchase of this book, you have been licensed one copy for personal use only. No part of this work may be reproduced, redistributed, or used in any form or by any means without prior written permission of the publisher and copyright owner. Ascencia Test Prep, Trivium Test Prep, Accepted, and Cirrus Test Prep are all imprints of Trivium Test Prep, LLC.

The PTCB was not involved in the creation or production of this product, is not in any way affiliated with Ascencia Test Prep, and does not sponsor or endorse this product. All test names (and their acronyms) are trademarks of their respective owners. This study guide is for general information only and does not claim endorsement by any third party.

Image(s) used under license from Shutterstock.com

TABLE OF CONTENTS

Online Resources vii
Introduction ix

PART I MEDICATIONS — 1

ONE: Pharmacology 3
Pharmacokinetics 3
Pharmacodynamics 5
Therapeutic Equivalence 8
Drug Classes 10
Side Effects and Adverse Reactions 14
Drug Interactions 15
Drug Administration 16
Drug Stability 17
Drug Storage 18

TWO: Drug Effects and Indications 3
The Cardiovascular System 21
The Respiratory System 26
The Nervous System 28
The Immune System 35
The Musculoskeletal System 40
The Digestive System 42
The Endocrine System 46
The Urinary System 49
The Reproductive System 51
The Integumentary System 55
Radiopharmaceuticals 57

PART II FEDERAL REQUIREMENTS — 59

THREE: Legal Guidelines 61
Regulatory Agencies and Organizations 61
Federal Legislation 62
HIPAA 65
Drug Recalls 67
Prescribing Authority 68

FOUR: Regulation of Controlled Substances 71
Drug Schedules 71
DEA Registration for Controlled Substances 72
Dispensing Controlled Substances 74
Inventory of Controlled Substances 79
DEA Inspections 83
Prescription Monitoring 84
Restricted Drug Programs 84

PART III PATIENT SAFETY AND QUALITY ASSURANCE 89

FIVE: Prescription Errors............ 91
- Types of Prescription Errors 91
- Error Prevention 92
- What to Do if an Error Occurs 99
- Pharmacist Intervention 102
- Reference Materials 103

SIX: Safety in the Workplace 107
- The Occupational Safety and Health Administration (OSHA) ... 107
- Hygiene and Cleaning Standards 108
- Hazardous Materials 115

PART IV ORDER ENTRY AND PROCESSING 121

SEVEN: Order Processing 123
- Prescription Processing 123
- Prescription Adjudication 132
- Filling, Packaging, and Labeling the Prescription Order 137
- Pharmacist Verification 143
- Dispensing Medication to Patients 144
- Refills and Prescription Transfers 146
- Inventory 148
- Compounding 150
- Institutional (Hospital) Pharmacies 156
- Medical Terminology 158

EIGHT: Pharmacy Math 163
- Measurement Systems........................ 163
- Ratio, Proportions, and Percentage........................ 166
- Specific Gravity 167
- Concentrations................................... 168
- Ratio Strength............................. 169
- Stock Solutions 170
- Liquid Dilutions 170
- Solid Dilutions 171
- Alligations............................ 171
- Pediatric Dosages.............................. 174

PART V PRACTICE TESTS 181

NINE: Practice Test One 183
- Answer Key 193

TEN: Practice Test Two 199
- Answer Key 209

ONLINE RESOURCES

Ascencia Test Prep includes online resources with the purchase of this study guide to help you fully prepare for your Pharmacy Technician Certification Exam.

Practice Tests

In addition to the practice tests included in this book, we also offer online exams. Since many exams today are computer based, getting to practice your test-taking skills on the computer is a great way to prepare.

Review Questions

Need more practice? Our review questions use a variety of formats to help you memorize key terms and concepts.

Flash Cards

A convenient supplement to this study guide, Ascencia's flash cards enable you to review important terms easily on your computer or smartphone.

Cheat Sheets

Review the core skills you need to master the exam with easy-to-read Cheat Sheets.

From Stress to Success

Watch From Stress to Success, a brief but insightful YouTube video that offers the tips, tricks, and secrets experts use to score higher on the exam.

Reviews

Leave a review, send us helpful feedback, or sign up for Ascencia promotions—including free books!

Access these materials at:

www.ascenciatestprep.com/ptcb-online-resources

INTRODUCTION

Congratulations on your choice to become a Certified Pharmacy Technician! Pharmacy technicians play an essential role in the practice of pharmacy and are vital for its future as an evolving field. Because of the growing responsibilities of the pharmacy technician, becoming certified signifies that the pharmacy technician has achieved the competence necessary to become a trusted member of the pharmacy team. It also helps the pharmacy technician stay up to date with the continuing education crucial to the progressive field of pharmacy technology. This guide will introduce you to the essential skills that are required to pass the certification exam. In this chapter, we will review the different roles and responsibilities of pharmacy technicians, what the Pharmacy Technician Certification Board (PTCB) is, and present and future opportunities available for certified pharmacy technicians.

What is a Pharmacy Technician?

Pharmacy technicians are a fundamental part of the pharmacy practice. As a pharmacy technician, you will be responsible for assisting the pharmacist. Almost anything that does not require the professional judgment of the pharmacist can be done by the technician. Under the direct supervision of a pharmacist, pharmacy technicians assist patients, interact with physicians and nurses, are responsible for the administrative responsibilities of the pharmacy, and help prepare prescriptions and compounded medications. Pharmacists rely on pharmacy technicians to fulfill the technical and production aspects of the pharmacy so they can focus more on patient care such as patient counseling activities and safe dispensing of medications.

QUALIFICATIONS

Starting in the mid-1990s, with the advancement of pharmacy technology and the growth of managed care, an urgent need for competent pharmacy technicians arose. At that time, the most basic qualifications for pharmacy technicians were that they be at least eighteen years of age with a high school diploma or GED and a clear criminal record, with no felonies or drug-related offenses. As the pharmacist's responsibilities grew, pharmacy technicians required more specific skill sets to help reduce errors and free up pharmacists to focus on patient care. In response, more pharmacies offered incentives for pharmacy technicians to voluntarily become certified through the PTCB. This, in turn, increased their knowledge and abilities, giving pharmacy technicians credibility and recognition for their skills.

As pharmacy technology advanced into the twenty-first century, many state boards of pharmacy made **national certification** a requirement following the completion of pharmacy technician programs at **vocational schools** or **on-the-job-training**. National certification is required by many states to prove that the technician has the necessary level of skill and knowledge to perform his or her duties. Maintaining certification also requires reassessment through continuing education (CE) hours.

As of 2016, forty-five states and the District of Columbia also require pharmacy technicians to be **registered** through their state department of health. Registration is granted by the government and requires an individual to be licensed to practice an occupation in that particular state. The technician must prove that he or she has attained the proper minimum requirements needed to perform the occupation safely. Failure to comply with these requirements could result in suspension or revocation of the technician's license.

Common Responsibilities of Pharmacy Technicians

Being a pharmacy technician requires a strong code of ethics. Pharmacy personnel are trusted professionals, and patients rely on the pharmacy staff to deliver a safe, high-quality product. **Professionalism**, or the competence expected of the professional, puts patients at ease; they know that pharmacy staff will take all precautions necessary to ensure the correct medication is being dispensed.

Communication skills are extremely important in pharmacy. Besides the patient, pharmacy technicians interact with physicians, nurses, and other staff to meet the patient's needs. Whether it be calling the physician's office for a refill or preparing an intravenous (IV) admixture, addressing any questions or concerns can be the difference between helping and hurting a patient. **Safety** should always come first.

Other roles and responsibilities of the pharmacy technician depend on the health care facility where she or he is employed. Pharmacy technicians are responsible for a multitude of tasks that may change at the pharmacist's discretion. In a retail pharmacy, a pharmacy technician must assist both customers and the pharmacist. Pharmacy technicians may receive a prescription from a patient, input the prescription information into the computer, fill the medication, call physicians' offices for refills, work with insurance companies, order medications, inventory the pharmacy, handle cash, and do housekeeping.

In ambulatory pharmacies, pharmacy technicians work more closely with the nurses and staff and less with the patient. The pharmacy technician may be required to unit-dose and fill medication orders, prepare IV admixtures, enter data, deliver medications to the nursing floors, stock automated dispensing machines, do inventory, and order medications.

As pharmacy technology progresses, so do the roles and responsibilities of pharmacy technicians. **Continuing education**, or ongoing education related directly to pharmacy, helps to ensure the pharmacy technician develops intellectually as new opportunities arise.

Healthcare Settings

Healthcare settings for pharmacy technicians continue to progress as new opportunities arise. The two most common settings for the pharmacy technician are **community**, or retail pharmacy and **ambulatory**, or hospital pharmacy. However, there are a number of other settings where pharmacy technicians are needed.

In the past decade, **managed care** has become a growing institution in healthcare. Pharmacy technicians take on a more administrative role when working in managed care. Their medical knowledge has made them an indispensable part of the team in finding cost-effective ways to deliver quality care through prescription benefit management (PBM). Many pharmacy technicians who work in managed care work in **call center** environments. They may help patients find cost-effective solutions to high prescription costs, schedule appointments for medication therapy management (MTM), or assist in **medication compliance** if a patient is having trouble taking his or her medication regularly.

Nuclear medicine, which requires working with radiopharmaceuticals, is a more advanced role of the pharmacy technician. Some facilities that work with radiopharmaceuticals, such as **cancer treatment centers**, prefer technicians who have experience or have been certified to work in nuclear medicine due to the high health risk from radioactive chemicals. Nuclear medicine technicians must adhere to specific guidelines to avoid contamination.

With the growing older population in the United States, many IV medications are dispensed at home. If a patient is on **hospice** end-of-life care or **home healthcare**, pharmacy technicians can prepare and deliver an IV infusion from a centralized location, and a nurse can administer the medication from the comfort of home. Some **rehabilitation** and **long-term care** facilities have in-house pharmacies to better assist patients, while others work with local pharmaceutical companies or nationally accredited companies to deliver medications to facilities. The companies will unit-dose patient-specific medications in blister packs or make patient-specific IV admixtures to dispense medications more efficiently.

Future of Pharmacy Technology

The future of pharmacy technology is very promising. As computer technology advances, so do the pharmacy technician's roles and responsibilities. There are now a number of fields experienced pharmacy technicians can enter to take on new and interesting responsibilities.

Telepharmacy is an exciting advancement in healthcare. With telepharmacy, telecommunications allows patients to receive pharmaceutical care in cases when they may not be able to have direct contact with a pharmacist. In telepharmacy, hospitals employ pharmacists who work remotely, inputting medication orders overnight. This cuts costs since the pharmacy is not required to stay open 24 hours a day. As educational requirements improve, telepharmacy opportunities are now being offered to highly qualified pharmacy technicians as well. The medication order is entered, and the pharmacist verifies the order when completed. In rural areas, some hospitals have also allowed pharmacy technicians to work independently in the pharmacy; working remotely, a pharmacist verifies the technician's work by reviewing images of the fill process.

As pharmacy technicians become more qualified and better educated, many are trusted to work in quality assurance to assist in developing methods to promote better **patient safety**. Some pharmacy technicians, alongside pharmacists, help train employees through seminars on medication safety and implement standards within the healthcare facility to avoid medication errors.

As requirements to become a pharmacy technician become more stringent, many state boards of pharmacy are requiring training through a vocational school. Consequently, there is a need for **educators** to teach these classes. Experienced pharmacy technicians can also become trainers at pharmaceutical companies for new hires and continuing education.

Being a **pharmaceutical sales representative** in the past used to require a bachelor's degree in pharmacy. Now, with higher educational standards for pharmacy technicians, these opportunities are open to them as well. Sales representatives promote medications and medical devices to healthcare professionals; employees must be well versed in the product they are advertising.

Pharmacy informatics focuses on medication-related data and knowledge within healthcare systems. It includes implementation, analysis, use, and storage of patient care and health outcomes. Although a career in informatics may require certain computer certifications and other degrees, there is a stark need for training in pharmacy software as new technologies develop. Growth in this field is exceptional; many employment opportunities are emerging.

National Certification

As explained above, national certification is now becoming a requirement of most state boards of pharmacy to ensure that the pharmacy technician has a strong knowledge base. This chapter will provide an overview of the Pharmacy Technician Certification Board (PTCB) and the skill sets needed to pass the Pharmacy Technician Certification Exam (PTCE).

The PTCB's **Pharmacy Technician Certification Exam (PTCE)** is accredited by the National Commission for Certifying Agencies (NCCA). To schedule a test, you must first get authorization from the PTCB showing you have met all the pre-qualifications. The PTCB offers two pathways to qualify for the exam:

- Pathway 1: Completion of a PTCB-recognized education or training program
- Pathway 2: Minimum 500 hours experience as a pharmacy technician

After you receive authorization and pay the $129 test fee, you can schedule a test online or by phone with Pearson-VUE Professional Testing Centers. When you arrive at the center, be sure to have photo identification to prove your identity. The testing center may also collect your palm vein image digitally for verification and to protect the integrity of the test. No personal items are allowed in the testing area; you will be assigned a locker to secure your items while you test. When you enter the testing area, an employee will sign you in to a computer workstation and hand you any other materials permitted only for testing purposes. You are monitored at all times while taking the test and cannot communicate with other test-takers. Any disruptive or fraudulent behavior can cause termination of testing.

The PTCE is a computer-generated multiple-choice exam that contains ninety questions. Of the ninety questions, eighty questions are scored and ten questions are unscored. There are four possible answers for each question, but only one is correct. The exam takes 2 hours. A score of 1400/1600 or better is required to pass the exam. The range of possible scores is between

1000 and 1600 and is based off of the Modified Angoff method of testing. You will officially know if you passed the test within 1 to 3 weeks after you take the exam. Within 6 weeks, you will be sent an official certificate and wallet card stating you are a certified pharmacy technician.

What is the PTCB?

The main governing organization for the Pharmacy Technician Certification Exam (PTCE) is the **Pharmacy Technician Certification Board (PTCB)**. The PTCB was created in 1995 by leaders in both the American Society of Health Systems Pharmacists (ASHP) and the American Pharmacist Association (APA). These leaders, realizing the need for a better way to educate pharmacy technicians on the skill sets essential to their profession, created a board of advisors who initiated a testing system that assesses the knowledge and abilities needed to perform pharmacy technician work responsibilities.

By passing the PTCE, pharmacy technicians are nationally accredited and receive the title of a Certified Pharmacy Technician, or CPhT. This accreditation proves to employers that its holder's knowledge will be beneficial to their company. The skill sets tested on the exam specifically correspond to required knowledge for performing technical and production duties in the pharmacy.

What You Need to Know to Pass the PTCE

To pass the PTCE, the PTCB requires knowledge of specific subjects related to work as a pharmacy technician. The subjects and the percentage of each subject that will be on the test are listed in the table below.

Pharmacy Technician Certification Exam Content Outline	
Content Area (% of test)	**Details**
Medications 40%	Generic names, brand names, and classifications of medications
	Therapeutic equivalence
	Common and life-threatening drug interactions and contraindications
	Strengths/dose, dosage forms, routes of administration, special handling and administration instructions, and duration of drug therapy
	Common and severe medication side effects, adverse effects, and allergies
	Indications of medications and dietary supplements
	Drug stability
	Narrow therapeutic index (NTI) medications
	Physical and chemical incompatibilities related to non-sterile compounding and reconstitution
	Proper storage of medications (e.g., temperature ranges, light sensitivity, restricted access)

continued on next page

PTCE Exam Content Outline (continued)

Content Area (% of test)	Details
Federal Requirements 12.5%	Federal requirements for handling and disposal of non-hazardous, hazardous, and pharmaceutical substances and waste
	Federal requirements for controlled substance prescriptions and DEA controlled substance schedules
	Federal requirements (e.g., DEA, FDA) for controlled substances
	Federal requirements for restricted drug programs and related medication processing
	FDA recall requirements
Patient Safety and Quality Assurance 25%	High-alert/risk medications and look-alike/sound-alike [LASA] medications
	Error prevention strategies
	Issues that require pharmacist intervention
	Event reporting procedures
	Types of prescription errors
	Hygiene and cleaning standards
Order Entry and Processing 25%	Procedures to compound non-sterile products
	Formulas, calculations, ratios, proportions, alligations, conversions, Sig codes (e.g., b.i.d., t.i.d., Roman numerals), abbreviations, medical terminology, and symbols for days supply, quantity, dose, concentration, dilutions
	Equipment/supplies required for drug administration
	Lot numbers, expiration dates, and National Drug Code (NDC) numbers Procedures for identifying and returning dispensable, non-dispensable, and expired medications and supplies

AFTER THE PTCE

After you pass the PTCE, you will receive your certification by mail. To keep your certification current, you will be required to re-certify every 2 years. Because CPhTs are expanding their roles to better support pharmacists, changes have taken place in 2015 and 2016. Since 2015, CPhTs have been required to submit pharmacy technician-specific continuing education (CE) hours. For reinstatement, pharmacy technicians must submit 20 CE hours. Of the 20 CE hours, 2 CE hours must be in pharmacy law, and 1 CE hour must be in patient safety. As of January 1, 2016, only 10 of the total 20 CE hours may be accredited by passing a college-based equivalent course with a grade of "C." Certificate holders must also pay a reinstatement fee every 2 years.

Depending on your state, you may also be required to re-register every 2 years. Registration is state specific, and it is important to check with your state board of pharmacy and/or department of health to determine the requirements for re-registration in your state. Most states require their own set of CE hours and a re-registration fee.

Due to the professional standards of working in a pharmacy, drug-related offenses and felonies as well as other disciplinary issues may cause suspension and revocation of your license and certification. Remember that you are a trusted professional and must abide by a set of ethical standards. When you become PTCB certified, you will take an oath to uphold the PTCB Code of Conduct.

THE CODE OF CONDUCT FOLLOWS:

PTCB is dedicated to providing and implementing appropriate standards designed to serve pharmacy technicians, employers, pharmacists, and patients. First and foremost, PTCB certificants and candidates give priority to the health interests and protection of the public, and act in a manner that promotes integrity and reflects positively on the work of pharmacy technicians, consistent with appropriate ethical and legal standards.

As pharmacy technicians, and under the supervision of a licensed pharmacist, PTCB certificants and candidates have the obligation to: maintain high standards of integrity and conduct; accept responsibility for their actions; continually seek to improve their performance in the workplace; practice with fairness and honesty; and, encourage others to act in an ethical manner consistent with the standards and responsibilities set forth below. Pharmacy technicians assist pharmacists in dispensing medications and remain accountable to supervising pharmacists with regard to all pharmacy activities, and will act consistent with all applicable laws and regulations.

A. Responsibilities Relating to Legal Requirements.

Each certificant/candidate must:

1. Act consistent with all legal requirements relating to pharmacy technician practice, including Federal, State, and local laws and regulations.
2. Refrain from any behavior that violates legal or ethical standards, including all criminal laws, Federal laws and agency regulations, and State laws and regulatory agency rules.

B. Responsibilities to PTCB/Compliance with Organizational Policies and Rules.

Each certificant/candidate must:

1. Act consistent with all applicable PTCB Policies and requirements.
2. Provide accurate, truthful, and complete information to PTCB.
3. Maintain the security and confidentiality of PTCB Examination information and materials, including the prevention of unauthorized disclosure of test items and format and other confidential information.
4. Cooperate with PTCB concerning conduct review matters, including the submission of all required information in a timely, truthful, and accurate manner.
5. Report to PTCB apparent violations of this Code upon a reasonable and clear factual basis.

C. Responsibilities to the Public and Employers.
Each certificant/candidate must:
1. Deliver competent, safe, and appropriate pharmacy and related services.
2. Recognize practice limitations and provide services only when qualified and authorized by a supervising pharmacist and consistent with applicable laws and regulations. The certificant/candidate is responsible for determining the limits of his/her own abilities based on legal requirements, training, knowledge, skills, experience, and other relevant considerations.
3. Maintain and respect the confidentiality of sensitive information obtained in the course of all work and pharmacy-related activities, as directed by the supervising pharmacist and consistent with legal requirements, unless: the information is reasonably understood to pertain to unlawful activity; a court or governmental agency lawfully directs the release of the information; the patient or the employer expressly authorizes the release of specific information; or, the failure to release such information would likely result in death or serious physical harm to employees and/or patients.
4. Use pharmacy technician credentials properly, and provide truthful and accurate representations concerning education, experience, competency, and the performance of services.
5. Provide truthful and accurate representations to the public and employers.
6. Follow appropriate health and safety procedures with respect to all pharmacy-related activities and duties.
7. Protect the public, employees, and employers from conditions where injury and damage are reasonably foreseeable.
8. Disclose to patients or employers significant circumstances that could be construed as a conflict of interest or an appearance of impropriety.
9. Avoid conduct that could cause a conflict of interest with the interests of a patient or employer.
10. Assure that a real or perceived conflict of interest does not compromise legitimate interests of a patient or employer, and does not influence or interfere with work-related judgments.

– Code of Conduct, Pharmacy Technician Certification Board, 2014, https://www.ptcb.org/resources/code-of-conduct

PART I

MEDICATIONS

PHARMACOLOGY

Pharmacology is the study of the origin, uses, preparation, and effects of drugs on body systems. The history of pharmacology is as ancient as the human race. Early humans used plants to cure disease and ease symptoms. As scientists gained knowledge of chemical elements and processes, they began to experiment with producing synthetic drugs. Today, pharmaceutical companies are able to supply synthetic substances in bulk and modify the chemical structures of drugs to improve efficacy and minimize side effects.

Pharmacokinetics

Pharmacokinetics is the branch of pharmacology that interprets what happens to a drug after it enters the body, from when it is administered to the point of its elimination. After administration, all drugs are processed by the body through the same general mechanisms: liberation, absorption, distribution, metabolism, and excretion (LADME).

Liberation is the release of a drug from its pharmaceutical formulation, meaning the active ingredient separates from other components. A drug's liberation can be modified to change the onset and duration of action.

Absorption is the process of a drug entering the blood. The term *bioavailability* describes the percentage of the drug that actually reaches circulation. Bioavailability is dependent on many factors, including the chemical form of the drug, its route of administration, and how it is metabolized.

IV drugs have a bioavailability of 100%: they immediately enter circulation without being broken down. Drugs taken through other routes must pass through cell membranes (e.g., mucous membranes in the mouth or nose) or the GI tract to enter circulation. This process reduces their bioavailability.

HELPFUL HINT:

Extended release formulations prolong the liberation process to extend the drug's duration of action.

Drugs taken orally are subject to the **first pass effect** (also called first pass metabolism)—the breakdown of drugs before they reach circulation. This process occurs mainly in the liver but can also occur in the stomach, intestines, lungs, and kidneys.

Drugs with a high first pass effect will have low bioavailability. Oral insulin, for example, has a bioavailability <1%: it is easily broken down in the stomach and cannot pass through the intestinal wall.

Distribution is the dispersion of a drug throughout the body's fluid and tissue. Because of variations in blood perfusion, tissue binding, regional pH, and cell membrane permeability, distribution is often uneven.

Volume of distribution (Vd) is a parameter that represents a drug's tendency to remain in the plasma or spread to different tissue. A medication with a high Vd tends to leave the plasma for other tissues. A drug with low Vd stays highly concentrated in the plasma.

Metabolism is the transformation of a drug's compounds into drug metabolites (i.e., the breakdown of the drug). This process occurs mainly in the liver, and the inactive metabolites are excreted in urine or bile.

Excretion is the elimination of a drug from the body. The kidneys filter and excrete water-soluble compounds. The liver can also release drug metabolites into bile, which travels to the intestines to be excreted. Excretion can be measured in several ways:

- Excretion can be measured as an amount of drug removed over a specific time period, but this measurement is not often used in clinical settings.
- **Clearance** describes the volume of plasma cleared of a drug during a specific time period (e.g., the clearance for atorvastatin is 625 mL/min).
- **Elimination half-life** is the time required for the drug to reach half its peak concentration (e.g., the half-life of atorvastatin is 7 hours).

> **HELPFUL HINT:**
>
> **Bioequivalence** means that different drug products result in equal concentrations in the plasma and tissues when given to the same patient.

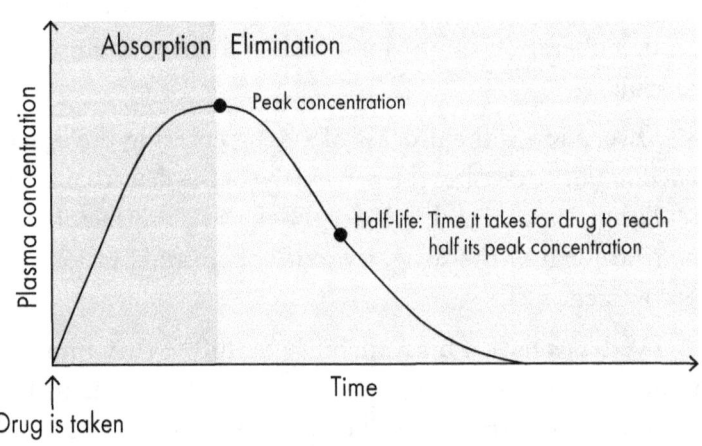

Figure 1.1. Elimination Half-Life

> **PRACTICE QUESTION**
>
> 1. Which of the following statements describes a drug with a high first pass effect?
>   A) liberated slowly to extend action
>   B) easily passes through membranes and into tissues
>   C) excreted by the kidneys
>   D) metabolized before it reaches circulation

Pharmacodynamics

Pharmacodynamics is the branch of pharmacology that studies how a drug affects the body. It includes the study of the mechanism through which drugs cause an effect and the relationship between dose and effect.

Receptors and Mechanisms of Action

The majority of drugs act on the system in two ways:
- mimicking or suppressing normal physiological processes in the body
- inhibiting the growth of certain microbial or parasitic organisms

Drugs cannot change the fundamental physiological processes that occur in the body—they can only change the rate at which they occur. Drug action occurs when the drug binds to receptors on a protein molecule in the body to activate or block a physiological process:

- An **agonist** binds to receptors and stimulates activity. For example, nitroglycerin is an agonist that results in the activation of enzymes which dilate blood vessels. Endogenous agonists (e.g., serotonin, epinephrine) are the molecules produced by the body that naturally bind to receptor sites.
- An **antagonist** binds to a receptor to block activity. For example, ACE inhibitors block the angiotensin-converting enzyme (ACE), which normally causes blood vessels to constrict. The result is dilation of the blood vessels.
- Some drugs are **partial agonists**, meaning they only partially activate receptors. Buprenorphine is a partial agonist that bonds to opioid receptors but does not fully activate them. It is used to lessen the effects of opioid withdrawal.
- An **inverse agonist** binds to a receptor to slow activity. It does not block the receptor in the same way as an antagonist; instead, it prevents the receptor from performing basal-level activity. Famotidine is an example of an inverse agonist: it decreases basal levels of gastric acid to prevent heartburn.

> **HELPFUL HINT:**
>
> **Anticholinergic** drugs block activity at acetylcholine receptors in the parasympathetic nervous system. They relax smooth muscles and are used to treat conditions like asthma, overactive bladder, and tremors. Some antipsychotics and SSRIs are also anticholinergic drugs.

A drug's **mechanism of action (MOA)** is the specific biochemical process that generates its effects. Examples of common MOAs include

- stimulating or blocking receptors (as agonists or antagonists);
- stimulating or suppressing enzyme or hormone synthesis; and
- affecting cell function or growth (e.g., antibiotics destroying the cell walls of bacteria).

The MOA for some medications is occasionally unknown. The medicine may have the desired therapeutic effect, but it is simply not known how the molecule interacts with receptors to achieve it.

> **PRACTICE QUESTION**
>
> 2. Naloxone is an opioid antagonist and reverses the effects of opioid overdose by
>   - **A)** acting as a central nervous system stimulant.
>   - **B)** removing opioids from the body.
>   - **C)** competitively binding to opioid receptors.
>   - **D)** reducing the production of endogenous opioids.

Therapeutic Index

Drug manufacturers closely study the behavior of drugs in the body to determine safe, effective dosing instructions. They must determine how much of a drug is needed for it to be effective; this amount must be balanced against the risk for adverse side effects. The resulting dose range is expressed as a therapeutic window or index.

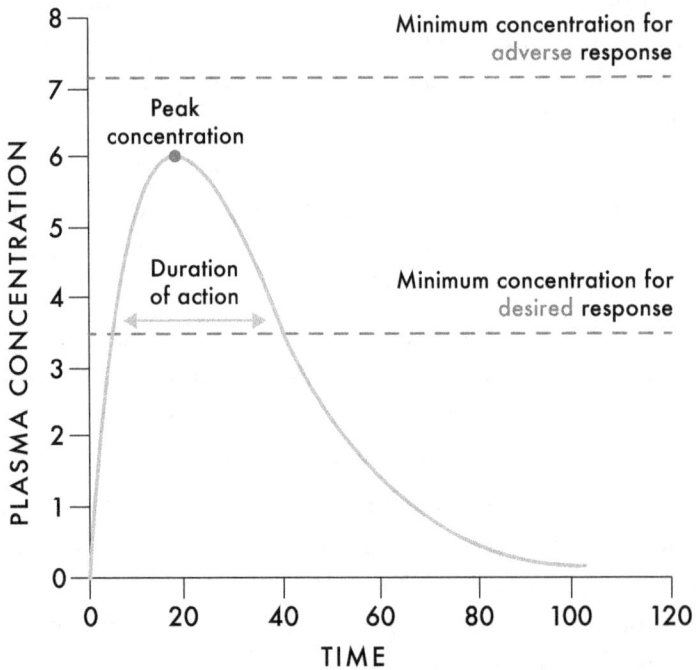

Figure 1.2. Therapeutic Window

As discussed above, drugs go through a process of liberation, absorption, and eventual metabolization and excretion. This process is reflected in the drug's **duration of action (DOA)**, which describes how long a drug is effective. **Peak concentration** occurs when the drug's plasma concentration is highest.

The **therapeutic window (TW)** describes the plasma concentration required for a medication to be effective without causing serious adverse effects. A concentration below the TW will not produce the desired effect; a concentration higher than the TW produces serious adverse effects. A drug's therapeutic window affects how the drug is prescribed and administered. For example, warfarin (Coumadin) has a very narrow therapeutic window; its use must be monitored so that plasma concentrations fall within range.

During drug development, researchers formulate a graph representing a **dose-response curve**, which plots responses to the drug against dosage. Three different doses are used in a dose-response curve:

- the **effective dose** (ED50), at which 50% of participants experience some therapeutic effect
- the **toxic dose** (TD50), at which 50% of participants experience some toxic effect
- the **lethal dose** (LD50), at which 50% of participants will die

The **therapeutic index (TI)** is the range of doses at which a medication is effective and has minimal adverse effects. TI is found by dividing the toxic dose (TD50) by the effective dose (ED50) as described in Figure 1.3.

HELPFUL HINT:

A **dose** is the amount of a drug given in a single administration. **Dosage** refers to the entire quantity of the drug prescribed, which accounts for the size and number of doses.

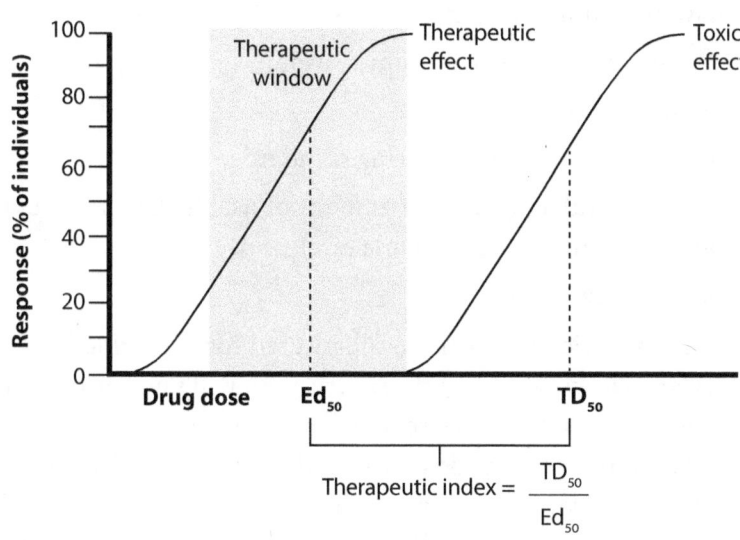

Figure 1.3. Therapeutic Index

> **PRACTICE QUESTION**
>
> 3. Dividing the toxic dose by effective dose will give which value?
>   A) therapeutic window
>   B) peak concentration
>   C) duration of action
>   D) therapeutic index

Therapeutic Equivalence

The **brand name** of a drug is the name it is given by the pharmaceutical company that funded its research and development. This company holds the drug's patent for up to 20 years after its initial development. When the patent expires, other pharmaceutical companies can produce the drug.

A **generic drug** is the therapeutic equivalent of the brand name of a drug. It must have the same active ingredient, strength, and dosage form as the brand-name drug, but the inactive ingredients do not need to be the same. Many generic drugs cost less to produce because generic manufacturers do not need to recoup the cost of research and development.

For the FDA to approve a generic drug, it must be **therapeutically equivalent** to the brand name, meaning it produces the same clinical effect and has the same safety profile. According to the FDA, therapeutic equivalent (generic) drugs must

- be as safe and effective as the brand name,
- have the same active ingredients,
- use the same route of administration,
- be the same dosage,
- meet the same manufacturing standards,
- be bioequivalent (the same amount of usable drug reaches the body's circulation at the same rate), and
- be correctly labeled.

Generally, generic drugs can be substituted for prescribed brand-name medications (and vice versa) when the substitution will save the patient money. In fact, many insurers and state regulations require this substitution. The *Orange Book: Approved Drug Products with Therapeutic Equivalence Evaluations* identifies approved brand-name drug products along with evaluations of their therapeutic equivalents. The *Orange Book* is approved by the FDA, updated daily, and available online.

In some circumstances, generic drugs cannot be substituted for brand-name medications. Brand-name medications with a narrow therapeutic index (NTI) usually cannot be substituted with generic drugs. Small changes in

HELPFUL HINT:

Therapeutic equivalent drugs do NOT need to have the same appearance, packaging, preservatives, or flavor.

dosages of NTI drugs can result in adverse events or therapeutic failure. Common NTI drugs include

- carbamazepine,
- cyclosporine,
- digoxin,
- levothyroxine,
- lithium carbonate,
- phenytoin, and
- warfarin.

Providers and patients can also request either brand-name or generic drugs. Patient requests should always be honored; however, the patient should be advised that the brand-name drug may be more expensive or not covered by insurance.

Dispense as written (DAW) codes play a significant role in pharmacy billing. A DAW code indicates the prescriber's instructions to third-party payers to dispense the exact medication as prescribed or instructions to substitute a generic equivalent. The code used when processing the prescription will influence how the third-party payer responds. There are ten DAW codes that can be used, but most insurance companies only recognize a few of them and strictly limit their use:

- DAW 0: No product selection is indicated. This code is used when it is acceptable to substitute the generic version of the drug.
- DAW 1: Substitutions are not allowed by the prescriber. This code is used when the doctor deems the brand-name medication to be medically necessary.
- DAW 2: The patient is requesting the brand-name version of the drug; this code is used when the patient will not accept the generic, but the doctor does not deem the brand-name medically necessary.
- DAW 3: The pharmacist has selected the brand name, although substitution is allowed.
- DAW 4: The generic version of the drug is not in stock; substitution is allowed.
- DAW 5: The brand-name version of the drug has been dispensed at the generic price; substitution is allowed.
- DAW 6: This is the override code.
- DAW 7: The brand-name drug is mandated by law; substitution is not allowed.
- DAW 8: The generic version of the drug is not available; substitution is allowed.
- DAW 9: Other

HELPFUL HINT:

If a prescription states "dispense as written" or "DAW," the pharmacy tech must dispense the exact medication as it is written on the prescription.

> **PRACTICE QUESTION**
>
> 4. A generic drug must have all the same characteristics as a brand-name drug EXCEPT its
>   - A) active ingredient.
>   - B) color.
>   - C) dosage.
>   - D) strength.

Drug Classes

A **drug class** is a group of related medications that have the same mechanism of action or are used to treat the same condition. Drugs within a single drug class usually have the same suffix, although the suffixes of older drugs may differ because grouping generic drugs by suffix is a relatively new concept.

Therapeutic substitution is the substitution of a prescribed drug with another medication that produces the same therapeutic effect (usually from the same class). Often this substitution is done when a brand-name medication has no generic version, but a different generic drug is available in the same class. Pharmacists may offer therapeutic substitutes in some states, but prescriber approval is always required.

HELPFUL HINT:

Pharmacy technicians are not authorized to make therapeutic substitutions.

TABLE 1.1. Drug Classes

Drug Class	Commonly Used Suffix	Purpose	Example(s) generic name (brand name)
angiotensin II receptor blockers (A2RBs)	–artan	block angiotensin II enzymes from specific receptor sites; help prohibit vasoconstriction	candesartan
angiotensin-converting enzyme (ACE) inhibitors	–pril	block the conversion of angiotensin I to angiotensin II; may reduce the chance of increased vasoconstriction or blood pressure	enalapril
alpha-adrenergic blockers	–azosin	relax the veins and arteries so blood can easily pass through; antihypertensives	terazosin

Drug Class	Commonly Used Suffix	Purpose	Example(s) generic name (brand name)
antibiotics	–cillin –cycline –floxacin –mycin	inhibit growth of or kill bacteria	penicillin amoxicillin ciprofloxacin moxifloxacin vancomycin
anticoagulants (blood thinners)	N/A	prevent blood clots	rivaroxaban (Xarelto) warfarin (Coumadin)
anticonvulsants	N/A	prevent seizures	carbamazepine (Tegretol) topiramate (Topamax)
antidepressants	N/A	treat depression and mood disorders	fluoxetine (Prozac) sertraline (Zoloft) bupropion (Wellbutrin, Zyban)
antihistamines	N/A	treat allergies	diphenhydramine (Benadryl)
antipsychotics	N/A	manage psychosis	aripiprazole (Abilify) lithium carbonate
antivirals	–vir	inhibit growth of or kill viruses	docosanol (Abreva) oseltamivir (Tamiflu)
barbiturates	–barbital	depress the central nervous system	amobarbital (Amytal Sodium) butabarbital (Butisol) phenobarbital (Nembutal)

TABLE 1.1. Drug Classes (continued)

Drug Class	Commonly Used Suffix	Purpose	Example(s) generic name (brand name)
benzodiazepines	–pam	reduce anxiety and relax muscles	alprazolam (Xanax) clonazepam (Klonopin) lorazepam (Ativan) diazepam (Valium)
beta blockers (B1s) or beta-adrenergic blocking agents	–olol	reduce blood pressure and improve blood flow	acebutolol (Sectral) atenolol (Tenormin) metoprolol (Lopressor) propranolol (Inderal)
calcium channel blockers	–pine	relax and widen blood vessels	amlodipine (Norvasc) felodipine (Plendil) diltiazem (Cardizem) nifedipine (Procardia)
corticosteroids	–olone –sone	reduce inflammation	dexamethasone (Decadron) prednisone (Sterapred)
potassium-sparing diuretics	–actone	increase the flow of urine and enhance the loss of sodium	spironolactone
loop diuretics	–emide	increase the flow of urine and enhance the loss of sodium	furosemide
histamine type-2 receptor antagonists (H2 blockers)	–tidine	reduce stomach acid	famotidine (PEPCID) ranitidine (Zantac)

Drug Class	Commonly Used Suffix	Purpose	Example(s) generic name (brand name)
HMG-CoA reductase inhibitors	–statin	inhibit cholesterol production	rosuvastatin (Crestor)
hypnotics	N/A	reduce anxiety and induce sleep	eszopiclone (Lunesta) zolpidem (Ambien)
immunosuppressants	N/A	suppress the immune system	adalimumab (Humira) methotrexate (Trexall)
local anesthetics	–caine	block sensation in a small area	lidocaine (Xylocaine, Lidoderm) benzocaine
neuromuscular blockers	–nium	paralyze skeletal muscles	pancuronium (Pavulon) rocuronium (Zemuron)
nonsteroidal anti-inflammatory drugs (NSAIDs)	N/A	reduce pain and inflammation	ibuprofen (Motrin, Advil) naproxen (Aleve, Naprosyn)
opioid pain relievers	–codone	block pain signals in brain	oxycodone (Percocet, OxyContin) morphine (Astramorph, Duramorph)
proton pump inhibitors	–razole	reduce stomach acid	esomeprazole (Nexium) lansoprazole (Prevacid) omeprazole (Prilosec)

CONTINUE

> **PRACTICE QUESTION**
>
> 5. Drugs in a drug class must have the following traits in common EXCEPT
>   A) the same targeted mechanism.
>   B) a similar mode of action.
>   C) the same active ingredient.
>   D) similar structures.

HELPFUL HINT:

A patient may continue taking a medication even if it results in negative side effects. Some adverse reactions (e.g., dry mouth, diarrhea) subside with time, and the benefits of the drug may outweigh the uncomfortable side effects. The patient should always check with the provider before discontinuing a medication.

Side Effects and Adverse Reactions

Adverse drug reaction is a broad term used to describe unwanted or dangerous effects caused by a specific medication. Most adverse drug reactions are dose related, but they can also be allergic or idiosyncratic (unexpected responses that are neither dose related nor allergic). Adverse drug reactions are one of the leading causes of morbidity and mortality in health care. They can be classified by severity as follows:

- mild (e.g., drowsiness)
- moderate (e.g., hypertension)
- severe (e.g., abnormal heart rhythm)
- lethal (e.g., liver failure)

Allergic reactions may cause itching, rash, airway edema with difficulty breathing, or a drop in blood pressure. Severe allergic reactions can cause **anaphylaxis**, which is a life-threatening condition requiring emergent care. An **idiosyncratic reaction** can cause almost any sign or symptom and usually cannot be predicted.

Adverse drug reactions are classified into six types, described in Table 1.2.

TABLE 1.2. Types of Adverse Drug Reactions		
Type	Description	Example
A augmented	predictable reactions arising from the pharmacological effects of the drug; dependent on dose	diarrhea due to antibiotics; hypoglycemia due to insulin
B bizarre	unpredictable reactions; independent of dose	hypersensitivity (anaphylaxis) due to penicillin
C chronic	reactions caused by the cumulative dose (the dose taken over a long period of time)	osteoporosis with oral steroids
D delayed	reactions that occur after the drug is no longer being taken	teratogenic effects with anticonvulsants

Type	Description	Example
E end of use	reactions caused by withdrawal from a drug	withdrawal syndrome with benzodiazepines
F failure	unexpected failure of the drug to work; often caused by dose or drug interactions	resistance to antimicrobials

PRACTICE QUESTION

6. Rifampin is an antibiotic used to treat tuberculosis. When taken with oral contraceptives, it can reduce estrogen levels and decrease the effectiveness of the contraceptive. This adverse reaction would be classified as

   A) A—augmented.
   B) B—bizarre.
   C) E—end of use.
   D) F—failure.

Drug Interactions

Medications may interact with other medications or health conditions. These **drug interactions** can increase or decrease the action of the drug, which changes the therapeutic effects of the medication. There are three main types of drug interactions: drug-drug, drug-disease, and drug-nutrient.

A **drug-drug interaction** can occur when a person takes multiple medications. The drugs may be duplicates, meaning they have a similar therapeutic effect. This type of interaction can result in toxicity or increased effect. Combining drugs with opposite effects may reduce the effectiveness of one or both medications.

Drug-disease interaction occurs when a medication taken for one disease causes or exacerbates a different disease. For example, calcium channel blockers (to treat hypertension) must be used cautiously in patients with chronic kidney disease because they can impair kidney function.

Drugs may interact with other consumable substances, including foods, alcohol, and nutritional supplements. These interactions are grouped together as **drug-nutrient interactions**. For example, alcohol and grapefruit juice both change the absorption and effectiveness of antibiotics.

Some drugs can also interact with laboratory tests in a **drug-laboratory interaction**. The drugs may alter the test specimen (e.g., blood, urine) or interfere with test reagents. Taking omeprazole, for example, can lead to false negatives on a urea breath test.

HELPFUL HINT:

Drug-drug interactions are common when patients take medications that contain multiple drugs. For example, a patient taking Norco and OTC Nyquil might not realize that both medications contain acetaminophen.

HELPFUL HINT:

Monoamine oxidase inhibitors (MAOIs) are a class of antidepressants that are effective in treating mood disorders but are rarely used due to their potential for drug-drug interactions. Most drugs that affect serotonin, norepinephrine, or dopamine levels are contraindicated for patients taking MAOIs.

PRACTICE QUESTION

7. Which of the following is an example of a drug-drug interaction?

    A) Taking omeprazole with clopidogrel may decrease the effectiveness of clopidogrel.

    B) Ibuprofen may cause or exacerbate gastrointestinal bleeding.

    C) Drinking grapefruit juice with simvastatin reduces the concentration of simvastatin in the blood.

    D) Antidepressants may cause suicidal thoughts or behaviors in children.

Drug Administration

One of the specific factors that influences a drug's bioavailability and how it distributes through the system is its **route of administration.** Pharmacy technicians should be familiar with common routes of administration and their abbreviations so that the correct drug can be dispensed:

- buccal (BUC): in the cheek
- inhalational (INH): through the mouth
- intramuscular (IM): into the muscle
- intranasal (NAS): through the nose
- intravenous (IV): into the vein
- oral (PO): by mouth
- rectal (PR): into the rectum
- subcutaneous (subcut): under the skin
- sublingual (SL): under the tongue
- transdermal (TOP): through the skin
- vaginal (PV): into the vagina

PRACTICE QUESTION

8. A patient has a prescription for nitroglycerin 0.4 mg SL. How should the patient be directed to take this medication?

    A) under the tongue

    B) in the cheek

    C) swallowed without chewing

    D) injected into the muscle

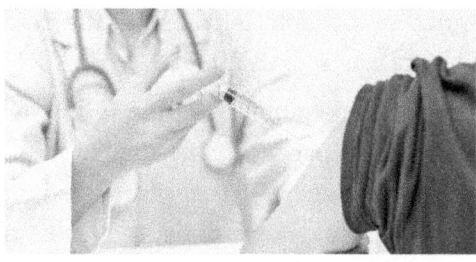
Intramuscular Injection

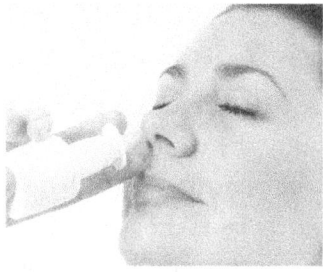
Intranasal Delivery

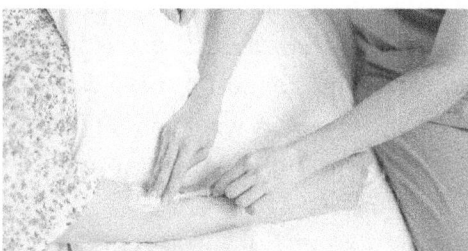
Intravenous Delivery

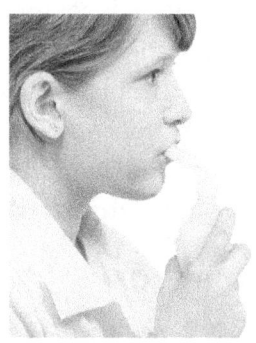
Inhalation

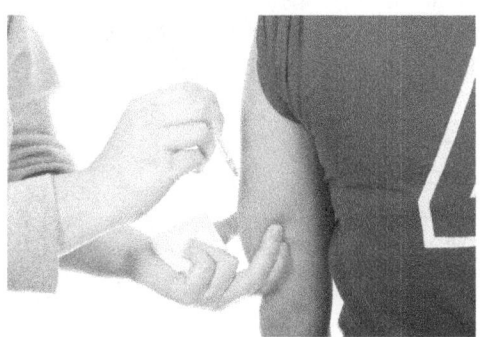
Subcutaneous Injection

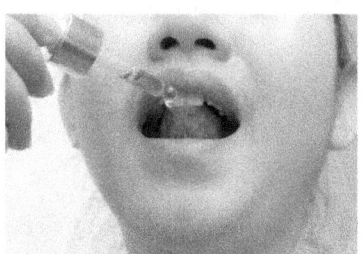
Sublingual Delivery

Figure 1.4. Routes of Administration

Drug Stability

Drugs degrade over time, so manufacturers put **expiration dates** on every product to ensure that medications will work properly when taken. The expiration date is usually a month and year, and the medication is considered usable through the end of the given month. For example, if the expiration date on a drug is 7/25, the last day it should be taken is 7/31/2025.

Once a drug has been removed from its packaging for compounding or repackaging, the expiration date on the original package is no longer valid. Instead, the pharmacy calculates a **beyond-use date (BUD)** that is included on the new drug label. For repackaged nonsterile solids or liquids, the BUD is one year after the repackaging date or the original expiration date, whichever comes first.

When a medication is compounded, it is only good for a limited amount of time due to degradation. These medications will have a BUD that is specific to the product. For example, reconstituted vancomycin must be used within 7 days. So the BUD for this compound made on 7/10/2025 would be 7/17/2025. The BUD must be included on the label for compounded medications and is usually written as "Discard After" or "Do Not Use After."

PRACTICE QUESTION

9. On 11/3/2021, a pharmacy technician uses a bottle of amoxicillin with an expiration date of 3/31/2022 to make an oral suspension. If the oral suspension must be used within 10 days, what beyond-use date should the technician put on the label?

    A) 11/3/2021
    B) 11/13/2021
    C) 3/31/2022
    D) 4/10/2022

Drug Storage

Drugs must be stored properly to ensure their integrity. Factors that may influence the rate at which drugs degrade include temperature, light, air, and moisture.

Drugs should be stored at the temperature recommended by the manufacturer. The packaging will state whether a drug should be kept at room temperature, refrigerated, or frozen.

Some drugs will degrade faster when exposed to light. Light-sensitive solids are usually coated to protect them from light or stored in opaque packaging. Light-sensitive liquids, including reconstituted drugs, should be stored in amber or opaque vials. Examples of drugs that should be protected from light include insulin, furosemide, and sumatriptan.

TABLE 1.3. Drug Storage Temperatures		
Room temperature (59°F – 86°F [15°C – 30°C])	**Refrigerated** (36°F – 46°F [2°C – 8°C])	**Frozen** (–13°F – 14°F [–25° – –10°C])
Most PO tablets and pills can be stored at room temperature.	• insulin • eye and ear drops (e.g., latanoprost) • antidiabetic injections (e.g., liraglutide, exenatide) • many biological drugs (e.g., adalimumab, etanercept) • vaccines, including flu, Tdap, Hep A and B, Gardasil9, and rotavirus vaccines • many cancer drugs (e.g., melphalan, chlorambucil) • calcitonin nasal spray • reconstituted antibiotics	• MMR vaccine • varicella vaccine • shingles vaccine • anthrax immune globulin • carmustine wafer • dinoprostone vaginal insert

PRACTICE QUESTION

10. A patient is picking up a prescription for amoxicillin, which the pharmacy technician has reconstituted. Where should the patient store this medication?

    A) a dry area at room temperature
    B) away from light sources
    C) a refrigerator
    D) a freezer

CONTINUE

ANSWER KEY

1. **D)** Drugs with a high first pass effect are metabolized (usually by the liver or GI tract) before they can reach circulation.

2. **C)** Naloxone is an opioid antagonist. It binds to opioid receptors and prevents opioid agonists (such as morphine and oxycodone) from binding to those sites.

3. **D)** Dividing the toxic dose (TD50) by the effective dose (ED50) provides the therapeutic index (TI). This is the range of doses at which a medication is effective and has minimal adverse effects.

4. **B)** The color of a drug does not affect its ability to treat its targeted disease or condition.

5. **C)** Drugs do not have to have the same active ingredient to be in the same drug class since each drug is chemically different.

6. **D)** Contraceptive failure caused by interaction between medications is an example of an adverse drug reaction of type F (failure of therapy).

7. **A)** Omeprazole (Prilosec) can decrease the effectiveness of clopidogrel (Plavix), which is a drug-drug interaction.

8. **A)** The abbreviation for sublingual is SL, meaning "under the tongue."

9. **B)** The beyond-use date should be 10 days after the solution is reconstituted, which would be 11/13/2021.

10. **C)** Reconstituted amoxicillin should be refrigerated.

2 DRUG EFFECTS AND INDICATIONS

The Cardiovascular System

The **cardiovascular system** circulates **blood**, which carries nutrients, waste, hormones, and other important substances dissolved or suspended in liquid plasma. Two of the most important components of blood are **white blood cells**, which fight infections, and **red blood cells**, which transport oxygen.

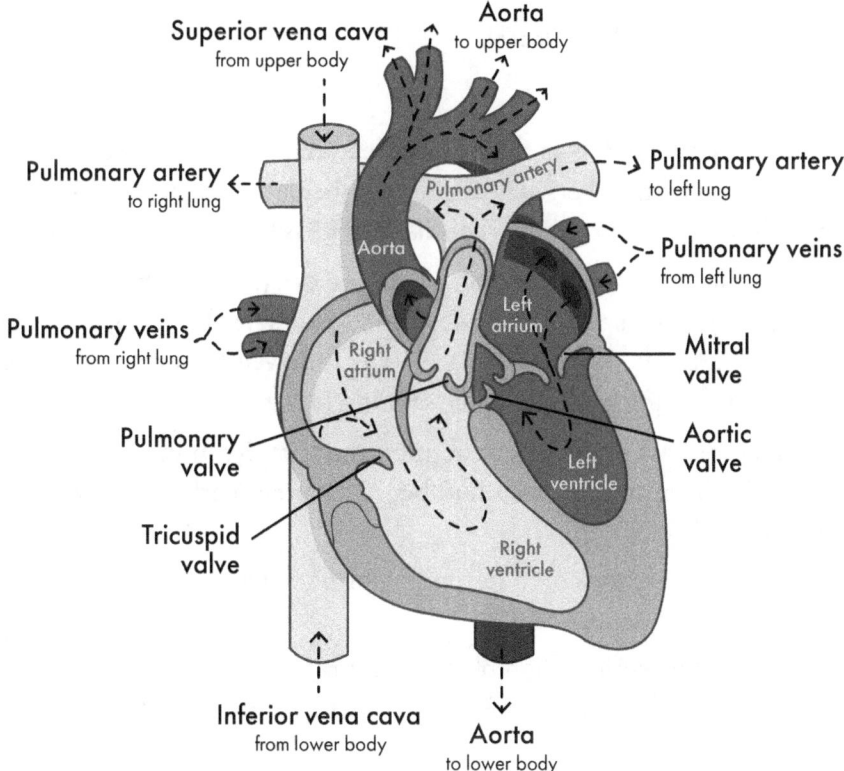

Figure 2.1. Anatomy of the Heart

Blood is circulated by the **heart**, which is a muscular organ. The human heart has four **chambers**: the right and left atria and the right and left ventricles, as shown in Figure 2.1. Each chamber is isolated by **valves** that prevent the backflow of blood once it has passed through.

Blood leaves the heart and travels throughout the body in **blood vessels**, which decrease in diameter as they move away from the heart and toward the tissues and organs. Blood exits the heart through **arteries**, which become **arterioles** and then **capillaries**, the smallest branch of the circulatory system in which gas exchange from blood to tissues occurs. Deoxygenated blood travels back to the heart through **veins**.

> **DID YOU KNOW?**
>
> Many cardiac medications work by relaxing blood vessels (to decrease blood pressure) or constricting blood vessels (to increase blood pressure).

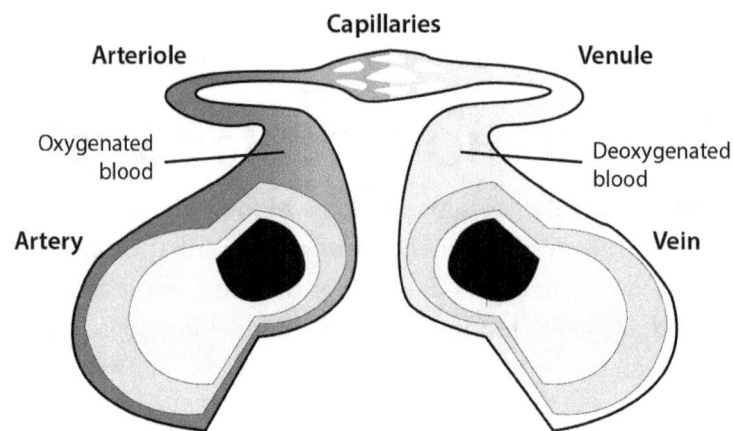

Figure 2.2. Blood Vessels

> **HELPFUL HINT:**
>
> Medications are available that either promote coagulation (e.g., tranexamic acid) or prevent coagulation (e.g., warfarin). Anticoagulants are a high-alert medication because they can result in severe bleeding.

Blood pressure (BP) is the pressure exerted by blood on vessel walls. It is expressed as two numbers. The higher number is the **systolic BP**, which is found when the heart is contracting. The **diastolic BP** is found when the heart relaxes.

Coagulation is the formation of a **blood clot** (thrombus) to stop bleeding. Clots begin when specialized cells called **platelets** clump together to block blood flow. The activation of platelets is followed by a complex cascade of reactions involving proteins called **clotting factors**.

Heart disease is the most common cause of death in the United States. This umbrella term includes a number of different pathologies that cause the heart to weaken or stop:

- **Atherosclerosis** is a hardening or narrowing of the arteries due to plaque deposits.
- **Hypertension** (high blood pressure) is a risk factor for heart disease, stroke, and kidney disease. (**Hypotension** is decreased blood pressure.)

- **Myocardial infarction** (heart attack) is the death of heart tissue, typically caused by lack of blood flow to heart muscles due to a thrombus that blocks blood vessels.
- **Angina** is a small or temporary blockage in the heart's blood vessels that does not lead to tissue death.
- **Heart failure** occurs when either one or both ventricles in the heart cannot efficiently pump blood. It is typically due to another disease or illness, most commonly atherosclerosis.
- **Dysrhythmia** is an abnormal heart rhythm.

TABLE 2.1. Cardiovascular Medications

Medication	Common Brand Names	Adverse Reactions and Interactions
ACE Inhibitors: *hypertension, heart failure*		
lisinopril	Prinivil, Zestril	**BBW**: fetal toxicity
benazepril	Lotensin	**ADR**: cough, hypotension, dizziness
enalapril	Epaned, Vasotec	
ramipril	Altace	**Interactions**: other medications that lower BP
Anticoagulants: *thrombus prevention*		
clopidogrel	Plavix	**BBW**: bleeding, abrupt discontinuation
warfarin	Coumadin; Jantoven	
apixaban	Eliquis	**ADR**: bleeding
rivaroxaban	Xarelto	**Interactions**: omeprazole/esomeprazole (clopidogrel), NSAIDs
aspirin	Bayer	
		Pregnancy: Category X (warfarin, rivaroxaban)
Angiotensin II Receptor Blockers (A2RBs): *hypertension, heart failure*		
losartan	Cozaar	**BBW**: fetal toxicity
losartan and hydrochlorothiazide	Hyzaar	**ADR**: dizziness, headache, fatigue
valsartan	Diovan	**Interactions**: potassium supplements, other drugs that lower BP
valsartan and hydrochlorothiazide	none	
		Pregnancy: Category D

continued on next page

HELPFUL HINT:

The 50 most prescribed medications are highlighted in the tables throughout this chapter.

HELPFUL HINT:

Some types of cholesterol worsen atherosclerosis. Statins (like Crestor and Zocor) lower cholesterol levels and reduce the risk of heart disease.

TABLE 2.1. Cardiovascular Medications (continued)

Medication	Common Brand Names	Adverse Reactions and Interactions
Beta Blockers: *hypertension, angina, migraine, anaphylaxis*		
metoprolol	Toprol-XL, Lopressor	**BBW**: abrupt discontinuation
carvedilol	Coreg	**ADR**: dizziness, fatigue, weight gain
atenolol	Tenormin	**Interactions**: other drugs that lower BP
propranolol	Inderal, Hemangeol	
nebivolol	Bystolic	
timolol	none	
Calcium Channel Blockers: *hypertension, angina, dysrhythmias*		
amlodipine	Amvaz, Norvasc	**ADR**: headache, edema, tiredness, dizziness
diltiazem	Cardizem	**Interactions**: other drugs that lower BP, grapefruit (nifedipine)
nifedipine	Procardia	
verapamil	Calan, Verelan	
amlodipine and benazepril	Lotrel	
HMG-CoA Reductase Inhibitors (statins): *high cholesterol*		
atorvastatin	Lipitor	**ADR**: muscle/joint pain
simvastatin	FloLipid, Zocor	**Interactions**: grapefruit/grapefruit juice, some antibiotics (e.g., cyclosporine, clarithromycin), some antifungals (e.g., itraconazole)
pravastatin	Pravachol	
rosuvastatin	Crestor	
lovastatin	Altoprev	
		Pregnancy: Category X
Other Antilipemics: *high cholesterol*		
fenofibrate	Tricor	**ADR**: abdominal/back pain, muscle/joint pain, headache, nausea, diarrhea
gemfibrozil	Lopid	**Interactions**: grapefruit juice, anticoagulants, other drugs that lower cholesterol, cyclosporine (ezetimibe)
ezetimibe	Zetia	
		Contraindications: liver or gallbladder disease

Medication	Common Brand Names	Adverse Reactions and Interactions
omega-3-acid ethyl esters (fish oil)	none	**ADR**: indigestion **Interactions**: anticoagulants **Contraindications**: fish or shellfish allergy
Vasodilators: *angina, hypertension*		
hydralazine	Apresoline, Dralzine	**ADR**: headache, nausea/vomiting/diarrhea **Interactions**: MAO inhibitors, other drugs that lower BP
isosorbide	none	**ADR**: dizziness, lightheadedness **Interactions**: other drugs that lower BP, sildenafil, alcohol
nitroglycerin	none	
Miscellaneous		
digoxin *dysrhythmias, heart failure*	Digitek, Digox, Lanoxin	**ADR**: nausea, diarrhea, headache, dizziness **Interactions**: macrolide antibiotics, azole antifungals, other antidysrhythmic drugs
amiodarone *dysrhythmias*	Nexterone, Pacerone	**BBW**: pulmonary toxicity **ADR**: nausea, vomiting, dizziness, vision problems **Interactions**: grapefruit juice

BBW: black box warning

ADR: adverse drug reactions

HELPFUL HINT:

Aspirin is an NSAID that also slows platelet aggregation, which prevents clotting. It is often prescribed to prevent thrombus formation (e.g., myocardial infarction, stroke), but can also be taken for pain, fever, or inflammation.

PRACTICE QUESTIONS

1. Drugs with the suffix *–pril* are
   - **A)** calcium channel blockers.
   - **B)** beta blockers.
   - **C)** fibric acid.
   - **D)** ACE inhibitors.

2. Vasodilators lower blood pressure by
   - **A)** reducing cholesterol levels.
   - **B)** preventing coagulation.
   - **C)** relaxing blood vessels.
   - **D)** resetting the heart's rhythm.

3. A pharmacy technician should alert the pharmacist to counsel a patient who has presented prescriptions for both
   A) clopidogrel and furosemide.
   B) nitroglycerin and tadalafil.
   C) atorvastatin and benzonatate.
   D) lisinopril and amoxicillin.

The Respiratory System

The **respiratory system** is responsible for the exchange of gases between the human body and the environment. Oxygen is brought into the body for use in glucose metabolism, and the carbon dioxide created by glucose metabolism is expelled.

Humans primarily take in air through the nose but can also do so through the mouth. Air travels down the **trachea**, **bronchi**, and **bronchioles** into the lungs. The **lungs** contain millions of small **alveoli** where oxygen and carbon dioxide are exchanged between the blood and the air.

HELPFUL HINT:

A **bronchospasm** is a sudden constriction of the bronchioles that restricts airflow and is most commonly caused by asthma or COPD. It is treated with inhaled albuterol, which reopens the airway.

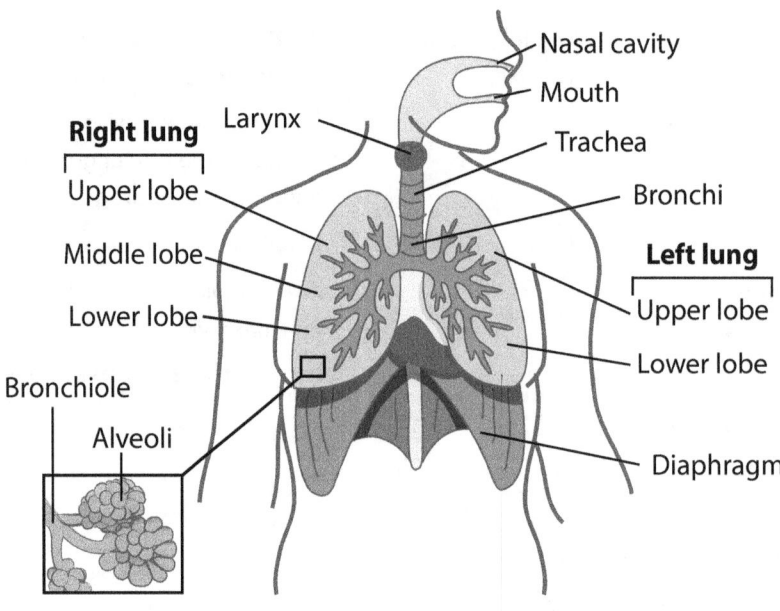

Figure 2.3. The Respiratory System

Respiratory disorders can be caused by infection or by pathophysiological processes that damage respiratory tract tissues:

- **Chronic obstructive pulmonary disease (COPD)** is a progressive restriction of airflow caused by constriction of airways and the destruction of lung tissue.
- **Asthma** is a chronic condition in which the airways narrow, swell, and produce excess mucus.

- Common **respiratory infections** include colds, influenza, and pneumonia. Children are at high risk for some more serious respiratory infections, including pertussis, croup, and bronchiolitis.

Many of the drugs used to treat respiratory problems can be purchased OTC in both adult and child formulations:

- **Expectorants**, such as guaifenesin (Mucinex), help loosen up and thin mucus to make coughs more productive.
- **Antitussives** relieve coughing. Dextromethorphan is a common OTC antitussive.
- **Decongestants** help to relieve stuffy noses. Phenylephrine is the most common drug used in OTC decongestant medicines, although pseudoephedrine (Sudafed, Claritin-D, Allegra-D) is more effective. **Pseudoephedrine** purchases are highly regulated because they can be used to manufacture methamphetamine. (See Chapter 2 for more on pseudoephedrine regulations.)

TABLE 2.2. Respiratory Medications

Medication	Common Brand Names	Adverse Reactions and Interactions
Bronchodilators: *asthma, COPD*		
albuterol	Ventolin HFA, Proventil HFA, Combivent Respimat, DuoNeb, ProAir HFA	**ADR**: headache, fast heart rate, dizziness, sore throat, nasal congestion **Interactions**: beta blockers, digoxin, MAOI, tricyclic antidepressants
montelukast	Singulair	**BBW**: neuropsychiatric symptoms **ADR**: respiratory infection, fever, headache, sore throat, cough
tiotropium	Spiriva	**ADR**: sore throat, cough, dry mouth, headache, visual disturbances **Interactions**: other anticholinergics
ipratropium and albuterol	Combivent Respimat	**ADR**: upper respiratory infection, sore throat, cough, headache **Interactions**: beta blockers, digoxin, MAOI, tricyclic antidepressants, other anticholinergics

continued on next page

TABLE 2.2. Respiratory Medications (continued)		
Medication	**Common Brand Names**	**Adverse Reactions and Interactions**
Bronchodilators and Corticosteroids: *asthma, COPD*		
fluticasone and salmeterol	Advair Diskus/HFA, AirDuo RespiClick	**BBW**: worsening asthma symptoms (formoterol) **ADR**: respiratory infection, sore throat, oral candidiasis, cough, headache, nausea, vomiting **Interactions**: beta blockers, diuretics, MAOI
budesonide and formoterol	Symbicort	
Miscellaneous		
benzonatate *cough*	Tessalon	**ADR:** sedation, headache, congestion, "chilly" sensation in chest **Counseling**: Swallow capsule whole.

BBW: black box warning
ADR: adverse drug reactions

PRACTICE QUESTIONS

4. Which of the following medications may be prescribed for asthma?
   A) montelukast
   B) carvedilol
   C) doxycycline
   D) zolpidem

5. Which auxiliary label should be affixed to a prescription bottle of benzonatate?
   A) Do not take this drug if you become pregnant.
   B) Do not eat grapefruit or drink grapefruit juice while taking this medication.
   C) Keep refrigerated.
   D) Do not crush or chew; swallow whole.

The Nervous System

The **nervous system** processes external stimuli and sends signals throughout the body. **Nerve cells**, or **neurons**, communicate through electrical impulses and allow the body to process and respond to stimuli. **Neurotransmitters**, such as serotonin, dopamine, and histamines, are molecules that carry communication between nerves. Many medications act by mimicking neurotransmitters (e.g., opioids) or by altering their levels (e.g., selective serotonin reuptake inhibitors).

The **central nervous system (CNS)** consists of the brain and spinal cord. It is where information is processed and stored. The **peripheral nervous system (PNS)** transmits information throughout the body using electrical signals.

The **autonomic nervous system** controls involuntary actions that occur in the body, such as respiration, heartbeat, digestive processes, and more. The **somatic nervous system** is responsible for the body's ability to control skeletal muscles and voluntary movement as well as some involuntary reflexes.

The autonomic nervous system is further broken down into the **sympathetic nervous system** and **parasympathetic nervous system**. The sympathetic nervous system is responsible for the body's reaction to stress. It induces a "fight-or-flight" response that increases heart rate and blood pressure. In contrast, the parasympathetic nervous system is stimulated by the body's need for rest or recovery.

HELPFUL HINT:

Serotonin syndrome is a set of symptoms (including fever, fast heart rate, and agitation) caused by excess serotonin. It may occur with the use of any serotonergic drug but is more common when multiple serotonergic drugs are combined.

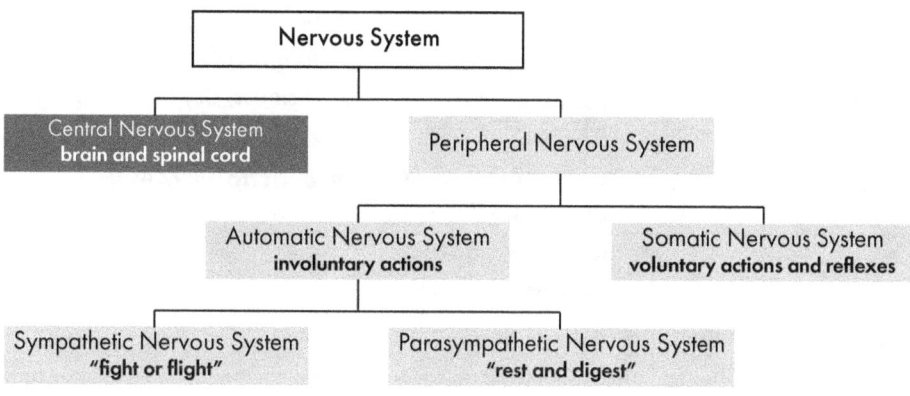

Figure 2.4. Divisions of the Nervous System

Many common nervous system disorders are caused by chronic degeneration of nervous system tissue. Disruptions in hormone levels, electrical activity, or blood flow in the brain can also cause neurological symptoms that can signal the following conditions:

- **Mental health conditions**, which may be treated with medications and include anxiety, depression, bipolar disorder, schizophrenia, attention deficit hyperactivity disorder (ADHD), and post-traumatic stress disorder (PTSD).
- **Migraines** are intense headaches accompanied by nausea and light sensitivity.
- **Seizure** is caused by abnormal electrical discharges in the brain that disrupt brain function and may cause convulsions. **Epilepsy** is a condition characterized by recurrent seizures.

HELPFUL HINT:

Sympathomimetic drugs mimic adrenaline (epinephrine) and stimulate the autonomic nervous system. They are used for shock, allergic reactions, and cardiac arrest.

Parasympathomimetic drugs mimic acetylcholine, a neurotransmitter, and activate the parasympathetic nervous system. Nicotine is a naturally occurring parasympathetic compound.

- **Alzheimer's disease** is characterized by the loss of memory and deteriorating cognitive function, usually later in life, due to the degeneration of neurons in the brain.
- Other degenerative nerve diseases include **multiple sclerosis (MS)**, **amyotrophic lateral sclerosis (ALS)**, and **Parkinson's disease.**
- **Stroke**, or **cardiovascular accident (CVA)**, occurs when a blood vessel in the brain ruptures or is blocked. The resulting lack of oxygen to the brain can result in significant brain damage or death.
- **Peripheral neuropathy** is impairment of the peripheral nerves. It is often caused by diabetes (diabetic neuropathy).

TABLE 2.3. Antidepressants

Drug Class	Common Drugs	Adverse Reactions and Interactions
dopamine/norepinephrine-reuptake inhibitors	bupropion (Wellbutrin, Zyban)	**BBW**: increased risk of suicidal thoughts/behaviors **ADR**: insomnia, headache, agitation, dizziness, drowsiness, dry mouth, nausea, vomiting **Interactions**: MAOIs
selective serotonin reuptake inhibitors (SSRIs)	sertraline (Zoloft), escitalopram (Lexapro), citalopram (Celexa), trazodone (Desyrel), fluoxetine (Prozac), paroxetine (Paxil)	
serotonin-norepinephrine reuptake inhibitors (SNRIs)	duloxetine (Cymbalta), venlafaxine (Effexor)	
tricyclic antidepressants	amitriptyline (Amitid, Amitril, Elavil, Endep), nortriptyline (Pamelor)	

BBW: black box warning
ADR: adverse drug reactions

TABLE 2.4. Nervous System Medications

Medication	Common Brand Names	Adverse Reactions and Interactions
Anticonvulsants (*also indicated for mood stabilization): *seizures, nerve pain*		
gabapentin	Gralise, Neurontin	**ADR**: drowsiness, dizziness, edema, angioedema (pregabalin), suicidal thoughts, emotional changes
pregabalin	Lyrica	
levetiracetam	Keppra, Roweepra, Spritam	**Interactions**: alcohol, other CNS depressants
lamotrigine*	Lamictal, Subvenite	**BBW**: skin rashes **ADR**: dizziness, headache, nausea, visual disturbances
carbamazepine*	Carbatrol, Epitol, Equetro, Tegretol	**Interactions**: other anticonvulsants, other CNS depressants, hormonal contraceptives **Pregnancy**: Category D (carbamazepine)
topiramate	Topamax	**ADR**: drowsiness, dizziness, cognitive problems, tingling, anorexia **Interactions**: other anticonvulsants, other CNS depressants **Pregnancy**: Category D
valproate (divalproex)*	Depakote	**BBW**: hepatotoxicity **ADR**: drowsiness, dizziness, headache, nausea and vomiting, visual disturbances **Interactions:** other anticonvulsants, other CNS depressants **Pregnancy**: Category D
phenytoin	Dilantin	**ADR:** visual disturbances, slurred speech, decreased coordination, confusion **Interactions**: oral contraceptives (reduces efficacy), some anticoagulants, statins **Pregnancy**: Category D

continued on next page

TABLE 2.4. Nervous System Medications (continued)

Medication	Common Brand Names	Adverse Reactions and Interactions
Atypical Antipsychotics: *mood disorders, schizophrenia*		
quetiapine fumarate	Seroquel	**BBW**: increased risk of suicidal thoughts/behaviors
aripiprazole	Abilify	**ADR**: drowsiness, dry mouth, dizziness, weakness, movement disorders
risperidone	Perseris, Risperdal	
Treatment for ADHD (†drug also indicated for hypertension)		
amphetamine and dextroamphetamine	Adderall	**BBW**: potential for abuse/dependence
methylphenidate	Ritalin	**ADR**: insomnia, headache, fast heartbeat, mood changes, decreased appetite, vomiting, dry mouth
dexmethylphenidate	Focalin	**Interactions**: MAOIs
lisdexamfetamine	Vyvanse	
clonidine†	Catapres, Duraclon, Kapvay	**ADR**: drowsiness, headache, fatigue, dizziness, dry mouth, skin rash
guanfacine†	Intuniv	**Interactions**: other CNS depressants
atomoxetine	Strattera	**BBW**: increased risk of suicidal thoughts/behaviors
		ADR: headache, insomnia, dry mouth, nausea, skin rash
		Interactions: MAOIs
Benzodiazepines: *anxiety, seizures, muscle spasms, insomnia, alcohol withdrawal*		
alprazolam	Xanax	**BBW**: risk of respiratory depression and death when used with opioids; risk of abuse/dependence
clonazepam	Klonopin	
lorazepam	Ativan	**ADR**: drowsiness, sedation, fatigue, memory impairment
diazepam	Diastat, Valium, Valtoco	
temazepam	Restoril	**Interactions**: alcohol, other CNS depressants

Medication	Common Brand Names	Adverse Reactions and Interactions
Nonsteroidal Anti-inflammatory Drugs (NSAIDs): *pain, fever*		
ibuprofen	Advil, Motrin	**BBW**: cardiovascular thrombotic events, GI bleeding **ADR**: abdominal pain, diarrhea, upset stomach **Pregnancy**: Category D (> 30 weeks)
naproxen	Aleve	
diclofenac	Cambia, Zipsor, Zorvolex	
celecoxib	Celebrex	
meloxicam	Mobic	
Opioids: *pain*		
acetaminophen and hydrocodone	Norco, Vicodin, Lortab	**BBW**: addiction, misuse, and abuse; respiratory depression; accidental ingestion; neonatal opioid withdrawal syndrome; risk from use with other CNS depressants **ADR**: constipation, lightheadedness, dizziness, nausea and vomiting **Interactions**: MAOI, serotonergic drugs, alcohol, other CNS depressants **Counseling**: may impair the ability to perform potentially hazardous activities
tramadol	Ultram	
oxycodone	Xtampza, OxyContin	
hydrocodone	Hysingla, Zohydro	
morphine	Arymo, Duramorph, Infumorph, Kadian, Mitigo, MS Contin	
Other Analgesics: *pain, fever*		
acetaminophen	Tylenol	**BBW:** hepatotoxicity **ADR**: nausea and vomiting, lightheadedness (butalbital), sedation (butalbital) **Contraindications**: hepatic impairment
butalbital and acetaminophen	Allzital, Bupap	
Treatment for Parkinson's Disease		
ropinirole	Requip	**ADR**: drowsiness, dizziness, hypotension, nausea, vomiting **Interactions**: MAOIs (carbidopa and levodopa)
pramipexole	Mirapex	
carbidopa and levodopa	Duopa, Rytary, Sinemet	
Treatment for Alzheimer's Disease		
donepezil	Aricept	**ADR**: nausea, diarrhea, insomnia, mood changes
memantine	Namenda	

continued on next page

TABLE 2.4. Nervous System Medications (continued)		
Medication	Common Brand Names	Adverse Reactions and Interactions
Other Psychiatric Drugs		
buspirone *generalized anxiety disorder*	Buspar	**ADR**: dizziness, drowsiness **Interactions**: alcohol
mirtazapine *mood disorders*	Remeron	**BBW**: increased risk of suicidal thoughts/behaviors **ADR**: drowsiness, dry mouth, weight gain, constipation **Interactions**: alcohol, other CNS depressants
lithium *bipolar disorder*	Lithobid	**BBW**: close monitoring required to prevent toxicity **ADR**: tremor, frequent urination, thirst, nausea **Interactions**: NSAIDs **Pregnancy**: Category D
Miscellaneous		
zolpidem *sleep disorders*	Ambien	**BBW**: complex sleep behaviors **ADR**: headache, drowsiness, dizziness **Interactions**: other CNS depressants
sumatriptan *migraine or cluster headache (acute)*	Imitrex	**ADR**: tingling, dizziness **Interactions**: other triptans, ergot-containing drugs **Contraindications**: MAOI use
latanoprost *elevated intraocular pressure*	Xalatan, Xelpros	**ADR**: pain, stinging, or redness in eyes **Counseling**: Wait 15 minutes after application to insert contact lenses.
brimonidine *rosacea, elevated intraocular pressure*	Mirvaso	**ADR** (topical): flushing, redness **ADR** (ophthalmic): dry mouth; pain, stinging, or redness in eyes
BBW: black box warning **ADR**: adverse drug reactions		

PRACTICE QUESTIONS

6. Which of the following would be prescribed for a patient to slow the progression of Alzheimer's disease?

    A) donepezil

    B) ropinirole

    C) diazepam

    D) benazepril

7. Which drug class suffix refers to benzodiazepines?

    A) –artan

    B) –pam

    C) –ine

    D) –olol

8. Which auxiliary label should be affixed to a prescription bottle of buspirone?

    A) Do not eat grapefruit or drink grapefruit juice while taking this medication.

    B) Medication should be taken with plenty of water.

    C) Do not take this drug if you become pregnant.

    D) May cause drowsiness.

The Immune System

The human **immune system** protects the body against bacteria and viruses that cause disease. The immune system includes both innate and adaptive systems. The **innate immune system** includes nonspecific defenses that work against a wide range of infectious agents. These nonspecific defenses include barriers to entry (e.g., skin), inflammation, and white blood cells (WBCs).

The **adaptive immune system** "learns" to respond only to specific invaders. The adaptive immune system relies on molecules called **antigens** that appear on the surface of pathogens to which the system has previously been exposed. **T cells** and **B cells** are activated by these antigens and destroy the invading cells. During an infection, **memory B cells** specific to an antigen are created, allowing the immune system to respond more quickly if the infection appears again.

Immune system disorders include autoimmune diseases, cancers, and infections. **Infections** can be caused by many different infectious agents, each of which are treated with a different type of medication.

> **DID YOU KNOW?**
>
> Memory B cells are the underlying mechanisms behind some vaccines, which introduce a harmless version of a pathogen into the body to activate the body's adaptive immune response.

TABLE 2.5. Infectious Agents

Agent	Description	Common Infections	Treatment
Bacteria	single-celled prokaryotic organisms	strep throat, urinary tract infections, wound infections, many food-borne illnesses	antibiotics

continued on next page

TABLE 2.5. Infectious Agents (continued)

Agent	Description	Common Infections	Treatment
Viruses	composed of a nucleic acid (DNA or RNA) wrapped in a protein capsid; they invade host cells and hijack cell machinery to reproduce	varicella (chicken pox), herpes zoster (shingles), herpes simplex virus, influenza, human immunodeficiency virus (HIV)	antivirals
Protozoa	single-celled eukaryotic organisms	giardia (an intestinal infection), trichomoniasis (a vaginal infection)	antiprotozoal drugs
Fungi	group of eukaryotic organisms that includes yeasts, molds, and mushrooms	athlete's foot, ringworm, oral and vaginal yeast infections	antifungals
Parasite	organism that lives in or on the human body and uses its resources	worms (e.g., tapeworms), flukes, lice, ticks	antiparasitic drugs

HELPFUL HINT:

Histamines are biological molecules that mediate immune response and act as neurotransmitters. Many OTC allergy medications contain **antihistamines** to block histamine activity. Antihistamines can also be used as sedatives, antiemetics, and antipsychotics.

The immune system of individuals with an **autoimmune disease** will attack healthy tissues. Autoimmune diseases (and the tissues they attack) include:

- psoriasis (skin)
- rheumatoid arthritis (joints)
- multiple sclerosis (nerve cells)
- lupus (kidneys, lungs, and skin)

Allergies are intense reactions by the immune system to harmless particles (e.g., dust, dog hair). The overreaction of the immune system can be mild (runny nose and watery eyes) or life-threatening (anaphylactic shock).

Immune system cancers include **Hodgkin's lymphoma** and **leukemia**.

TABLE 2.6. Antibiotics

Antibiotic Class	Common Drugs	Adverse Reactions and Interactions
penicillins	amoxicillin (Augmentin), penicillin	**BBW**: tendon rupture (fluroquinolones)
macrolides	azithromycin (Zithromax), clarithromycin, erythromycin	**ADR**: diarrhea, nausea, photosensitivity (tetracyclines), tooth discoloration (tetracyclines)
tetracyclines	doxycycline, tetracycline	**Interactions**: anticoagulants, antidiabetics
lincosamide	clindamycin (Cleocin)	
cephalosporin	cefdinir, cephalexin (Keflex)	
fluoroquinolones (quinolones)	ciprofloxacin, levofloxacin (Levaquin), moxifloxacin (Avelox), ofloxacin (Floxin)	
sulfonamide	trimethoprim-sulfamethoxazole, co-trimoxazole (Bactrim)	
N/A	nitrofurantoin *urinary tract infections*	
aminoglycosides	gentamicin (Garamycin), tobramycin (Tobrex)	**BBW**: nephrotoxicity and neurotoxicity **ADR**: respiratory depression, lethargy, confusion, visual disturbances
N/A	metronidazole (Flagyl) *bacterial and protozoal infections*	**ADR**: headache, nausea, vaginitis **Contraindications**: alcohol use

BBW: black box warning
ADR: adverse drug reactions

CONTINUE

DRUG EFFECTS AND INDICATIONS

TABLE 2.7. Immune Medications

Medication	Common Brand Names	Indications	Adverse Reactions and Interactions
Antivirals			
valacyclovir	Valtrex	herpes zoster	**ADR**: headache, nausea, abdominal pain
oseltamivir	Tamiflu	influenza	
acyclovir	Zovirax	herpes simplex virus, herpes zoster, varicella	
Corticosteroids			
fluticasone	Flonase (nasal), Flovent (oral inhalant)	asthma, COPD (oral inhalation) allergies (nasal) dermatitis (topical) inflammation, autoimmune conditions (oral tablet)	**ADR** (nasal/oral inhalation): headache, nasal/throat irritation, nose bleed, cough, worsening of infections **ADR** (oral tablet): fluid retention, hyper/hypoglycemia, hypertension, changes in behavior/mood, weight gain, worsening of infections **Interactions** (oral tablet): antidiabetics, anticoagulants, oral contraceptives, NSAIDs
prednisone	Sterapred (oral tablet)		
triamcinolone	Nasacort (nasal)		
prednisolone	Millipred (oral tablet), Orapred ODT (oral tablet)		
beclomethasone	QVAR RediHaler (oral inhalant), QNASL (nasal)		
hydrocortisone	Cortaid (topical)		
methylprednisolone	Medrol (oral tablet)		
budesonide	Rhinocort (nasal), Entocort (oral tablet)		
mometasone	Asmanex (oral inhalant)		

Medication	Common Brand Names	Indications	Adverse Reactions and Interactions
Histamine H1 Antagonists			
loratadine	Alavert, Claritin	allergies	**ADR**: drowsiness, nasal/throat irritation, dry mouth, muscle pain **Interactions**: other CNS depressants
cetirizine	Zyrtec		
levocetirizine	Xyzal Allergy		
promethazine	Phenergan, Promethegan	allergies, nausea/vomiting, motion sickness	
hydroxyzine	Vistaril	anxiety, allergies, nausea/vomiting	
meclizine	Dramamine	motion sickness	
Immunosuppressants			
methotrexate	Otrexup, Rasuvo, Trexall, Xatmep	cancer, arthritis, psoriasis	**BBW**: fetal toxicity, severe or fatal adverse reactions **ADR**: nausea, fatigue, stomach upset, increased risk of infection **Pregnancy**: Category X
adalimumab	Humira	Crohn's disease, rheumatoid arthritis, psoriasis, ulcerative colitis	**BBW**: risk of serious infection **ADR**: infection, headache, rash
Miscellaneous			
hydroxychloroquine	Plaquenil	lupus, malaria, rheumatoid arthritis	**ADR**: blurred vision, blistering or peeling of skin, dizziness, nausea, vomiting **Interactions**: digoxin, insulin, antidiabetic drugs, antiepileptics

continued on next page

TABLE 2.7. Immune Medications (continued)

Medication	Common Brand Names	Indications	Adverse Reactions and Interactions
Miscellaneous			
fluconazole	Diflucan	fungal infections	**ADR**: headache, nausea, abdominal pain **Interactions**: antidiabetics, anticoagulants, benzodiazepines

BBW: black box warning
ADR: adverse drug reactions

PRACTICE QUESTIONS

9. Patients who have previously had an allergic reaction to azithromycin should have a note in their profile about an allergy to which class of antibiotics?

    A) macrolides
    B) tetracyclines
    C) quinolones
    D) penicillins

10. Which of the following medications is an immunosuppressant?

    A) valacyclovir
    B) methotrexate
    C) cefdinir
    D) carbamazepine

The Musculoskeletal System

The skeletal system is made up of over 200 different **bones**, which are stiff connective tissues in the human body. The bones have many functions, including

- protecting internal organs,
- synthesizing blood cells,
- storing necessary minerals, and
- providing the muscular system with leverage to create movement.

The point at which a bone is attached to another bone is called a **joint**. Various connective tissues join the parts of the skeleton together to other systems, including ligaments, tendons, and cartilage.

The primary function of the **muscular system** is movement: muscles contract and relax, resulting in motion. The muscular system consists of three types of muscle: cardiac, visceral, and skeletal.

- **Cardiac muscle** is only found in the heart. It contracts involuntarily, creating the heartbeat and pumping blood.
- **Visceral**, or **smooth muscle** tissue is found in many of the body's essential organs, including the stomach and intestines. It contracts involuntarily to move nutrients, blood, and other substances throughout the body.
- **Skeletal muscle** is responsible for voluntary movement and, as the name suggests, is linked to the skeletal system.

Most musculoskeletal system disorders are caused by the degeneration of tissue or damage to muscles or bones from trauma.

- **Arthritis** is inflammation in joints.
- **Gout** is inflammation and pain in joints caused by a buildup of uric acid.
- **Osteoporosis** is poor bone mineral density due to the loss or lack of production of calcium content in bone cells, which makes bones more likely to fracture.
- **Osteomyelitis** is an infection in the bone.
- **Muscular dystrophy (MD)** is a genetically inherited condition that results in progressive muscle wasting, which limits movement and can cause respiratory and cardiovascular difficulties.
- Muscle **cramps** are involuntary muscle contractions (or **spasms**) that cause intense pain.

TABLE 2.8. Musculoskeletal Medications

Medication	Common Brand Names	Adverse Reactions and Interactions
Muscle Relaxants and Antispasmodics: *muscle spasm*		
cyclobenzaprine	Flexeril	**BBW**: abrupt discontinuation (baclofen)
tizanidine	Zanaflex	**ADR**: drowsiness, dizziness, dry mouth, nausea and vomiting
baclofen	Gablofen, Lioresal, Ozobax	**Interactions**: alcohol, other CNS depressants, MAOIs, serotonergic drugs
methocarbamol	Robaxin	**Contraindications**: use of MAOIs (cyclobenzaprine), use of ciprofloxacin or fluvoxamine (tizanidine)

continued on next page

TABLE 2.8. Musculoskeletal Medications

Medication	Common Brand Names	Adverse Reactions and Interactions
Miscellaneous		
alendronate osteoporosis	Binosto, Fosamax	**ADR**: headache, upset stomach, musculoskeletal pain **Interactions**: calcium supplements, antacids, NSAIDs **Counseling**: Take with water 30 minutes before first food of the day.

BBW: black box warning
ADR: adverse drug reactions

PRACTICE QUESTIONS

11. A patient presents a new prescription for cyclobenzaprine. The pharmacy technician should alert the pharmacist to a potential interaction if the patient is currently prescribed which of the following medications?

    A) Nexium
    B) Januvia
    C) Zoloft
    D) Ortho Tri-Cyclen

12. Which auxiliary label should be affixed to a prescription bottle of alendronate?

    A) Do not take antacids within one hour of this medication.
    B) Do not eat grapefruit or drink grapefruit juice while taking this medication.
    C) Do not take this drug if you become pregnant.
    D) Do not drink alcoholic beverages while taking this medication.

The Digestive System

The **digestive system** is responsible for the breakdown and absorption of food necessary to power the body. The digestive system starts at the **mouth**. Chewed and lubricated food travels from the mouth through the **esophagus**, which leads to the **stomach**. In the stomach, food is mixed with powerful acidic liquid for further digestion. The resulting **chyme** travels to the **small intestine**, where nutrients are absorbed.

The small intestine then transports food to the **large intestine**, which absorbs water and produces feces. At the end of the large intestine are the **rectum** and **anus**, which are responsible for the storage and removal of feces.

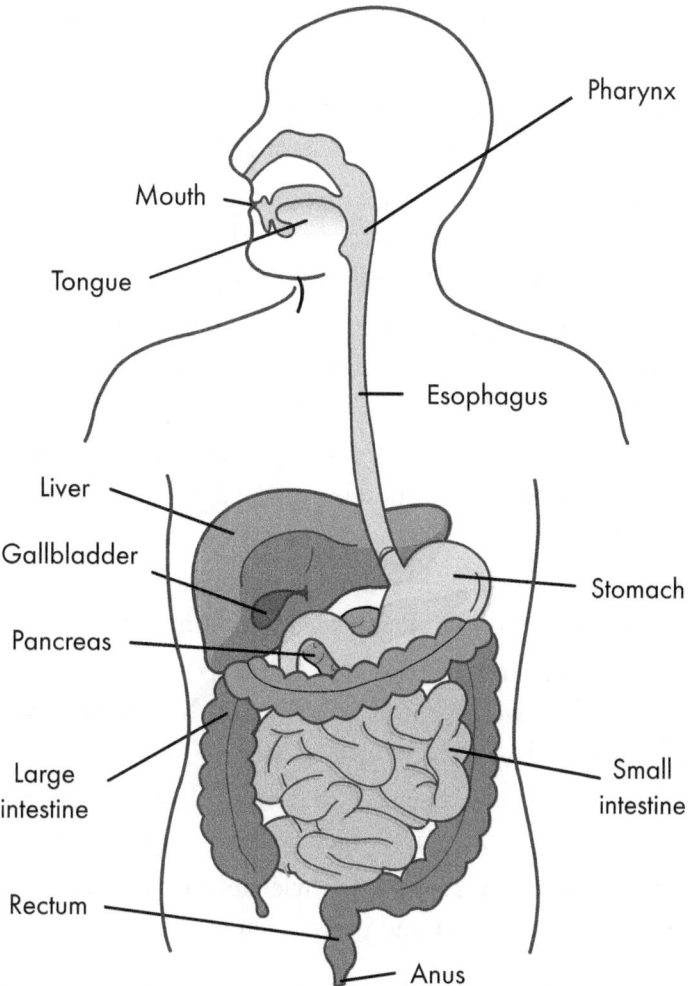

Figure 2.5. The Digestive System

The digestive system also includes accessory organs that aid in digestion:

- **salivary glands**: produce saliva, which begins the process of breaking down starches and fats
- **liver**: produces bile, which helps break down fat in the small intestine (The liver also plays an important role in the metabolism of many proteins and carbohydrates.)
- **gallbladder**: stores bile
- **pancreas**: produces pancreatic juice, which neutralizes the acidity of chyme and digestive enzymes

Common gastrointestinal disorders include infections, autoimmune disorders, and liver disease:

- **Heartburn** occurs when stomach acid moves into the esophagus.
- **Food poisoning** occurs when an acute infection (bacterial or viral) affects the lining of the digestive system and the resulting immune response triggers the body to void the contents of the digestive system.

- **Irritable bowel syndrome (IBS)** refers to recurrent abdominal pain, bloating, diarrhea, or constipation.
- **Crohn's disease** is an inflammatory bowel disorder that occurs when the immune system attacks the digestive system.
- **Cirrhosis** is a chronic disease in which the liver has permanent scarring and loses cells, impairing normal functioning. The most common cause of cirrhosis is alcohol abuse.

Many of the drugs used for the digestive system are available OTC and may alleviate digestive symptoms developed from heartburn, diet, gas, nausea, and food poisoning:

- **Antacids** are used primarily for heartburn but also as a calcium supplement. Some common brands of antacids are Tums and Rolaids.
- **Antidiarrheal drugs** help reduce or stop diarrhea. A common OTC antidiarrheal drug is loperamide (Imodium A-D).
- **Laxatives** treat constipation. OTC laxatives include bisacodyl (Dulcolax), polyethylene glycol (MiraLAX), and sennoside (Milk of Magnesia, Ex-Lax).
- **Stool softeners**, like docusate sodium (Colace), soften the stool and do not cause as much urgency and cramping as laxatives do.
- **Fiber supplements**, such as methylcellulose (Metamucil), help to keep the body regular and prevent constipation.

TABLE 2.9. Digestive Medications

Medication	Common Brand Names	Adverse Reactions and Interactions
Antiemetics: *nausea and vomiting*		
ondansetron	Zofran	**ADR**: headache, constipation, and diarrhea **Interactions**: serotonergic drugs
prochlorperazine	Compro	**ADR**: drowsiness, dizziness, blurred vision, hypotension **Interactions**: other CNS depressants
doxylamine and pyridoxine	Diclegis	**ADR**: drowsiness **Interactions**: other CNS depressants

Medication	Common Brand Names	Adverse Reactions and Interactions
Histamine H2 Antagonist: *heartburn, GERD*		
ranitidine	Zantac	**ADR**: headache, constipation, diarrhea, nausea, vomiting **Interactions**: warfarin
famotidine	Pepcid	
Proton Pump Inhibitors: *heartburn, GERD*		
omeprazole	Prilosec	**ADR**: headache, abdominal pain, nausea, diarrhea, vomiting **Interactions**: digoxin, clopidogrel, benzodiazepines, warfarin
pantoprazole	Protonix	
esomeprazole	Nexium	
lansoprazole	Prevacid	
Supplements		
potassium	none	**ADR**: nausea, vomiting, flatulence, abdominal pain/discomfort, and diarrhea **Interactions**: potassium-sparing diuretics
ergocalciferol (vitamin D)	Deltalin, Drisdol, Ergocal	none
ferrous sulfate (iron)	none	**BBW**: accidental overdose in children **ADR**: darkened stool, abdominal pain, heartburn, constipation, nausea, vomiting
folic acid	FA-8	none
cyanocobalamin (vitamin B-12)	none	**ADR**: headache, infection, weakness
Miscellaneous		
dicyclomine *irritable bowel syndrome*	Bentyl	**ADR**: dry mouth, nausea, vomiting, constipation, dizziness, blurred vision **Interactions**: other anticholinergics **Counseling**: may impair the ability to perform potentially hazardous activities

continued on next page

TABLE 2.9. Digestive Medications (continued)

Medication	Common Brand Names	Adverse Reactions and Interactions
phentermine *obesity*	Adipex-P, Lomaira	**ADR**: restlessness, dizziness, dry mouth **Interactions**: alcohol, MAOI, insulin **Pregnancy**: Category X **Counseling**: may impair the ability to perform potentially hazardous activities

BBW: black box warning
ADR: adverse drug reactions

PRACTICE QUESTIONS

13. Antiemetics are taken to prevent
    A) vomiting.
    B) diarrhea.
    C) constipation.
    D) gas.

14. Which of the following medications is a proton pump inhibitor?
    A) misoprostol
    B) famotidine
    C) sucralfate
    D) pantoprazole

HELPFUL HINT:

One of the most prescribed medications in the US is levothyroxine (Synthroid), a manufactured form of the hormone *thyroxine*. It is prescribed for patients with underactive thyroids.

The Endocrine System

The endocrine system is made up of **glands** that regulate numerous processes throughout the body by secreting chemical messengers called **hormones**. Hormones regulate a wide variety of bodily processes, including metabolism, growth and development, sexual reproduction, the sleep-wake cycle, and hunger. Important endocrine organs and their functions are described below:

- The **pancreas** produces insulin and glucagon, which regulate blood sugar levels.
- The **thyroid gland** controls metabolism.
- The **pituitary gland** controls growth and basic functions, such as temperature and blood pressure.
- The **adrenal glands** produce adrenaline (epinephrine).

- The **parathyroid gland** controls calcium and phosphate levels in the blood.
- The **ovaries** (female) and **testes** (male) produce hormones related to sexual functioning.

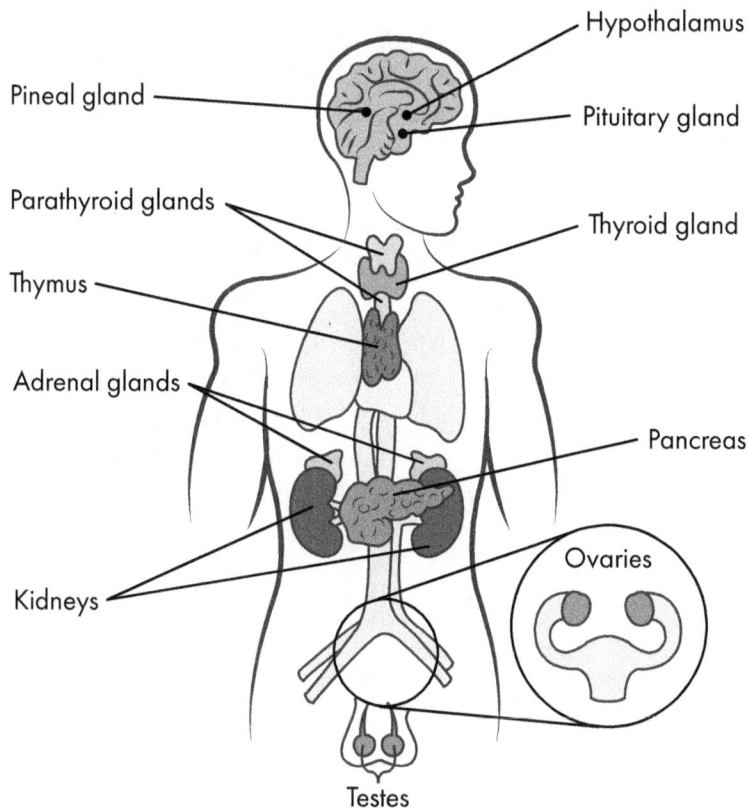

Figure 2.6. The Endocrine System

Disruptions in hormone production can affect multiple systems throughout the body:

- **Diabetes mellitus** is a metabolic disorder that affects the body's ability to produce and use **insulin**, a hormone that regulates the cellular uptake of glucose (sugar). Diabetes mellitus is classified as type 1 or type 2.
- **Hypothyroidism** occurs when insufficient thyroxine is produced and can result in fatigue, weight gain, and cold intolerance.
- **Hyperthyroidism** occurs when too much thyroxine is produced and can cause anxiety, mood swings, weight loss, and palpitations. Grave's disease is a specific cause of hyperthyroidism common in women over 40.
- **Adrenal insufficiency** (Addison's disease) is the chronic underproduction of steroids.

- **Cushing syndrome** is caused by exposure to high cortisol levels over an extended period of time due to overproduction of cortisol from the adrenal glands.
- **Hypercalcemia** is a treatable condition in which the parathyroid glands become overactive, causing the blood to have a high calcium level.

TABLE 2.10. Endocrine Medications

Medication	Common Brand Names	Adverse Reactions and Interactions
Antidiabetics: *diabetes*		
metformin	Fortamet, Glucophage	**ADR:** hypoglycemia, diarrhea, nausea, headache **Interactions:** alcohol, miconazole (glimepiride) **Counseling:** Take with food (metformin); Take 30 minutes before food (glipizide).
glipizide	Glucotrol	
glimepiride	Amaryl	
sitagliptin	Januvia	
pioglitazone	Actos	
liraglutide	Saxenda, Victoza	
glyburide	Glynase	
canagliflozin	Invokana	
linagliptin	Tradjenta	
sitagliptin and metformin	Janumet	
Insulins: *diabetes*		
insulin glargine	Lantus	**ADR:** hypoglycemia, injection site reactions **Interactions:** other insulin products
insulin aspart	Fiasp, Novolog	
insulin human (insulin regular)	Humulin, Novolin	
insulin detemir	Levemir	
insulin lispro	ADMELOG, Humalog	
Miscellaneous		
Levothyroxine (synthetic thyroxine) *hypothyroidism*	Levoxyl, Synthroid, Tirosint, Unithroid	**BBW:** weight reduction **ADR:** dysrhythmias, trouble breathing, headache, nervousness, irritability, weight loss **Interactions:** iron supplement, calcium supplement, antacids **Counseling:** Take with water 30 minutes before eating.

Medication	Common Brand Names	Adverse Reactions and Interactions
propylthiouracil *hyperthyroidism*	none	**BBW**: hepatotoxicity **ADR**: upset stomach, nausea, vomiting, headache, drowsiness, hair loss **Interactions**: anticoagulants, beta blockers **Pregnancy**: Category D

BBW: black box warning
ADR: adverse drug reactions

PRACTICE QUESTIONS

15. Which of the following is a common adverse reaction to levothyroxine?
    A) drowsiness
    B) constipation
    C) weight loss
    D) dry mouth

16. Which of the following is NOT a type of manufactured insulin?
    A) lispro
    B) detemir
    C) glargine
    D) dulaglutide

The Urinary System

The **urinary system** excretes water and waste from the body and is crucial for maintaining the balance of water and salt in the blood (also called electrolyte balance). The main organs of the urinary system are the **kidneys**, which perform several important functions:

- filter waste from the blood
- maintain the electrolyte balance in the blood
- regulate blood volume, pressure, and pH

Nephrons in the kidneys filter the blood and excrete the waste products as **urine**. Urine then passes through the ureters into the urinary bladder and exits through the **urethra**.

Common urinary system conditions that may require medication include infections, incontinence, and fluid/electrolyte imbalances:

- **Urinary incontinence**—loss of bladder control—is a common problem, especially in women over 40, and can range from slight to severe incontinence.

HELPFUL HINT:

Diuretics alter the function of nephrons, causing the kidneys to absorb and excrete more water. They are used to treat **edema** (swelling due to fluid buildup) caused by heart, lung, or kidney disease.

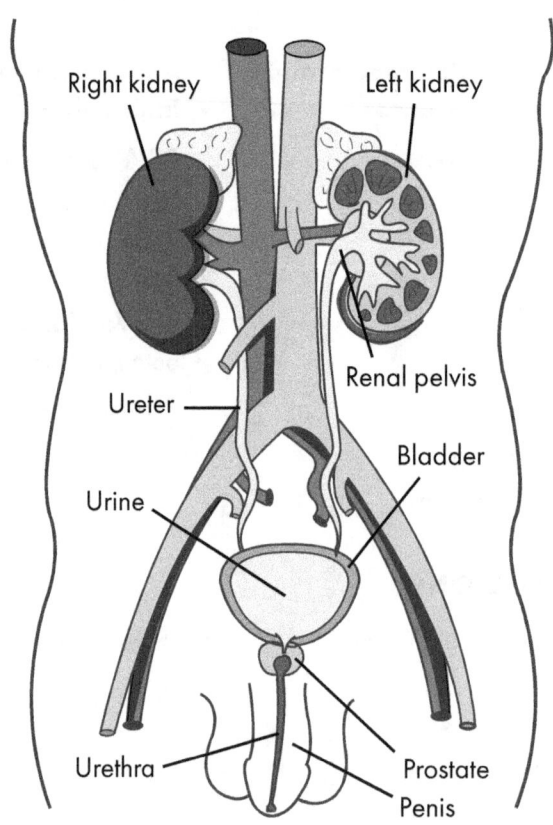

Figure 2.7. The Urinary System

- **Renal calculi** (kidney stones) are hardened mineral deposits that form in the kidneys and cause pain and urinary symptoms.
- **Urinary tract infections (UTIs)** can occur in the lower urinary tract (bladder and urethra) or in the upper urinary tract (kidneys and ureters).
- **Renal failure** is the loss of kidney function that leads to buildup of waste in the bloodstream. It can be acute or chronic.

TABLE 2.11. Urinary Medications		
Medication	**Common Brand Names**	**Adverse Reactions and Interactions**
Diuretics: *hypertension, edema*		
hydrochlorothiazide	Microzide	**BBW**: fluid/electrolyte loss (furosemide), pregnancy (lisinopril)
furosemide	Lasix	
spironolactone	Aldactone, CaroSpir	**ADR**: hypotension, weakness, dizziness, blurred vision
chlorthalidone	none	
hydrochlorothiazide and triamterene	Dyazide, Maxzide	**Interactions**: alcohol, other antihypertensive drugs, NSAIDs
hydrochlorothiazide and lisinopril	Zestoretic	

Medication	Common Brand Names	Adverse Reactions and Interactions
Treatment of Overactive Bladder		
oxybutynin	Ditropan XL, Gelnique, Oxytrol	**ADR**: constipation, dry mouth, dizziness, drowsiness
trospium	Trosec	**Interactions**: anticholinergic drugs
mirabegron	Myrbetriq	**ADR**: hypertension, nose and throat irritation, dry mouth, headache
		Interactions: digoxin
Miscellaneous		
allopurinol *gout*	Lopurin, Zyloprim, Aloprim	**ADR**: rash, nausea, vomiting, drowsiness
		Interactions: anticoagulants
		Counseling: may impair the ability to perform potentially hazardous activities

BBW: black box warning
ADR: adverse drug reactions

PRACTICE QUESTIONS

17. Which of the following medications may be prescribed to treat edema caused by liver failure?

    A) spironolactone

    B) benazepril

    C) oxybutynin

    D) pravastatin

18. Which auxiliary label should be affixed to a prescription bottle of oxybutynin?

    A) Chew tablets before swallowing.

    B) May cause drowsiness/dizziness.

    C) Medication should be taken with plenty of water.

    D) Do not take this drug if you become pregnant.

The Reproductive System

The **male reproductive system** produces **sperm**, or male gametes, and passes them to the female reproductive system. Sperm are produced in the **testes** (also called testicles), which are housed in a sac-like external structure called the **scrotum**. During sexual stimulation, sperm mixes with fluids from the

seminal vesicles, **prostate**, and **Cowper's gland**. The mix of fluids and sperm, called **semen**, travels through the urethra and exits the body through the **penis**, which becomes rigid during sexual arousal.

The main hormone associated with the male reproductive system is **testosterone**, which is released mainly by the testes. Testosterone is responsible for the development of the male reproductive system and male secondary sexual characteristics, including muscle development and facial hair growth.

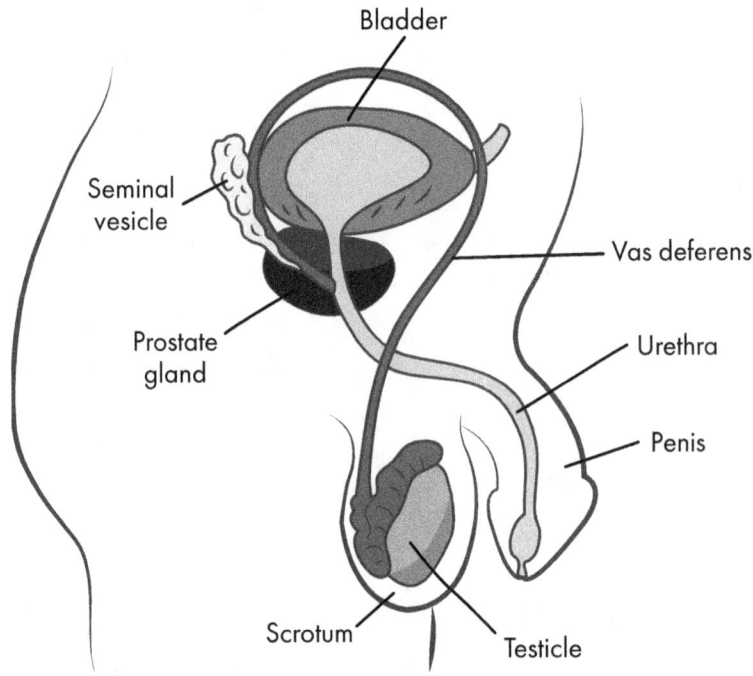

Figure 2.8. The Male Reproductive System

The **female reproductive system** produces **eggs**, or female gametes, and gestates the **fetus** during pregnancy. Eggs are produced in the **ovaries** and travel through the **fallopian tubes** to the **uterus**, which is a muscular organ that houses the fetus during pregnancy. The uterine cavity is lined with a layer of blood-rich tissue called the **endometrium**. If no pregnancy occurs, the endometrium is shed monthly during **menstruation**.

Fertilization occurs when the egg absorbs the sperm. After fertilization, the new **zygote** implants itself in the endometrium, where it will grow and develop over thirty-eight weeks (roughly nine months). During gestation, nutrients and waste pass between the fetus and mother via the **umbilical cord**, which is attached to the **placenta**. During labor, uterine contractions push the baby through the **cervix** and out of the **vagina**.

> **DID YOU KNOW?**
>
> Most oral contraceptive pills prevent pregnancy by stopping **ovulation** (the release of eggs from the ovaries).

The female reproductive cycle is controlled by several different hormones, including **estrogen** and **progesterone**.

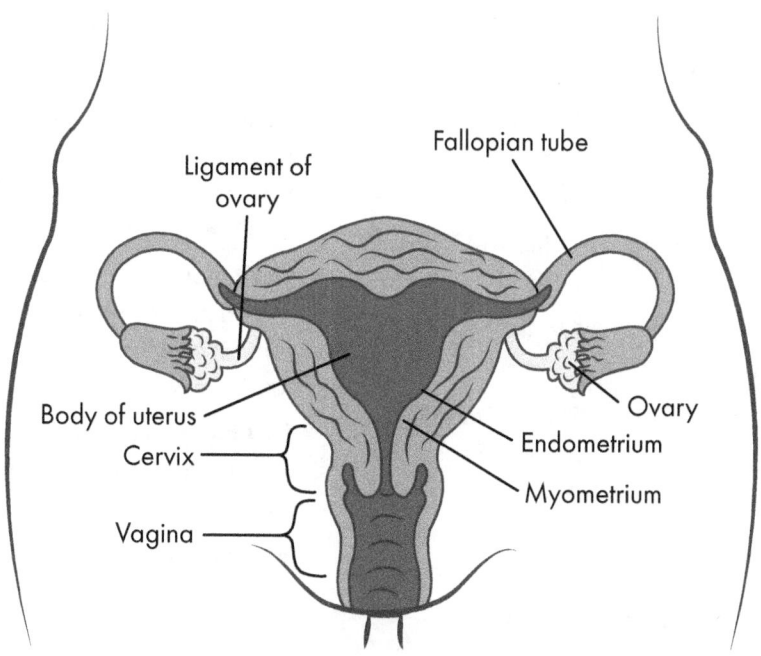

Figure 2.9. The Female Reproductive System

Patients may require prescription medications to manage infections, cancers, and dysfunction of the reproductive systems:

- **Sexually transmitted infections (STIs)** occur in both males and females. Common STIs include chlamydia, gonorrhea, genital herpes, human papillomavirus (HPV), and syphilis.
- **Endometriosis** is a painful disorder in which the tissue that lines the uterus grows outside the uterus.
- **Menopause** is the natural decline in the reproduction of hormones in women, typically when they reach their forties or fifties.
- **Benign prostatic hypertrophy** (BPH) is an age-associated condition in which the prostate gland enlarges, causing urinary difficulty.
- **Erectile dysfunction** (ED) is when a man cannot achieve or keep an erection strong enough for sexual intercourse.
- **Prostate cancer** afflicts the male prostate.
- **Breast cancer**, although most common in women, can afflict men as well.

HELPFUL HINT:

Alpha2-adrenergic agonists (suffix –ine) act on the central nervous system and are used to treat a wide range of conditions, including BPH, hypertension, muscle spasms, and alcohol/opioid withdrawal.

→ CONTINUE

TABLE 2.12. Reproductive Medications

Medication	Common Brand Names	Adverse Reactions and Interactions
Contraceptives		
ethinyl estradiol and norethindrone	Cyclafem 7/7/7, Femhrt, Loestrin, Ortho-Novum	**BBW**: increased risk of cardiovascular disease with smoking, increased risk of endometrial and breast cancer **ADR**: nausea, vomiting, headache, menstrual irregularities, weight change, breast tenderness **Interactions**: some anticonvulsants (e.g., topiramate), St. John's wort **Pregnancy**: Category X
ethinyl estradiol and norgestimate	Ortho Tri-Cyclen, Sprintec, TriNessa	
ethinyl estradiol and drospirenone	Ocella, Yasmin, Zarah	
ethinyl estradiol and levonorgestrel	Plan B One-Step, Jolessa, Seasonique, Mirena	
ethinyl estradiol and desogestrel	Apri, Kariva	
ethinyl estradiol and etonogestrel	NuvaRing	
norethindrone	Camilla, Errin	
Hormones		
Estradiol (estrogen) *low estrogen, osteoporosis prophylaxis, symptoms of menopause*	none	**BBW**: increased risk of endometrial cancer, breast cancer, and cardiovascular disease **ADR**: edema, headache, mood changes, rash, breast tenderness, nasal or throat irritation
Testosterone *breast cancer, delayed puberty, hypogonadism*	none	**BBW**: blood pressure increases, secondary exposure **ADR**: hypertension, blister or irritation at application site **Interactions**: anticoagulants
Progesterone *assisted reproductive technology, amenorrhea*	Crinone, Endometrin, Prometrium	**BBW**: increased risk of breast cancer and cardiovascular disorders **ADR**: edema, mood changes, nausea, breast tenderness **Interactions**: anticoagulants

Medication	Common Brand Names	Adverse Reactions and Interactions
Treatment of BPH (*also indicated for hypertension)		
tamsulosin	Flomax	**ADR**: orthostatic hypotension, sexual disorder, dizziness, headache
doxazosin*	Cardura	
terazosin*	none	
finasteride	Propecia, Proscar	
Treatment of Erectile Dysfunction		
sildenafil	Revatio, Viagra	**ADR**: headache, flushing, upset stomach, abnormal vision, congestion, nausea
tadalafil	Cialis	**Interactions**: anti-hypertensives
vardenafil	Levitra	**Contraindications**: nitrate use

BBW: black box warning
ADR: adverse drug reactions

PRACTICE QUESTIONS

19. Which of the following is a BPH medication?
    A) buserelin
    B) terazosin
    C) progesterone
    D) clomiphene

20. Which OTC product may reduce the effectiveness of hormonal contraceptives?
    A) phenylephrine
    B) NSAIDs
    C) iron supplements
    D) St. John's wort

The Integumentary System

The **integumentary system** refers to the skin (the largest organ in the body) and related structures, including the hair and nails. The **skin** is composed of three layers: the epidermis (outer layer), dermis, and hypodermis (inner layer).

The skin has several important roles. It houses nerves, and it acts as a barrier to protect the body from injury, the intrusion of foreign particles, and the loss of water and nutrients. It also produces vitamin D and helps thermoregulation.

Most integumentary disorders that require prescribed medications are bacterial, fungal, or parasitic infections. The skin can also be damaged by trauma, which may require antibiotics or analgesics:

- **Acne** is the most common skin infection. Although it is most prevalent in adolescents, acne can happen at any age.
- **Staphylococcus** (staph) **infection** is caused by an accumulation of the bacteria *staphylococcus*, normally found on the skin or nose. It is very contagious. **Methicillin-resilient *Staphylococcus aureus*** (MRSA) can only be treated with certain kinds of antibiotics.
- **Fungal infections** are caused by an overgrowth of fungus. *Candida* is the most common. Symptoms include a skin rash and itching.
- **Rashes** are itchy, inflamed skin usually caused by allergic reactions.
- **Scabies** is caused by a tiny mite that burrows into the skin.
- **Rosacea** is a chronic condition that causes redness and small, pus-filled bumps on the face. It tends to affect fair-skinned women.
- **Impetigo** is a highly contagious skin infection that causes sores and is mainly seen in children.
- **Skin cancer** is caused by an abnormal growth of cells on the skin and presents in many forms.
- **Sunburns** can be very painful, cause chills or fevers, and lead to sun poisoning.

TABLE 2.13. Integumentary Medications

Medication	Common Brand Names	Adverse Reactions and Interactions
Topical Antibiotics		
bacitracin, neomycin, and polymyxin B	Neosporin	**ADR**: burning, stinging, rash
mupirocin	Centany	
Topical Antifungals		
miconazole	Lotrimin	**ADR**: itching, rash
nystatin	Nyamyc, Nystop	
tolnaftate	Tinactin	
ADR: adverse drug reactions		

PRACTICE QUESTION

21. Which of the following would be prescribed to treat a skin infection caused by *Candida albicans*?

    A) benzocaine

    B) anthralin

    C) imiquimod

    D) nystatin

Radiopharmaceuticals

Radiopharmaceutical drugs have a radioactive compound and are used for diagnostic and therapeutic purposes. As with all pharmaceuticals, a standard is required for implementing and developing these drugs.

Most radiopharmaceuticals are used for diagnostic imaging, but they can also be used for chemotherapy and radiation in cancer patients. Chemotherapy radiopharmaceuticals include strontium 89 (Metastron), samarium 153 (Quadramet), and radium-223 (Xofigo) for bone cancers; radioactive iodine for thyroid cancer; and phosphorus 32 for brain tumors.

Monoclonal antibodies, or **radio-labeled antibodies**, are manufactured versions of immune system proteins with radioactive atoms that only attach to their target. This treatment is used for non-Hodgkin's lymphoma.

PRACTICE QUESTION

22. Which of these is NOT a radiopharmaceutical?

    A) monoclonal antibodies

    B) radium 450

    C) phosphorus 32

    D) radium 223

ANSWER KEY

1. **D)** ACE inhibitors, such as benazepril, fosinopril, and quinapril, have the *–pril* suffix.
2. **C)** Vasodilators relax blood vessels, reducing the force of the heart and the pressure of the blood against the vessel walls.
3. **B)** Nitroglycerin should not be taken with erectile dysfunction medications such as tadalafil (Cialis).
4. **A)** Montelukast (Singulair) is an inhaled bronchodilator prescribed for the treatment of asthma.
5. **D)** Benzonatate should be swallowed whole to prevent numbing of the mouth and throat.
6. **A)** Donepezil is a cognition-enhancing medication used to slow the progression of Alzheimer's disease.
7. **B)** The suffix *–pam* refers to benzodiazepines.
8. **D)** Buspirone is an anti-anxiety medication that may cause drowsiness.
9. **A)** Azithromycin is a macrolide antibiotic.
10. **B)** Methotrexate is an immunosuppressant prescribed to treat cancer and some autoimmune conditions.
11. **C)** Sertraline (Zoloft) is an SSRI. Combining cyclobenzaprine and a serotonergic drug may lead to serotonin syndrome.
12. **A)** Antacids decrease the absorption of alendronate (Fosamax), so the drugs should not be taken together.
13. **A)** Antiemetics prevent nausea and vomiting.
14. **D)** Pantoprazole is a proton pump inhibitor.
15. **C)** Levothyroxine is a synthetic thyroid hormone that increases metabolism, which may result in weight loss.
16. **D)** Dulaglutide (Trulicity) is an antidiabetic, not an insulin.
17. **A)** Spironolactone is a diuretic used to treat edema caused by liver failure.
18. **B)** Oxybutynin is an anticholinergic drug that may cause drowsiness or dizziness.
19. **B)** Terazosin is an alpha-adrenergic blocker prescribed to treat benign prostatic hypertrophy or hypertension.
20. **D)** Taking St. John's wort can reduce the effectiveness of hormonal contraceptive pills.
21. **D)** Nystatin is an antifungal used to treat *Candida* infections.
22. **B)** Radium 450 is not a radiopharmaceutical.

PART II

FEDERAL REQUIREMENTS

3 LEGAL GUIDELINES

Regulatory Agencies and Organizations

The **US Food and Drug Administration (FDA)** is part of the US Department of Health and Human Services. It approves applications for new drugs and medical devices and investigates the improper use and misbranding of agricultural goods and services used for food and drugs.

The **Drug Enforcement Agency (DEA)** is part of the US Department of Justice. The DEA enforces the Controlled Substances Act to prevent the diversion and abuse of both controlled substances and chemicals regulated by the FDA. The DEA is involved in every aspect of the handling and distribution of controlled substances and regulated chemicals.

The **Bureau of Alcohol, Tobacco, Firearms and Explosives (ATF)** is a federal organization within the US Department of Justice. The ATF combats terrorism, arson, and violent crime. It also regulates alcohol, tobacco, firearms, and explosives.

Each state has its own **Board of Pharmacy (BOP)** that regulates the practice of pharmacy. State BOPs mainly focus on the public's health and the implementation and enforcement of state pharmacy laws.

The **Centers for Medicare & Medicaid Services (CMS)** manages Medicare, Medicaid, the Children's Health Insurance Program (CHIP), and the health insurance exchanges.

The **US Pharmacopeial Convention (USP)** is a nonprofit organization that sets standards for the strength, purity, quality, and identity of medicines, dietary supplements, and food. The USP sets standards for preparing compounds.

> **HELPFUL HINT:**
>
> **MedWatch** is the FDA's safety and adverse event reporting program.

The Joint Commission is a nonprofit organization whose main function is to enhance patient safety and quality of care in institutional environments. The Joint Commission accredits hospitals through yearly inspections for compliance and national patient safety goals.

The **Institute for Safe Medication Practices (ISMP)** is a nonprofit that operates a medication error reporting system and issues regular alerts for recurring medication errors.

> **PRACTICE QUESTION**
>
> 1. Which of the following agencies is responsible for monitoring the handling and distribution of controlled substances?
>   A) Centers for Medicare & Medicaid Services
>   B) Drug Enforcement Agency
>   C) Food and Drug Administration
>   D) the State Board of Pharmacy

Federal Legislation

Drug manufacturing, labeling, and distribution is regulated by a wide array of federal legislation and guidelines. While these are not likely to be directly tested on the exam, it can be helpful to understand how the history of drug regulation has affected work in today's pharmacy.

HELPFUL HINT:

An **act** is legislation passed by Congress and signed by the president. Before an act is passed into law, it is called a **bill**. An **amendment** is the altering of an act or bill that is already in place or being processed.

TABLE 3.1. Federal Legislation

Name	Description
Pure Food and Drug Act of 1906	requires all manufacturers to properly label a drug with truthful information and prove its effectiveness through scientific methods; prohibits the adulteration and misbranding of food and drugs in interstate commerce
Harrison Narcotics Tax Act of 1914	created in response to international treaties to stop the recreational use of opium; requires practitioners to be registered and document the use and dispensing of narcotics; restricts and taxes the sale and distribution of products used to prepare controlled substances (e.g., opium and coca leaves)
Food, Drug, and Cosmetic Act of 1938	bans false product claims and requires that products include package inserts with directions and exact labeling; requires addictive substances to be labeled, "Warning: May be habit forming"; gave legal status to the FDA and created the USP and National Formulary

Name	Description
Durham-Humphrey Amendment of 1951	added more labeling requirements, including "Caution: Federal law prohibits dispensing without a prescription"; requires that prescription and OTC drugs be distinguished
Kefauver-Harris Amendment of 1962	a reaction to the Thalidomide Tragedy; requires manufacturers to provide proof of a drugs' effectiveness and safety before approval; requires disclosure of accurate side effect information; prevents generic drugs from being marketed under new trade names
Comprehensive Drug Abuse and Prevention Act of 1970/ Controlled Substances Act (CSA)	requires strict record keeping and physical security of certain drug types; divides controlled substances into five classes (schedules) based on their accepted use, potential for abuse, and accepted safety under medical supervision; discussed in Chapter 4
Poison Prevention Packaging Act of 1970	requires manufacturers and pharmacies to secure all medications (both prescription and OTC) in containers with childproof caps/packaging
Occupational Safety and Health Act (OSHA) of 1970	aims to ensure worker and workplace safety, including an environment that prevents toxic chemical exposure, excessive noise, mechanical dangers, unsanitary conditions and stress from heat or cold; discussed in Chapter 6
Medical Device Amendment of 1976	establishes three regulatory classes for medical devices: Class I (general controlled devices with low risk for human use); Class II (performance-standard devices with moderate risk for human use); Class III (the most regulated—high risks for human use, requires premarket approval applications equivalent to a new drug application)
Resource Conservation and Recovery Act of 1976	gives the Environmental Protection Agency (EPA) complete authority in the disposal of hazardous substances, including their generation, transportation, treatment, storage, and disposal
Orphan Drug Act of 1983	regulates orphan drugs (pharmaceuticals developed specifically for rare diseases); passed to help develop treatments for orphan diseases such as Huntington's disease, Tourette's syndrome, muscular dystrophy, and ALS

continued on next page

TABLE 3.1. Federal Legislation (continued)	
Name	Description
Drug Price Competition and Patent Term Restoration Act of 1984	encourages the manufacture of generic drugs; formed the modern system of generic drug regulation in the US; outlines the process for drug companies to file an **abbreviated new drug application (ANDA)** to receive approval of a generic drug by the FDA (Figure 3.1.)
Prescription Drug Marketing Act of 1987	helps prevent counterfeit drugs by providing legal safeguards in the pharmaceutical chain of distribution; designed to prevent the sales of discontinued, counterfeit, misbranded, subpar, and expired prescription drugs
Omnibus Budget Reconciliation Act of 1990	related to COBRA, which allows for continuing coverage and group health care plan benefits for employees and families based on qualifying issues and events when benefits would otherwise be terminated
FDA Safe Medical Devices Act (1990)	implemented medical device reporting (MDR) of serious incidents that occur from the use of medical devices; a post-market surveillance tool used by the FDA to monitor performance, potential safety issues, and benefit-risk assessments of the devices
Anabolic Steroids Control Act of 1990	amended the CSA to require penalties for trainers and advisors who recommend anabolic steroid use; added anabolic steroids as a CIII schedule drug
Americans with Disabilities Act of 1990	civil rights law that protects against discrimination based on a disability; requires employers to make reasonable accommodations to employees with disabilities
Dietary Supplement Health and Education Act of 1994	defines and regulates dietary supplements under the FDA's Good Manufacturing Practices
FDA Modernization Act (1997)	updated the Food, Drug, and Cosmetic Act to include technological, trade, and public health issues more relevant to the twenty-first century
Medicare Prescription Drug Improvement and Modernization Act of 2003	gives low-income patients the option of a prescription drug discount card; helps increase access to medical treatments and reduces unnecessary hospitalizations associated with noncompliance in taking prescription drugs

Name	Description
Dietary Supplement and Nonprescription Drug Act of 2006	amends the Food, Drug, and Cosmetic Act by requiring the reporting of adverse events caused by dietary supplements and nonprescription drugs, including abuse of and withdrawals from the drug, overdose of the drug, and failure of the drug's expected pharmacological action
Patient Protection and Affordable Care Act of 2010	also known as the Affordable Care Act or Obamacare; aims to increase health care quality and affordability by lowering the costs of insurance and the number of uninsured persons in the US; requires insurance companies to cover all individuals with new minimum standards regardless of pre-existing conditions
Drug Quality and Security Act of 2013	modifies the Food, Drug, and Cosmetic Act; outlines steps to build an electronic tracking system to identify and trace specific prescription drugs distributed in the US

There are regulatory agencies and organizations that work both independently and together to enforce and/or help regulate the pharmacy laws, acts, and amendments. Pharmacy laws are complex and constructed of both federal and state requirements. Each agency and organization has a specific role in regulating drugs and the manufacturers, suppliers, and distributors of medication. Other agencies or organizations regulate the licensing, accreditation, and discipline of the pharmacy practice. The combination of pharmacy laws and the regulatory agencies and organizations which enforce and regulate them helps deliver consumers the safest products available.

PRACTICE QUESTION

2. Which amendment requires "Caution: Federal law prohibits dispensing without a prescription" to be placed on all prescription labels?
   A) the Kefauver-Harris Amendment of 1962
   B) the Orphan Drug Act of 1983
   C) the Durham-Humphrey Amendment of 1951
   D) the Pure Food and Drug Act of 1906

HIPAA

In 1996, the US federal government enacted the **Health Insurance Portability and Accountability Act (HIPAA)**. HIPAA's primary purposes are to guarantee health insurance access, portability, and renewal. It limits the exclusion of some preexisting conditions and prohibits discrimination based on a person's health status.

HIPAA also regulates the security of protected health information, which must be kept confidential to protect the patient's privacy. HIPAA defines **protected health information (PHI)** as any information that allows a patient to be identified, including

- patient and family names;
- geographic areas;
- dates of birth, death, admission, and discharge;
- telephone and fax numbers;
- home and email addresses;
- social security numbers;
- health plan beneficiary members;
- vehicle, device, and equipment numbers;
- medical records and account numbers;
- photographs;
- biometric identifiers; and
- any unique identifying number, code, or characteristic.

In most cases, an **authorization form** signed by the patient is required prior to the release of any PHI. HIPAA allows for the disclosure of PHI without a signed authorization form when that information will be used for treatment, payment, or health care operations (e.g., care planning, customer service, etc.). This provision allows providers to consult each other regarding a patient's care, provide referrals, and coordinate care with third parties.

Pharmacy technicians are subject to HIPAA regulations and have a duty to protect patient PHI. Some general guidelines are explained below, but each pharmacy will have its own HIPAA compliance regulations:

- Technicians can only access patient PHI that is necessary for their work.
- Patient information should only be communicated on a need-to-know basis and only with parties directly involved in patient care (e.g., the prescriber, the pharmacist).
- Pharmacy technicians should not discuss sensitive information around other customers; if PHI must be discussed with a patient, the patient should be directed to the consultation window and spoken to quietly.
- When sending patient-sensitive information electronically, the information must be converted to a non-readable format through encryption.

- Access to patient information should be limited only to the health care providers who have permission to access it.
- All computers in the pharmacy should be password protected. This means workers must sign in and out of computers with a password each time they use them to access PHI.
- Any electronic release of information among health care providers must be approved by the patient.

> **PRACTICE QUESTION**
>
> 3. Under HIPAA, which of the following questions is the pharmacy technician able to answer?
>   A) A prescribing physician asks if a prescription for a patient has been filled.
>   B) The husband of a customer asks if his wife has recently filled any prescriptions.
>   C) The technician's friend asks if her son has filled his most recent prescription.
>   D) A lawyer asks about the prescription history of a client.

Drug Recalls

Sometimes a manufacturer will issue a **recall** of a particular drug batch because the product has been determined to be harmful. Reasons for a recall include defective products, contamination, incorrect labeling, FDA interference, or improper production.

In these cases, the manufacturer will send **recall notices** to the pharmacy. The pharmacy must act on these immediately to prevent the consumer from receiving the recalled drug. Notices will provide specific information about the product, including the drug name, lot number, and the reason for the recall.

Pharmacies have specific policies and procedures in place to ensure that the recalled drug is pulled from the shelves, documented, and returned. These include notifying the manufacturer and the FDA of compliance with removing the recalled drug.

Recalled medications should be removed from inventory and placed in a designated area until they are returned or disposed of as required by the recall notice. Technicians must check all inventory, including shelving in the pharmacy and med units, and automated drug dispensing systems located in the institutional pharmacy. If the recalled product is not in stock, the pharmacy must still send the recall form back to the FDA and manufacturer stating this fact.

The pharmacy is also required to contact affected patients if the pharmacy dispensed the recalled product. In these cases, the pharmacy or doctor's office may contact the patient to check the lot number of the dispensed medication. If the patient received a recalled product, the patient is asked to return the medication for a replacement. The pharmacy then must contact the manufacturer for replacement of the drug.

> **HELPFUL HINT:**
> Lot numbers are critical to a recall because they identify the defective batch of the drug.

> **HELPFUL HINT:**
> A current listing of drug recalls is available online at www.fda.gov/Drugs/Drugsafety/DrugRecalls.

There are three levels of recalls, which can be conducted by the FDA or the manufacturer. The levels are determined by the urgency and severity of the recall:

- **Class I recall:** There is a probability that use of or exposure to the product could cause serious health consequences or death.
- **Class II recall:** The product may cause temporary or reversible health problems, and there is a remote probability of serious adverse health consequences.
- **Class III recall:** The product is not likely to cause adverse health consequences but has violated FDA regulations.

FDA market withdrawals can happen when a product has a minor violation that does not require legal action; however, the product must still be removed from the market to correct the violation.

> **PRACTICE QUESTION**
>
> 4. A Class II recall occurs when
>
>   **A)** the product is not likely to cause an adverse event but has violated FDA regulations.
>
>   **B)** a product has a minor violation that does not require legal action, but the product still must be removed from the market to correct the violation.
>
>   **C)** the product may cause temporary health problems, and there is a remote probability of an adverse health event.
>
>   **D)** there is a probability that the use of or exposure to the product could cause an adverse event, health consequences, or death.

HELPFUL HINT:

Lot numbers are critical to a recall because they identify the defective batch of the drug.

HELPFUL HINT:

In some states, pharmacists have been given prescriptive authority to fill oral contraceptives.

Prescribing Authority

Prescribing authority is the legal authority to prescribe drugs. The scope of prescribing authority varies by licensure and differs from state to state:

- Physicians have full authority to prescribe drugs within the guidelines of the state where they practice.
- Physician assistants and nurse practitioners also have broad prescribing authority, although they are prevented from prescribing controlled substances in some states.
- Other health care providers, including psychiatrists, dentists, veterinarians, and some nurses, have a narrower prescribing authority related to their specific fields.
- Nurses (RN, LPN, LVN) and technicians do not have prescribing authority.

Pharmacy technicians have no prescribing authority, but pharmacists do have some limited authority in certain circumstances. Independent prescriptive authority is not given to pharmacists in any state, but most states do allow pharmacists to initiate or adjust drug therapies in collaboration with physicians. This normally happens in in-patient settings.

> **PRACTICE QUESTION**
>
> 5. Which of the following providers is able to prescribe controlled medications in most states?
>
>   A) pediatric registered nurse
>   B) paramedic
>   C) physician assistant
>   D) licensed vocational nurse

ANSWER KEY

1. **B)** The Drug Enforcement Agency (DEA) is responsible for monitoring the handling and distribution of controlled substances.

2. **C)** The Durham-Humphrey Amendment of 1951 requires prescription labels to state "Caution: Federal law prohibits dispensing without a prescription."

3. **A)** The pharmacy technician can release a fill history to the prescribing physician because this information is used for medical treatment. Providing information in the other scenarios would be violation of the Health Insurance Portability and Accountability Act (HIPAA)—unless the patient has authorized the information's disclosure.

4. **C)** A Class II recall occurs when the product may cause temporary health problems and there is a remote probability of an adverse health event.

5. **C)** A physician assistant can prescribe controlled substances in most states.

4 REGULATION OF CONTROLLED SUBSTANCES

Drug Schedules

Controlled substances are drugs the government strictly regulates. Prescribers must follow specific rules that differ from those for noncontrolled drugs. The **Controlled Substances Act (CSA) (1970)** strictly controls the manufacture, possession, sale, and use of controlled substances. These include opioids, stimulants, depressants, hallucinogens, anabolic steroids, and other regulated chemicals.

The Drug Enforcement Administration (DEA), responsible for enforcing the CSA, can prosecute any violators on both domestic and international levels. Individuals who handle, store, order, or distribute controlled substances must be registered with the DEA and have a DEA number.

The CSA categorizes opioids into **schedules** based on misuse potential and safety. The schedules range from CI – CV:

- **Schedule I (CI)** are illegal drugs that do not have any medical value, pose severe safety concerns, and have the most misuse potential. These drugs include heroin, LSD, Ecstasy, mescaline, MDMA, GHB, psilocybin, methaqualone, khat, and bath salts. On a federal level, marijuana is considered to be a CI opioid, but some state laws have changed to allow marijuana for medical and/or recreational use.
- **Schedule II (CII)** are legal drugs with a high potential for misuse. Although CII drugs have medical value, they are used under severe restrictions. These medications include cocaine, methamphetamine, methadone, hydromorphone, meperidine, oxycodone, fentanyl, and combination products with less than 15 mg of hydrocodone per dosage unit.

HELPFUL HINT:

When a state-controlled substance law is more stringent than federal law, the State Board of Pharmacy (BOP) requires pharmacies to adhere to the stricter state requirements.

HELPFUL HINT:

The drug schedule is imprinted on the stock bottles of controlled substances. For example, a stock bottle for alprazolam 0.5 mg tablets has an imprint of "CIV."

- **Schedule III (CIII)** are legal drugs with the potential for misuse but which are less misused and safer than CII opioids. They have low to moderate potential for physical misuse but a high potential for psychological misuse. These medicines include products containing less than 90 mg of codeine per dosage unit (such as acetaminophen with codeine), ketamine, anabolic steroids, and testosterone.
- **Schedule IV (CIV)** are legal drugs with a low potential for physical misuse and moderate potential for psychological misuse, such as tranquilizers and sleeping medicines. These medications include carisoprodol; tramadol; dextropropoxyphene; and benzodiazepines such as alprazolam, diazepam, and lorazepam.
- **Schedule V (CV)** are legal drugs with a low potential for physical and psychological misuse. They are usually low-dose opioids or stimulants combined with other medications, such as cough preparations with less than 200 mg of codeine per 100 mL, diphenoxylate/atropine, and pregabalin.

PRACTICE QUESTION

1. Which of the following medications is a Schedule IV drug?
   - **A)** cocaine
   - **B)** marijuana
   - **C)** diazepam
   - **D)** hydrocodone

DEA Registration for Controlled Substances

The DEA enforces the CSA to prevent the diversion and misuse of controlled substances and chemicals regulated by the FDA. The DEA is involved in every aspect of the handling and distribution of controlled substances and regulated chemicals. It requires accurate record keeping and compliance from pharmacies, wholesalers, and distributors.

The DEA restricts access to controlled substances by requiring all entities that prepare, handle, or distribute controlled substances to fill out an application for **DEA registration**. Such entities include physicians, drug distributors, drug importers, drug exporters, drug manufacturers, and pharmacies. The DEA registration form for new applications is **DEA Form 224. DEA Form 224a** is for renewal applications.

When the DEA approves registration, the entity receives a **DEA registration number**, which is necessary for dispensing and distributing controlled substances. DEA numbers are also used in pharmacy billing; some insurance claims may be denied if the DEA number is incorrect. Pharmacy technicians must know how to verify a DEA number and can do so by calculating the DEA formula, described below:

A patient drops off a prescription for a controlled substance: morphine IR 30 mg tablets. The physician's name is Dr. Mae Long, and her DEA number is AL2455562.

To verify that the DEA number is correct, use the following **DEA formula**:

1. A valid DEA number consists of 2 letters, 6 numbers, and 1 check digit at the end.

2. The first letter of the DEA number is the **DEA registrant** type. Some registrants only have the authorization to distribute or manufacture; others are only allowed to use controlled substances in research and labs. Still others, such as practitioners, can write prescriptions for patients. Pharmacy technicians typically encounter DEA numbers that begin with *A*, *B*, *C*, or *M*. A complete list of registrant types follows:

A.	deprecated (used by older entities)
B.	hospital or clinic
C.	practitioner
D.	teaching institution
E.	manufacturer
F.	distributor
G.	researcher
H.	analytical lab
J.	importer
K.	exporter
L.	reverse distributor
M.	mid-level practitioner
P. – U.	opioid treatment program
X.	Suboxone/Subutex prescribing program

3. The second letter is the first letter of the practitioner's last name. In the example, this is "L."

4. To verify the number, add the first, third, and fifth numbers in the DEA number: $2 + 5 + 5 = 12$.

5. Next, add the second, fourth, and sixth numbers and multiply by 2: $4 + 5 + 6 = 15$; $15 \times 2 = 30$.

REGULATION OF CONTROLLED SUBSTANCES

6. Finally, add the sums of the previous two steps: 12 and 30. The last digit in this total should match the last digit in the DEA number: 12 + 30 = 42. The last digit in the DEA number is 2: AL2455562.

PRACTICE QUESTION

2. Which DEA registrant type is used for a hospital or clinic?
   A) B
   B) M
   C) L
   D) A

> **CHECK YOUR UNDERSTANDING**
>
> Practice by analyzing these DEA numbers: AW3284065, AG4342793, FN5623740, AR5472612, and BN6428521.

Dispensing Controlled Substances

Electronic Prescriptions

Electronic prescribing for controlled substances (EPCS) uses software tools that meet all DEA standards. EPCS increases patient safety, adherence, and staff productivity while decreasing fraud.

The **Substance Use-Disorder Prevention that Promotes Opioid Recovery and Treatment for Patients and Communities (SUPPORT) Act** was signed into law in 2018. It requires e-prescriptions for all Schedule II – V controlled substances prescribed under Medicare Part D. As part of their compliance, most states now require EPCS for all controlled prescriptions. When filling e-prescriptions for controlled substances, pharmacies must verify the following information:

- date received and signed on
- date issued
- patient's name and address
- drug name
- strength
- dosage form
- quantity
- directions for use
- indication
- number of refills
- practitioner's name and address
- DEA registration number
- electronic signature

Next, the technician checks the patient's profile, paying particular attention to duplicate drug therapies. Patients taking multiple controlled substances can suffer serious or even fatal reactions. Duplicate drug therapies could also indicate that a patient with dependency issues may be trying to fill multiple prescriptions from different physicians. Any questionable circumstances should be brought to the pharmacist's attention.

> **PRACTICE QUESTION**
>
> 3. Which of the following requires EPCS for Schedule II – V controlled substances?
>   A) DEA
>   B) Federal Food, Drug, and Cosmetic Act
>   C) HIPAA
>   D) SUPPORT Act

HARD-COPY PRESCRIPTIONS

Providers who do not meet the technology standards for EPCS may still use hard-copy prescriptions, but they must be verified by the pharmacy technician at drop-off. When the patient drops off a controlled prescription, the pharmacy technician must check for the information listed below—especially for CII drugs—to ensure the physician has correctly written the prescription:

- date the prescription was written
- patient's full name and address
- prescriber's name, full address, phone number, and DEA number
- directions for use
- quantity
- number of refills (if allowed)
- manual signature of prescriber

The technician should closely examine the hard copy. Any discrepancies could signify a forged or fraudulent prescription.

After the technician receives a controlled prescription, the DEA number should be verified as explained above. If there are any discrepancies or questions about the prescription's validity or if the DEA number is not verifiable, the pharmacist should be notified. The pharmacist will verify the prescription by calling the prescriber. Finally, the technician can check the patient's profile for drug duplications or other issues (as described in Electronic Prescriptions above).

HELPFUL HINT:

Pharmacies must keep electronic prescription records for at least 2 years. Some states mandate electronic prescriptions and may require more than 2 years of record keeping.

HELPFUL HINT:

Most prescription pads are tamper-resistant; if an individual tries to copy a prescription, "VOID" appears on the prescription's background.

→ CONTINUE

REGULATION OF CONTROLLED SUBSTANCES 75

PRACTICE QUESTION

4. Which information does NOT need to be checked on a controlled prescription when the patient drops it off?

    A) manual signature of the prescriber
    B) date the prescription was written
    C) patient's full name and address
    D) patient's signature

Prescription Requirements by Schedule

In states that mandate electronic prescribing, CII prescriptions must be signed by the prescriber either manually or electronically. There is no federal policy stating when a CII prescription expires, but many states have time limits (30 days to 6 months). CII prescriptions can only be written for a 30-day supply and cannot have refills. The prescriber must write a new prescription for additional fills.

For schedules CIII – CV, the physician must sign the original prescription. When refilling CIII – CV drugs, the physician can write up to 6 months of additional refills (the original fill plus 5 refills). If the patient needs a refill and none are left on the original prescription, the physician must write a new one.

Prescriptions for controlled substances must be kept in the pharmacy for at least 2 years. Electronic prescriptions can be stored electronically. Paper prescriptions can be filed using one of three separate prescription file systems:

- **Three-file system:** The pharmacy keeps three files. One is used exclusively for CII prescriptions, one for CIII – CV prescriptions, and one for noncontrolled prescriptions.
- **Two-file system:** One file contains only CII prescriptions; the other includes all other prescriptions. Because the second file contains both controlled and noncontrolled medications, the DEA requires that controlled drugs are stamped with a red "C" in the lower-right-hand corner of CIII – CV prescriptions.
- **Alternative two-file system:** All controlled substances are placed in one folder; noncontrolled medications are in another folder. The CIII – CV prescriptions must still be stamped "C" in the lower-right-hand corner.

HELPFUL HINT:

The DEA allows a 90-day prescription for CII drugs; however, each prescription must be separate, list the earliest date it can be filled, and comply with state laws.

HELPFUL HINT:

It is essential to check the last refill date on a controlled substance. Trying to refill the prescription too early could indicate that the patient is either not complying with the directions or misusing the medication.

PRACTICE QUESTION

5. Which of the following is true of a Schedule II prescription?

    A) Prescriptions for Schedule II drugs can be called in.
    B) Federal regulations do not allow pharmacies to fill Schedule II prescriptions after 30 days.
    C) Schedule II drug prescriptions cannot be refilled.
    D) The maximum allowed supply for a Schedule II drug prescription is 60 days.

Filling and Dispensing Prescriptions for Controlled Substances

Pharmacy technicians can fill prescriptions for controlled substances. Filling, packaging, and dispensing these substances is done similarly as for other drugs, with some additional protocols:

- Most pharmacy practices require the pharmacist and technicians to double-count and initial the quantity of a controlled substance on the label, verifying that the quantity was counted twice to avoid discrepancies and inventory issues.
- Scheduled substances must be held in storage cabinets that meet federal and state security guidelines. In some pharmacies, technicians may need to ask the pharmacist for access to these cabinets.
- Federal guidelines require all controlled substance labels to state, "Caution: Federal law prohibits the transfer of this drug to any person other than the patient for whom it was prescribed."
- In most situations, patients picking up controlled substances must show identification and sign a log.

PRACTICE QUESTION

6. To verify that a controlled substance medication is counted correctly, the pharmacist and the pharmacy technician must

  A) double-count and initial the quantity of the medication.
  B) call the prescriber to verify the prescription.
  C) use an automatic pill counting machine.
  D) count the medication in front of the patient.

Transferring Prescriptions for Controlled Substances

Laws regarding the transfer of controlled substances differ among states. Some states allow a one-time refill for CIII – CV controlled substances between in-state pharmacies. The transfer must be done between two pharmacists—technicians are not able to transfer these prescriptions. The pharmacists in charge of the transferring and receiving must follow federal and state guidelines for recording all information related to the transfer.

The receiving pharmacist must create an electronic record for the prescription with the pharmacist's name and the information transferred with the prescription. The original and transferred prescription(s) must be maintained for a period of 2 years from the date of the last refill.

It is less common for a state to allow a refill transfer for a controlled substance from out of state. In states that do allow such transfers, doing so is at the pharmacist's discretion.

> **PRACTICE QUESTION**
>
> 7. An original and transferred prescription must be maintained for a period of 2 years from the date
>   A) the prescription was written by the physician.
>   B) the prescription was first filled.
>   C) the prescription was transferred.
>   D) of the last refill.

EMERGENCY DISPENSING AND PARTIAL FILLS

The physician may call in a verbal rather than a written prescription only in an emergency and under special circumstances. **Emergency dispensing** is done when a physician determines that a CII drug is required as soon as possible and there is no alternative treatment (for example, if a patient is in hospice). The pharmacist fills the prescription in **good faith**, which means the physician is expected to send a written or electronic, signed prescription within 7 days or less, depending on state laws. Other guidelines for emergency dispensing follow:

- Emergency dispensing can be done if a physician is out of the area and cannot give the pharmacist a written prescription.
- The physician must provide the pharmacist with the patient's name and address; drug name, dosage, and strength; dosage form; route of administration; and physician's name, address, phone number, and DEA number. The pharmacist must document the information.
- The quantity dispensed can only be enough to sustain the patient during the emergency period, which should not exceed 3 days.
- The pharmacist must document on the prescription that it was dispensed in an emergency.
- The pharmacist must verify the physician's authority.
- After the verbal prescription, the physician must submit a written or electronic prescription to the pharmacist within 7 days with the statement **"Authorization for Emergency Dispensing"** written on it. The DEA must be informed if the physician fails to complete these steps.
- The written or electronic copy must be filed with the verbal prescription.
- There might be additional requirements based on the BOP regulation of the state where the CII drug was dispensed.

If the pharmacy does not have enough of a drug in stock to fill the full quantity of the CIII – CV prescription, the pharmacist can provide a **partial fill** until the rest of the prescription can be filled. In these cases, the pharmacist may prorate the prescription's price, and the patient can request a refill when needed. Otherwise, the pharmacy may owe the additional quantity to the patient, and, when the drug is available, the patient can pick up the additional quantity at no charge. In this event, the pharmacist must mark on the label the number of pills given and the amount owed to the patient.

The pharmacist may also partially fill CII prescriptions, but if the remaining quantity cannot be dispensed within 72 hours, the physician must be notified and write a new prescription for the additional quantity. Partial fills must be noted on the hard copy of the prescription along with the amount filled.

PRACTICE QUESTION

8. Which of the following is NOT a valid reason for dispensing an emergency oral prescription?
   - **A)** The patient is terminally ill or in hospice.
   - **B)** A Schedule II drug is required as soon as possible.
   - **C)** The patient did not refill his medication before it expired.
   - **D)** The prescriber determines there is no alternative method of treatment.

Inventory of Controlled Substances

Storage and Security Requirements

All controlled substances are stored in a way that obstructs theft or drug diversion. The higher the class of the controlled substance, the more stringent the storage and security requirements.

CI substances, although very rarely used, must be securely locked in a cabinet with controlled accessibility. **Controlled accessibility** is the use of security features that control access to a certain resource. CI drugs are only used in scientific and clinical research.

CII drugs must also be stored securely. They are closely monitored and locked in specially engineered safety cabinets. Some methods for preventing theft and ensuring security in a health care setting include

- electronic alarm systems,
- self-closing and automatic locking doors,
- key- and/or password-control systems,
- allowing authorized personnel only, and
- using security officers in high-crime areas.

CIII – CV drugs must be stored securely as well, but the guidelines are less strict. The drugs can be stored alongside noncontrolled drugs. Security is maintained by ensuring that the drug storage area is accessible only to authorized personnel who need keys or passwords to enter the facility.

PRACTICE QUESTION

9. Which of the following is NOT a way to control theft and drug diversion?
   A) storing all drugs together in a central location
   B) controlled accessibility via key cards
   C) self-locking doors
   D) electronic alarm systems

Perpetual Inventory

Perpetual inventory is required for all CII drugs. Although most pharmacy inventory is done electronically, perpetual inventory of CII drugs is done by hand. The inventory log must be signed by a pharmacist when a CII drug has been received into inventory, dispensed to a patient, or disposed of. Perpetual inventories must be reconciled and verified every 10 days to avoid counting discrepancies.

On a CII perpetual inventory log, the name of the drug, the item number, and the sheet number are listed at the top of the page. The sheet is divided into three sections that state when the drug is ordered, received, and sold:

- In the "ordered" section, the pharmacist states the date ordered, the order number, the vendor, and the quantity.
- When the order is received, the pharmacist marks the date and the quantity in the "received" section. If the drug is back-ordered, the back-order box is marked and/or the date the vendor expects the drug to be available is stated.
- The pharmacist writes the date, order number, and quantity dispensed in the "sold" section. After each drug has been entered as ordered, received, and sold, the pharmacist calculates the quantity balance, signs the log, and adds any necessary comments.

HELPFUL HINT:

CIII – CV drugs may be estimated unless the bulk container holds more than 1,000 units; then it must have an exact count.

PRACTICE QUESTION

10. What is NOT documented on a perpetual inventory log?
    A) details of the CII order placed with the drug manufacturer
    B) the patient to whom the CII drug was prescribed
    C) the date that CII drugs are received from the drug manufacturer
    D) the quantity of CII drugs dispensed during a transaction

Perpetual Inventory Control

ITEM				ITEM NO			SHEET NO		
Ordered				Recieved			Sold		
Date	Order No	Vendor	Qty	Date	Qty	Backorder	Due Date	Date	Order No	Qty

Figure 4.1. Perpetual Inventory Control Log

Ordering and Receiving Controlled Substances

Pharmacists are responsible for ordering CII medications because the process requires a DEA number. CII ordering requires **DEA Form 222**. The distributor cannot process the order if the form is filled out incorrectly. When filling out DEA Form 222, the pharmacist must include the following specific information:

- company name and address
- order date
- name of drug
- order number of the item (up to 10 items per form)
- quantity of packages of the item needed
- package size of the item needed
- purchaser's (pharmacist's) signature
- registrant's DEA number

Pharmacists must also receive the CII orders, at which time they verify that the order is complete and log the order in the perpetual inventory book. CII drug records must be complete, accurate, and kept for 2 to 5 years, depending on the state where the pharmacy is located. CII records are kept separately from all other records.

HELPFUL HINT:

A pharmacy may distribute a CII drug to another pharmacy or health care setting only when those entities are DEA registrants that use DEA Form 222 to request the drug.

> **PRACTICE QUESTION**
>
> 11. Which is NOT required on DEA Form 222 when a pharmacist orders CII drugs?
>   A) order number
>   B) number of packages
>   C) size of the package
>   D) physician's DEA number

Non-Dispensable Controlled Substances

In the course of regular business, pharmacies will have controlled substances in stock that cannot be dispensed to patients. These medications may be expired, damaged, or otherwise unusable (e.g., remaining medication in a single-use vial). The DEA requires that these controlled substances be destroyed to be "non-retrievable"—they cannot be used or transformed back into a controlled substance.

Most pharmacies use a reverse distributor that collects and destroys unusable controlled substances. The reverse distributor might come to the pharmacy to collect these medications, or the pharmacy might package and ship the medications using DEA Form 222.

In limited cases, the pharmacy might choose to destroy controlled substances. When this occurs, the pharmacy must complete **DEA Form 41**. The form must be kept on file for 2 years, but must only be submitted to the DEA if requested. Two people must witness the destruction of drugs. Approved witnesses include pharmacists, nurses, other eligible health care practitioners, and law enforcement officers.

HELPFUL HINT:

Reverse distributors must be used for medications dispensed to a patient that the patient returns to the pharmacy, or for any medications for which the pharmacy needs reimbursement.

> **PRACTICE QUESTION**
>
> 12. When must Form 41 be submitted to the DEA?
>   A) immediately
>   B) within 1 week
>   C) within 1 month
>   D) when requested

Theft or Loss of Controlled Substances

Any theft or loss of a controlled substance must be documented, and the pharmacist must contact the local DEA office. Significant losses must be reported immediately. For smaller losses or thefts of controlled substances, pharmacists fill out **DEA Form 106**. The form includes

- the pharmacy's name, address, phone number, and DEA number;
- the date of loss or theft;
- a list of items stolen or lost;

- local police department information; and
- information about the container and labels with a description and costs.

Copies of DEA Form 106 are then sent to the state BOP, the local police, and the DEA.

PRACTICE QUESTION

13. Whom should the pharmacist contact FIRST if a controlled substance is lost or stolen?
    A) local police
    B) DEA
    C) State Board of Pharmacy
    D) Bureau of Alcohol, Tobacco, Firearms, and Explosives

DEA Inspections

DEA inspections are mandated by the CSA and require administrative search warrants. Before entering a DEA-registered business, the inspectors must state the purpose of the inspection and identify themselves. During consensual inspections, the DEA checks the accuracy of DEA- and state BOP-required controlled substances record keeping. (DEA inspections are usually performed with a representative of the BOP.) The inspectors also check for correct and up-to-date DEA registrants, certifications, and registrations.

Proper controlled substance records make the inspection quick and efficient. Records checked include all invoices and receipts for orders, receiving, distribution, inventory, DEA Form 222, and the file systems for those CII and CIII – CV prescriptions filled. Records are kept on file for at least 2 years—sometimes longer, depending on state requirements.

In emergencies, dangerous health situations, or if the inspection is of a special state statute category, DEA agents may not have an administrative search warrant but still must identify themselves and their purpose. Pharmacy technicians are required to refer agents to the pharmacist-in-charge immediately.

HELPFUL HINT:

When DEA inspectors identify themselves, the pharmacy technician must refer them to the pharmacist-in-charge; otherwise, the DEA agent will give the pharmacy a negative mark for noncompliance during the inspection.

PRACTICE QUESTION

14. What must the pharmacy technician do immediately if DEA agents identify themselves for an inspection?
    A) retrieve all records needed for the inspection
    B) allow the agents into the pharmacy and start showing them around
    C) show the inspectors where the file system is located
    D) refer the agents to the pharmacist

Prescription Monitoring

Many states now participate in a **prescription drug monitoring program (PDMP)**. These programs identify the possible misuse and diversion of controlled substances. The monitoring programs not only identify discrepancies within a patient's controlled prescription history but can also find discrepancies with prescribers and pharmacies in the dispensing of controlled drugs.

The statewide electronic database is used by regulatory, administrative, and law enforcement agencies. The DEA is not involved in state monitoring programs.

The **National Alliance for Model State Drug Laws (NAMSDL)** states that PDMPs

- support access to legitimate medical use of controlled substances;
- identify and deter or prevent drug misuse and diversion;
- facilitate and encourage the identification of, intervention with, and treatment of persons with an addiction to prescription drugs;
- inform public health initiatives by outlining use and misuse trends; and
- educate individuals about PDMPs and the use, misuse and diversion of, and addiction to prescription drugs.

Some states have begun to participate in national programs that monitor the prescription histories of potential drug misusers across state lines. One of these is **NABP PMP InterConnect**, in which more than forty states currently participate.

> **PRACTICE QUESTION**
>
> 15. Which is NOT a purpose of the PDMP?
>
>   **A)** to track patients with chronic pain and deter them from taking opioids
>
>   **B)** to support access to legitimate medical use of controlled substances
>
>   **C)** to identify and deter or prevent drug misuse and diversion
>
>   **D)** to inform public health initiatives by outlining use and misuse trends

Restricted Drug Programs

Restriction on Sales of Products Containing Ephedrine and Pseudoephedrine

The **Combat Methamphetamine Epidemic Act of 2005 (CMEA)** regulates the over-the-counter sales of **ephedrine** and **pseudoephedrine**, chemicals commonly used to produce methamphetamine. In retail pharmacies, enforcing the CMEA requirements is an important task of the pharmacy technician.

CMEA is an amendment to the CSA. The act ensures a sufficient supply of ephedrine and pseudoephedrine for medical purposes while deterring illegal uses of the drugs. The act requires pharmacies to specifically manage products that contain these drugs:

- Retailers must place products containing ephedrine and pseudoephedrine out of direct customer access.
- Customers must purchase these products at the pharmacy counter.
- Employees must ask customers for their photo ID and signature and keep this information in sales logbooks. (Prescription drugs are exempt from logbook requirements.)
- Retail customers may buy no more than 3.6 g of ephedrine or pseudoephedrine products a day. They also may not buy more than 9 g of these products every 30 days (or 7.5 g by mail order).
- Sellers of ephedrine and pseudoephedrine must obtain self-certification, and employees must receive the required training.

PRACTICE QUESTION

16. Which of the following is NOT a requirement of the CMEA?

    A) A 30-day supply of medication containing ephedrine or pseudoephedrine is limited to 9 g.

    B) Sellers must obtain self-certification and have training.

    C) Patients are required to have a prescription to receive ephedrine and pseudoephedrine.

    D) Products containing ephedrine and pseudoephedrine must be shelved away from customers.

CHECK YOUR UNDERSTANDING

If a single Sudafed pill contains 30 mg of pseudoephedrine, how many pills could a patient buy every 30 days if the limit is 9 g?

Risk Evaluation and Mitigatxion Strategies

When a drug has adverse effects that may outweigh the therapeutic benefits, the FDA requires a manufacturer to develop **Risk Evaluation and Mitigation Strategies (REMS)**. The purpose of REMS is to decrease the occurrence and severity of a drug's possible serious adverse effects. There are different types of REMS, but most include communication literature and protocols for health care providers. Information about the drug's risks is outlined in the package inserts, which are given to everyone involved, including patients, health care providers, and the pharmacy.

A pharmacy that dispenses medications with REMS must do so according to the requirements of the REMS. Pharmacists—and sometimes technicians—may require additional training according to REMS specifications. For example, clozapine has REMS because it may lead to neutropenia (low white blood cell count). To dispense clozapine, the pharmacy must be certified and staff must obtain a **Predispense Authorization** from the clozapine REMS program for each patient.

> **PRACTICE QUESTION**
>
> **17.** Risk Evaluation and Mitigation Strategies (REMS) are regulated and enforced by which entity?
>
> **A)** FDA
>
> **B)** DEA
>
> **C)** drug manufacturer
>
> **D)** prescribing provider

ANSWER KEY

1. **C)** Benzodiazepines, including diazepam, are classified as Schedule IV drugs.

2. **A)** The letter B (option A) is used for a hospital or clinic.

3. **D)** Under Medicare Part D, the SUPPORT Act (Substance Use-Disorder Prevention that Promotes Opioid Recovery and Treatment for Patients and Communities) requires EPCS for Schedule II – V controlled substances.

4. **D)** The patient's signature is not required on a controlled prescription.

5. **C)** Schedule II drugs cannot be refilled.

6. **A)** In most pharmacies, the pharmacist and the pharmacy technician must double-count and initial the labels of controlled substance medications.

7. **D)** Original and transferred prescriptions must be maintained for a period of 2 years from the date of the last refill.

8. **C)** An expired prescription is not a valid reason to dispense an emergency prescription.

9. **A)** Controlled substances should be stored separately from other drugs to prevent theft and diversion. Schedule II drugs must be kept in a locked safety cabinet where they are accessible only by key or password.

10. **B)** Patient names are not listed on the perpetual inventory log.

11. **D)** The registrant's DEA number is required, not the physician's.

12. **D)** Form 41 only needs to be submitted when requested.

13. **B)** The pharmacist should immediately contact the Drug Enforcement Administration (DEA).

14. **D)** Pharmacy technicians should immediately refer the inspectors to the pharmacist-in-charge.

15. **A)** A prescription drug monitoring program (PDMP) is not used to track patients who have chronic pain and deter them from taking opioids.

16. **C)** In many states, patients do not need a prescription to purchase products containing ephedrine or pseudoephedrine.

17. **A)** The FDA can require manufacturers to develop Risk Evaluation and Mitigation Strategies (REMS) and may take action against participants who do not adhere to them.

PART III

PATIENT SAFETY AND QUALITY ASSURANCE

5 PRESCRIPTION ERRORS

Types of Prescription Errors

Medication errors are preventable events that lead to the misuse of medications and possible harm to the patient. They are one of the most common errors in the health care industry and can occur at any step in the care process, from diagnosis to medication administration. A **prescription error** is a medication error in the prescription itself. A **dispensing error** occurs when the patient does not receive the medication as ordered in the prescription. Medication errors may also occur when drugs are not stored or administered properly. Pharmacy technicians should be familiar with the most common errors that occur in pharmacies:

- **Abnormal doses** occur when the prescribed dose and/or frequency is not consistent with the manufacturer's dosing recommendation. The abnormal dose can result in over/underdose, leading to adverse reactions or a failure in treatment. The pharmacist must be alerted to abnormal doses so the prescriber can correct it.

- **Early refills**—when a patient requests the pharmacy refill a medication before it is due to be refilled—may indicate the patient is taking the medication incorrectly. Pharmacists should be alerted to early refills so they can consult with the patient. If a physician changes a prescription in the middle of a patient's therapy without informing the pharmacy, the pharmacy will need to contact the patient's third-party payer and refill the medication with the updated instructions.

- Patients may be dispensed an **incorrect quantity** of a medication due to counting or clerical errors (e.g., misreading a prescription).
- Medications may be dispensed to the **incorrect patient** if all of the patient's information has not been correctly collected and verified.
- The **incorrect drug** may be dispensed due to technician error. This error is more likely to occur with drugs that have similar names or that are shelved close together.
- **Drug preparation errors** occur when the drug is not prepared as prescribed. Technicians must be especially aware of this type of error during compounding.
- A **deteriorated drug error** occurs when an expired drug is used or the chemical or physical potency and integrity of the drug has been compromised (e.g., it has not been stored properly).
- A **compliance error** occurs when a patient does not take the medication as directed.

> **HELPFUL HINT:**
> Each year, nearly 1.5 million medication errors occur in the United States. In pharmacies, it is estimated that nearly 2% of all written prescriptions contain some form of medication error.

PRACTICE QUESTION

1. A patient was dispensed a 30-day supply of a medication and has requested a refill after 15 days. The pharmacy technician should
   - A) fill the prescription as requested.
   - B) tell the patient that the prescription cannot be refilled early.
   - C) alert the pharmacist.
   - D) call the patient's insurance provider.

Error Prevention

Look-Alike/Sound-Alike Drug Names

Look-alike/sound-alike medications (LASA or SALAD medications) are an increasing problem for health care professionals. There are a large number of brand-name and generic drugs available and currently in development, and some of these drug names sound or are spelled similarly. These similarities can cause health care professionals to mistakenly dispense or administer the wrong drug.

Some contributing factors to misreading LASA drugs include similar packaging, interruptions while preparing the drug, bad lighting, and incorrect placement of stock bottles on the shelf. To resolve these factors and avoid confusion, the FDA and the Joint Commission developed the following strategies and requirements:

- **Tall man lettering** should be used on labels. When drugs have similar names, they are differentiated by capitalizing the dissimilar letters (e.g., ClomiPHENE and ClomiPRAMINE).

> **HELPFUL HINT:**
> Complete and current lists of LASA drugs are available at these websites: www.usp.org, www.ismp.org, and www.fda.gov/medwatch.

- The Joint Commission requires that all LASA medications, along with chemicals and reagents that can be mistaken for drugs, be kept away from other products.
- The Joint Commission also requires that a written policy be displayed in the health care setting specifying necessary precautions and procedures when ordering LASA drugs.
- Health care facilities must define which drugs and products used in the facility qualify as high-risk and develop policies and procedures for the drug or product throughout the dispensing process.
- Finally, health care settings must identify and produce an annual review of all LASA drugs used in the facility.

Pharmacy staff can be proactive in preventing LASA errors by doing the following:

- Pharmacy staff must not store LASA drugs alphabetically with other drug products; they should place LASA drugs on a separate shelf or in another area of the pharmacy.
- Pharmacy staff must undergo training on the precautions taken with LASA drugs to avoid prescribing errors.
- Pharmacy staff should change the appearance of LASA drugs by using techniques such as bold typing, color coding, highlighting, circling, or tall man lettering to emphasize dissimilar parts of the drug name. The same method must be used throughout the chosen medication management system, including the computer system, medication administration records (MARs), and in nursing unit med rooms and bins.
- Pharmacy staff must apply auxiliary labels that warn about LASA drugs.
- Pharmacy staff must avoid abbreviations when entering, filling, or dispensing LASA drugs.
- Pharmacy staff must add a prompt in the pharmacy computer system that warns when LASA drugs are dispensed.

PRACTICE QUESTION

2. Which of the following strategies is used to prevent look-alike/sound-alike (LASA) medication errors?

   A) placing LASA medications in similar packaging

   B) using tall man lettering

   C) using abbreviations

   D) storing all LASA medications on the same shelf

TABLE 5.1. Look-Alike/Sound-Alike Drugs

FDA List of Generic LASA Drugs (full)	ISMP List of LASA Drugs (most common)
acetaZOLAMIDE/acetoHEXAMIDE	ALPRAZolam/LORazepam/clonazePAM
buPROPion/busPIRone	aMILoride/amLODIPine
chlorproMAZINE/chlorproPAMIDE	lamiVUDine/lamoTRIgine
clomiPHENE/clomiPRAMINE	AVINza/INVanz
cycloSERINE/cycloSPORINE	carBAMazepine/OXcarbazepine
DAUNOrubicin/DOXOrubicin	CeleBREX/CeleXA
dimenhyDRINATE/diphenhydrAMINE	clonazePAM/cloNIDine/cloZAPine/cloBAZam/KlonoPIN
DOBUTamine/DOPamine	DEPO-Medrol/SOLU-Medrol
glipiZIDE/glyBURIDE	diazePAM/dilTIAZem
hydrALAZINE/hydrOXYzine/HYDROmorphone	DULoxetine/FLUoxetine/PARoxetine
medroxyPROGESTERone/methylPREDNISolone/methylTESTOSTERone	ePHEDrine/EPINEPHrine
niCARdipine/NIFEdipine	fentaNYL/SUFentanil
prednisoLONE/predniSONE	guaiFENesin/guanFACINE
risperiDONE/rOPINIRole	HumaLOG/HumuLIN
sulfADIAZINE/sulfiSOXAZOLE	LaMICtal/LamISIL
TOLAZamide/TOLBUTamide	levETIRAcetam/levOCARNitine/levoFLOXacin
vinBLAStine/vinCRIStine	metFORMIN/metroNIDAZOLE
	NexAVAR/NexIUM
	NovoLIN/NovoLOG
	OLANZapine/QUEtiapine
	oxyCODONE/HYDROcodone/OxyCONTIN/oxyMORphone
	penicillAMINE/penicillin
	PriLOSEC/PROzac
	raNITIdine/riMANTAdine
	sAXagliptin/SITagliptin/SUMAtriptan
	SEROquel/SINEquan
	TEGretol/TRENtal
	tiaGABine/tiZANidine
	traMADol/traZODone
	valACYclovir/valGANciclovir
	ZyPREXA/ZyrTEC

ABBREVIATION ERRORS

Although using abbreviations in the pharmacy saves time and improves efficiency, **abbreviation errors** can also result in misinterpretations, especially if two abbreviations are similar. The Joint Commission has created an official "Do Not Use" list of abbreviations that can lead to medication errors. The list applies to all orders, pre-printed forms, and medication-related documentation—either handwritten or electronic.

TABLE 5.2. Official "Do Not Use" Abbreviation List

Do Not Use	Potential Problem	Use Instead
U, u (unit)	mistaken for 0 (zero), the number 4 (four), or cc	unit
IU (International Unit)	mistaken for IV (intravenous) or the number 10 (ten)	International Unit
Q.D., QD, q.d., qd (daily) Q.O.D., QOD, q.o.d, qod (every other day)	mistaken for each other period after the Q mistaken for I and the O mistaken for I	daily every other day
Trailing zero (X.0 mg)* Lack of leading zero (.X mg)	missed decimal point	X mg 0.X mg
MS MSO$_4$ and MgSO$_4$	can mean morphine sulfate or magnesium sulfate confused for one another	morphine sulfate magnesium sulfate

*Exception: A trailing zero may be used only where required to demonstrate the level of precision of the value being reported (e.g., laboratory results or catheter/tube sizes). It may not be used in medication orders or other medication-related documentation.

TABLE 5.3. Additional Abbreviations, Acronyms, and Symbols*

Do Not Use	Potential Problem	Use Instead
> (greater than) < (less than)	misinterpreted as the number 7 (seven) or the letter L confused with one another	greater than less than

continued on next page

TABLE 5.3. Additional Abbreviations, Acronyms, and Symbols* (continued)

Do Not Use	Potential Problem	Use Instead
Abbreviations for drug names	misinterpreted due to similar abbreviations for multiple drugs	full name of drug
Apothecary units	unfamiliar to many practitioners confused with metric units	metric units
@	mistaken for the number 2 (two)	the word at
cc	mistaken for U (units) when poorly written	mL (preferred), ml, or milliliters
μg	mistaken for mg (milligrams)	mcg, micrograms

*for possible future inclusion in the "Do Not Use" abbreviation list

PRACTICE QUESTION

3. Which of the following dosages is written incorrectly?

   A) 10 mg
   B) 1 mg
   C) 0.1 mg
   D) 1.0 mg

CHECK SYSTEMS

Preventing medication errors is one of the pharmacist's highest priorities. Pharmacy technicians play a crucial role in preventing errors by assisting the pharmacist with routine tasks so that the pharmacist can focus on verifying prescription orders. Pharmacy technicians also help the pharmacist by being vigilant and checking their and the pharmacists' work through multiple **check systems**.

The first check system is at **prescription drop-off**. Technicians stationed at the drop-off window work with the patient. They gather important information needed to accurately enter the prescription and alert the pharmacist to any issues requiring the pharmacist's attention.

During prescription entry, technicians can use their knowledge and experience to prevent medication errors and enhance patient safety. However, the main tool to protect patient safety during prescription entry is the **drug utilization review (DUR)**. The pharmacy's software will analyze the entered prescription and identify any possible issues. Possible reasons for DUR alerts include

- drug-drug interactions;
- therapeutic duplications (when multiple prescribed drugs are in the same drug class or have the same function in the body);
- drug duplication (when multiple prescribed drugs contain the same active ingredient);
- incorrect dosages;
- allergies or adverse drug reactions;
- drug-disease interactions;
- special circumstances for administration;
- drug-patient interactions (e.g., contraindications for pregnancy or age); and
- formulary substitutions.

The results from a DUR are categorized as mild, moderate, or severe. Pharmacists must use their judgment to assess how each alert should be handled. Technicians must work with pharmacists to decide if the warning can be overridden or if the provider must intervene.

Depending on the pharmacy's policies and procedures, some technicians may be allowed to carry out certain overrides—for instance, if a patient is going on vacation and needs an early refill. If the technician gets an authorization code from the third-party payer allowing the early refill, the pharmacy's policies and procedures may allow the technician to override the prescription.

The first check during the **dispensing process** occurs when the fill technician checks the hard copy or electronic prescription against the prescription label that was generated by the order entry technician. This way, the fill technician is double checking the order entry technician's work for errors and possibly preventing a dispensing error.

Dispensing errors can happen if the fill technician incorrectly reads the label—for example, one consequence could be choosing the incorrect LASA drug from the shelf. A technician might also be rushed and choose the correct drug but not the correct strength. In these cases, it is crucial to check the National Drug Code (NDC) number and the illustration on the label. Tools like barcode technology and vial-filling systems that count out the number of pills needed when the label is generated can help the technician prevent errors.

HELPFUL HINT:

All clinical alerts from the pharmacy's software system, including interactions, allergies, and duplications, must be reported to the pharmacist.

The next check system is the **pharmacist-verification process**. The pharmacist thoroughly checks the prescription order from order entry through the dispensing process. Through scanning and barcode technology, the pharmacy software system will alert the pharmacist to any issues that require reconciliation. The pharmacist will then check the NDC number with the stock bottle, check the labeling for accuracy, and make sure the drug is correct by verifying the illustration image.

The last check system—**point of sale**—is at the checkout counter. Technicians must take a number of important steps in this stage to prevent errors. Checks at point of sale include

- using a second identifier (usually address, phone number, or DOB) in addition to the name to correctly identify the patient;
- verifying the quantity of prescriptions for pickup to ensure no medications have been overlooked or not yet filled; and
- referring patients to the pharmacist for high-risk medications or changes in medication dosages or strengths.

HELPFUL HINT:

Pharmacies place notes on the bag or use other internal protocols that direct technicians to refer patients to a pharmacist for counseling.

PRACTICE QUESTION

4. A pharmacy technician incorrectly reads a label and prepares a prescription for warfarin 5 mg instead of warfarin 2.5 mg. Which of the following multiple-check systems has failed?

   A) data entry
   B) verification
   C) drop-off
   D) dispensing

High-Alert Medications

In institutional settings, **high-alert medications** may cause significant harm to a patient if they are used in error. Although these drugs are not consistently prescribed wrong, when they are, the results can be much more devastating for the patient. There are no legal requirements for pharmacies to meet when dispensing high-alert medications; however, most institutions will have protocols in place to ensure that these medications are dispensed with no errors. High-alert medications include:

- heparin
- opioids
- potassium chloride injections
- insulin
- chemotherapeutic agents
- neuromuscular blocking agents

PRACTICE QUESTION

5. Which of the following medications is NOT a high-alert medication?
   A) neuromuscular blocking agents
   B) heparin
   C) insulin
   D) penicillin

What to Do if an Error Occurs

Error Reporting

Whenever technicians commit or discover a medication error, they must inform their supervisor immediately. Failure to inform supervisors of an error can be grounds for dismissal.

To help prevent future medication errors, technicians should also report errors to either the FDA's **MedWatch** program or the ISMP **National Medication Errors Reporting Program**. Both programs help the FDA, manufacturers, and pharmacy professionals implement protocols to prevent recurring errors. MedWatch is a voluntary reporting program for the FDA that allows health care professionals, patients, and others to anonymously report medication errors and adverse effects. The Institute for Safe Medication Practices (ISMP) is a nonprofit organization that focuses on collecting and reporting on medication errors.

Reports on medication errors can be filed online for both programs. When reporting the error, the technician should include

- an explanation of what went wrong, contributing factors, and how the error was discovered;
- the name(s) of the medication, the form, dosage strength, and manufacturer's name; and
- supplemental information, like pictures or labels.

Sometimes, a medication error *almost* happens—but ultimately does not. These events are called **near-misses**. Even though the error did not occur (and thus no patients were harmed), it is still considered an error and should be reported similarly.

HELPFUL HINT:

Although pharmacy technicians cannot counsel a patient who may have experienced a medication error, they can encourage patients to consult with the pharmacist.

PRACTICE QUESTION

6. A patient who picked up a medication returns the next day and tells the technician that she received the wrong medication and states that she didn't take any of it. The technician should
   A) immediately inform the pharmacist of the error.
   B) file a near-miss report.
   C) dispense the patient's correct prescription.
   D) try to find out why the patient received the wrong medication.

Error Analysis

If an error does occur, it is important to focus on its cause and how to improve the work habits that contributed to the problem. Systemic reviews can identify common factors that lead to errors. Pharmacies can then develop and implement strategies to improve the quality of pharmacy workflow and limit mistakes. This process is referred to as **continuous quality improvement (CQI)**.

Failure mode and effects analysis (FMEA) is an ongoing quality improvement process carried out by health care organizations. FMEA helps pharmacies inspect new products and services to determine points of possible failure and the effects of the failure before any error can actually happen. FMEA is a proactive process that determines steps that can be taken to avoid errors before the product or service is purchased. For example, to reduce medication errors, a multidisciplinary team will use FMEA to assess new drugs before considering placement of the drug in the health care organization's formulary. To complete the process, a series of steps must be taken:

- **Step One:** The multidisciplinary team first determines how the product is to be used. This will be deliberated thoroughly, from purchasing to administering the drug. Questions that would be considered include: What type of patient needs the drug? Who would prescribe the drug? How is the drug stored? How is the drug prepared and administered?

- **Step Two:** While discussing how the drug is used, the team then examines possible failures of the drug, including whether the labeling of the drug could be mistaken for another similarly packaged drug, if the drug could be mistaken for another drug, or if errors could occur during the administration of the drug.

- **Step Three:** After identifying any failures in the process, the team then determines the likelihood and consequences of the mistake. What adverse events could happen if the patient receives the drug at the wrong time, dose, route of administration, or rate?

- **Step Four:** The team factors in any pre-existing conditions in potential recipients of the drug and any processes already in place that may cause an error before the drug reaches the patient. Then, team members use their individual, specialized knowledge to account for human factors to determine the effectiveness of the drug.

- **Step Five:** If any significant errors occur during the evaluation, the team takes actions to detect, prevent, or minimize consequences. Some examples include using a different product, requiring dosing and concentration methods, using warning systems such as auxiliary labels or computer alerts, requiring specific drug

---

CHECK YOUR UNDERSTANDING

Despite safeguards to avoid confusion among LASA drugs, a technician entered the wrong drug. The pharmacist catches the mistake during the verification process. What can the technician do in the future to avoid making the same mistake again?

preparations in the pharmacy, and requiring specific data in the software systems before processing orders.

Root cause analysis (RCA) is used to determine the cause of an error after it has occurred. RCA involves breaking down a process, identifying elements that contributed to a mistake, and devising methods to avoid future errors. Conducting an RCA involves the following steps:

1. Identify events and gather essential information.
2. Form a structured inquiry team with a leader and team members who understand the process under investigation.
3. Determine what happened: collect and organize factual information about the event.
4. Identify relevant factors that increased the likelihood of the event occurring.
5. Determine the root causes that lead to the event.
6. Identify changes that can be implemented to prevent future events.
7. Make plans to measure and evaluate the success of the changes implemented.

When initiating a CQI project, the **FOCUS-PDCA** cycle can be used as well. FOCUS stands for the following:

- **Find** the improvement opportunity.
- **Organize** a group to help in the improvement process.
- **Clarify** current knowledge of the process.
- **Understand** the cause and effect in the process.
- **Select** which improvement needs to take place.

PDCA stands for the following:

- **Plan** the action needed to solve the problem.
- **Do** the action needed to solve the problem.
- **Check** to be sure the action works properly by studying the results.
- **Act** on the action: proceed with implementing the solution.

> **DID YOU KNOW?**
>
> The FMEA helps identify trends in potential errors with drug products and services based on past use experience and informational media tools, such as the *ISMP Medication Safety Alert!* newsletters. The newsletters can be viewed at http://www.ismp.org/newsletters.

PRACTICE QUESTION

7. The goal of root cause analysis is to
   A) punish employees who incorrectly dispense medication.
   B) identify adverse drug effects.
   C) prevent future medication errors.
   D) improve customer satisfaction.

Pharmacist Intervention

In some situations, the customer may need to speak directly to the pharmacist to ensure that medications are dispensed and administered properly. Situations that require pharmacist consultation are discussed below:

- **Consultations on drug indication, action, administration, interactions, or adverse effects:** Technicians are NOT allowed to counsel patients on these issues. When patients need such information, technicians must legally (mandated by the OBRA-90 law) offer patients the opportunity to consult with the pharmacist on duty.
- **Issues flagged during a DUR:** Only the pharmacist can override clinical alerts from a DUR.
- **New prescriptions:** Most state pharmacy boards require pharmacists to counsel patients receiving new prescriptions. The pharmacist ensures that the patient understands the type of medication prescribed and how to take it properly.
- **Consultations on OTC drugs:** Pharmacists can make medicine recommendations, explain proper dosages, and warn patients about potential interactions and side effects.
- **Therapeutic substitution:** Technicians are NOT authorized to make therapeutic substitutions or to explain the substitution to the patient.
- **Misuse or issues with adherence:** The pharmacist should be alerted if the patient appears to be missing drugs or not adhering to instructions for use.
- **Drug allergies:** Patients should speak to the pharmacist about their drug **allergies** and include details such as the time, duration, and allergy symptoms they experienced.
- **Post-immunization follow-up:** Patients with questions about vaccines or vaccine side effects should be directed to the pharmacist.

HELPFUL HINT:

Most OTC medications that treat common cold symptoms are NOT safe for patients with high blood pressure.

PRACTICE QUESTION

8. A patient is picking up a refill for an albuterol inhaler. Which of the following patient questions must be answered by the pharmacist?

   A) "Is a spacer included with the prescription?"
   B) "How many doses can I take in one day?"
   C) "Will my insurance cover the name-brand version of this drug?"
   D) "How many refills do I have left?"

Reference Materials

In the pharmacy, technicians have access to a variety of reference materials available in several different formats; some can also be accessed on the internet. Because reference materials are often consulted during pharmacy work, it is important for technicians to familiarize themselves with this information. Learning to correctly use these materials can help prevent errors in the pharmacy and ensure that prescriptions are verified and filled accurately.

- *American Drug Index*: Available in print and online, the *American Drug Index* is a reference source that identifies and describes thousands of prescription drugs in a dictionary format.
- *American Hospital Formulary Service Drug Information*: This publication provides drug information with therapeutic guidelines and off-label uses. It is written and published by pharmacists and is also available online.
- *Drug Facts and Comparisons*: This is a book that compiles information on 22,000 prescription and 6,000 OTC products and lists products by therapeutic categories. *Drug Facts and Comparisons* includes actions of drugs, warnings and precautions, interactions, adverse reactions, administration and dosage, contraindications and indications, dosages, and brand and generic names. It is also available online.
- *Geriatric Dosage Handbook*: Written by Todd P. Semla, this dictionary-formatted source gives geriatric-sensitive dosing information as well as information about drug interactions and dosing in older adults. In addition, it includes a risk assessment of drugs that should be avoided or used with caution in older adults. It is also available in PDF format.
- **Goodman and Gilman's** *The Pharmacological Basis of Therapeutics*: This pharmacology textbook, nicknamed the *Blue Bible*, was first published in 1941 and emphasizes the relationship between pharmacotherapy and pharmacodynamics. It is also available in PDF format.
- *Handbook of Nonprescription Drugs*: This book contains information on nonprescription drugs and self-care. It includes pharmacotherapy, medical foods, nutritional supplements, nondrug and preventative measures, and therapies unrelated to the use of prescription drugs. It is available in PDF format.
- *Ident-A-Drug*: This online and print pill identifier presents drugs by shape, imprints, and color. The website provides drug illustrations along with brand and generic names, manufacturers, and purposes.

- **Martindale's *The Complete Drug Reference*:** This is an unbiased and evaluated resource book on drugs used internationally. It also provides international disease reviews and drug preparations.
- ***Micromedex Healthcare Evidence and Clinical Xpert*:** This online database includes evidence-based, referenced information on drugs, diseases, acute care, toxicology, and alternative medicines for health care professionals.
- ***Orange Book: Approved Drug Topics with Therapeutic Equivalence Evaluations*:** Also known as the *List*, the *Orange Book* identifies approved drug products along with evaluations of therapeutic equivalents (generic drugs). The *Orange Book* is approved by the FDA, updated daily, and available online.
- ***Pediatric and Neonatal Dosage Handbook*:** Because pharmacodynamics and pharmacokinetics change extensively through infancy to adolescence, this handbook by Jane Hodding and Donna M. Kraus gives important dosing information and evaluations for the management of pediatric patients by health care professionals.
- ***The Pharmacy Technician's Pocket Drug Reference*:** This small, portable book provides brand and generic drug names, illustrations, therapeutic classes, dosage forms and strengths, and therapeutic uses.
- ***The Physician's Desk Reference (PDR)*:** The PDR is a compilation of annually updated manufacturers' prescribing information (package inserts) on prescription drugs. The PDR is also available online.
- ***Red Book: Pharmacy's Fundamental Reference*:** Available in print and online, the *Red Book* is a resource on drug pricing. It includes information about prescription pricing and order entry, forecasting, competitive analysis, formulary development management, claims adjudications, processing, reimbursement information, and average wholesale price (AWP) policies.
- **Trissel's *Handbook on Injectable Drugs*:** This reference book gives extensive information on injectable drugs available in the US and internationally. It explains in detail how to prepare, store, and administer injectable drugs. The handbook also gives information on drug stability and compatibility.
- **The United States Pharmacopeial (USP) Convention's *Pharmacopeia*:** A body of information on the standards of strength, purity, and quality of drugs, this publication was made a legal standard in 1907 and is revised periodically. It is also available online.

- *United States Pharmacopeia-National Formulary (USP-NF):* This is a compilation of both the USP and the National Formulary; it includes standards for botanicals, excipients, and other similar products. In 1975, the USP and NF were combined into one book.

PRACTICE QUESTION

9. Which reference material identifies approved drug products and includes evaluations of therapeutic equivalents (generic drugs)?

    A) the Red Book
    B) Ident-A-Drug
    C) the Orange Book
    D) The Physician's Desk Reference

ANSWER KEY

1. **C)** The pharmacist should be alerted to early refill requests.

2. **B)** Tall man lettering helps differentiate LASA medications from each other.

3. **D)** To help avoid medication errors, trailing zeroes (the zero after the decimal point) should not be used.

4. **D)** Pharmacy technicians may incorrectly read the prescription label during the dispensing process when selecting the drug.

5. **D)** Penicillin is not a high-alert medication.

6. **A)** All medication errors should be immediately reported to the pharmacist.

7. **C)** Root cause analysis is performed to identify how an error occurred so that it can be prevented from occurring again.

8. **B)** Questions about drug administration, such as dosing, should be directed to the pharmacist.

9. **C)** The *Orange Book* identifies approved drug products and includes evaluations of therapeutic equivalents (generic drugs).

SAFETY IN THE WORKPLACE

The Occupational Safety and Health Administration (OSHA)

Hazards exist in all workplace settings. Employees must know the policies and procedures at their workplaces to protect themselves and others. In pharmacies, workplace safety policies and procedures are determined primarily by OSHA but may also come from the Board of Pharmacy (BOP) and the individual pharmacy.

The Occupational Safety and Health Administration (OSHA) was established in 1970 to ensure safe working conditions in the United States. As part of the US Department of Labor, OSHA establishes mandatory workplace safety regulations and monitors the workplace to ensure compliance with these regulations.

OSHA requires that employers keep the workplace free of all recognized hazards that can cause serious injury and/or death. Employers must follow certain steps to guarantee the safety and health of their employees. OSHA may inspect any workplace to ensure proper steps and protocols are being followed. It can cite or discipline any business that does not comply with safety standards.

OSHA requires employees to abide by health and safety standards that apply to their job specifications and that were agreed to at the time of hire. Pharmacy technicians should follow these important health and safety standards:

- Observe warning labels on biohazard packaging and containers.

- Bandage any breaks in skin or lesions on hands before gloving.
- Do not recap, bend, or break contaminated needles or other sharps.
- Minimize splashing, spraying, or splattering of hazardous chemicals or infectious materials.
- If exposed skin comes in contact with bodily fluids, scrub with soap and water as soon as possible; if the eyes are contaminated, flush with water, preferably at an eye station.
- Decontaminate contaminated materials before reprocessing or place them in biohazard bags and dispose of them according to policies and procedures.
- Do not keep food or drink in refrigerators, freezers, or cabinets, or on countertops or shelves that can be exposed to blood, bodily fluids, or hazardous chemicals.
- Do not use mouth pipetting or suck blood or other harmful substances from tubing.
- Use hemostats to attach or remove scalpel blades from handles.

OSHA regulations that apply to the pharmacy setting include the Hazard Communication Standard and the Bloodborne Pathogens Standard. OSHA also addresses workplace safety issues not specific to pharmacies, including fire safety, emergency plans, environmental standards, latex allergies, work-related musculoskeletal injuries, ergonomics, and violence in the workplace. OSHA provides information, training, and education to help the implementation and continuity of required policies.

PRACTICE QUESTION

1. What is an important OSHA health and safety standard that pharmacy technicians should follow?
    - **A)** Use gloved hands to remove scalpel blades from handles.
    - **B)** Recap contaminated needles.
    - **C)** Bandage lesions on hands before gloving.
    - **D)** Immediately dry skin that was exposed to bodily fluids.

Hygiene and Cleaning Standards

The Chain of Infection

When an organism establishes an opportunistic relationship with a host, the process is called **infection**. This begins with the transmission of organisms and ends with the development of an infectious disease. Infections can be caused by many different infectious agents:

- **Bacteria** are single-celled prokaryotic organisms that are responsible for many common infections, such as strep throat, urinary tract infections, and food-borne illnesses.
- **Viruses** are composed of a nucleic acid (DNA or RNA) wrapped in a protein capsid. They invade host cells and hijack cell machinery to reproduce. Viral infections include the common cold, influenza, and human immunodeficiency virus (HIV).
- **Protozoa** are single-celled eukaryotic organisms. Protozoan infections include giardia (an intestinal infection) and African sleeping sickness.
- **Fungi** are eukaryotic organisms that include yeasts, molds, and mushrooms. Common fungal infections are athlete's foot, ringworm, and oral and vaginal yeast infections.
- Parasitic diseases are caused by **parasites** that live in or on the human body and use its resources. Common human parasites include worms (e.g., tapeworms), flukes, and ectoparasites like lice and ticks, which live on the outside of the body.

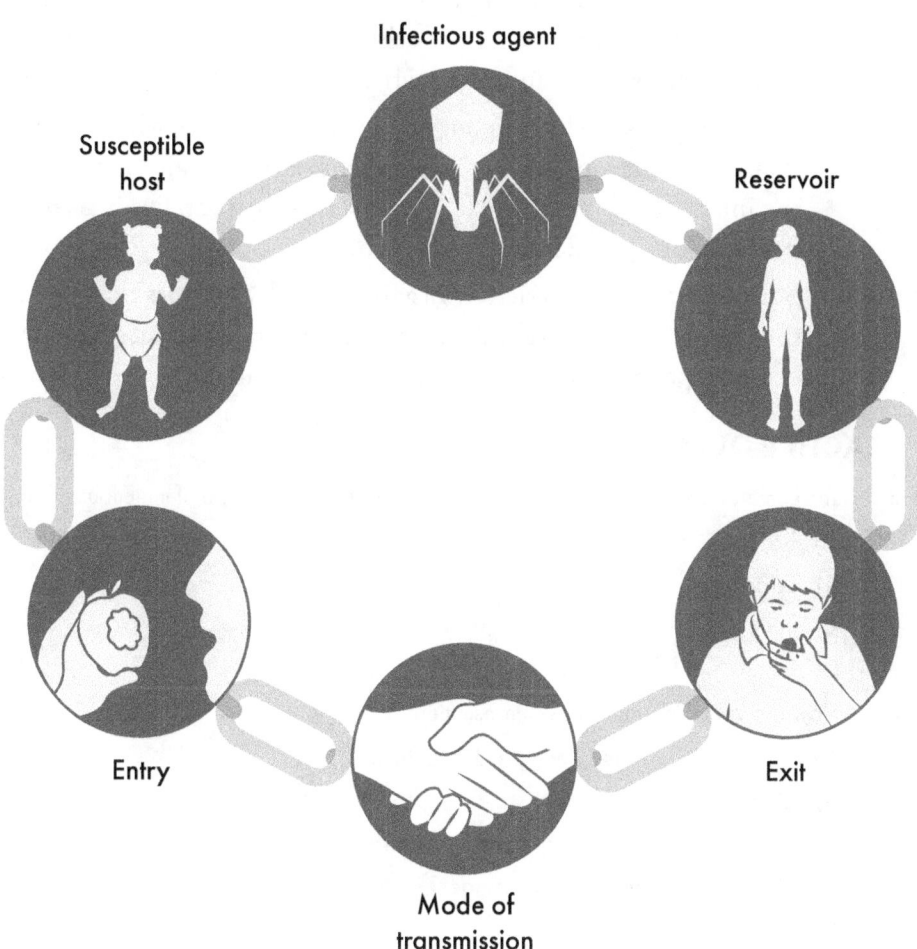

Figure 6.1. Chain of Infection

Infections travel from person to person via the **chain of infection**, which starts with a causative organism (e.g., a bacteria or virus). The organism needs a **reservoir**—a place to live—that is either biological, such as people or animals, or environmental. For example, in a medical office, equipment and office surfaces may act as reservoirs. To spread, the infectious agent needs a way to **exit** the reservoir, such as being expelled as droplets during a sneeze.

For the chain of infection to continue, the infectious agent must encounter a susceptible **host**—a person who can become infected. Finally, the infectious agent needs a way to enter the host, such as through inhalation or drinking contaminated water. There are different **modes of transmission** for infectious agents:

- **Direct contact** is transmission between an infected person and another from physical contact with blood or other bodily fluids (e.g., transmission of herpes during sexual intercourse).
- **Indirect contact** is transmission through a nonbiological reservoir (e.g., drinking water contaminated with giardia).
- **Droplets** are infectious agents trapped in moisture that are expelled when an infected person sneezes or coughs. They can enter the respiratory system of other people and cause infection (e.g., transmission of influenza when an infected person sneezes).
- Some droplets are light enough to remain airborne, which means that people may inhale infectious agents from the air long after the initial cough or sneeze (e.g., measles, which can live in **airborne droplets** for up to 2 hours).
- Some diseases are carried by organisms called **vectors** that spread the disease; the infection does not require direct physical contact between people (e.g., mosquitoes carrying malaria).

HELPFUL HINT:

Infectious disease precautions are categorized based on how the disease is transmitted. For example, droplet precautions require only a surgical mask, but airborne precautions require an N-95 respirator to prevent transmission.

PRACTICE QUESTIONS

2. The common cold, influenza, and HIV are caused by which type of infectious agent?
   - **A)** bacteria
   - **B)** protozoan
   - **C)** virus
   - **D)** fungus

3. How are vector-borne diseases transmitted?
   - **A)** Fluids are transferred during direct contact.
   - **B)** Small droplets are inhaled.
   - **C)** Contaminated water is consumed.
   - **D)** Organisms carry the infectious agent.

Infection Control

Infection control is the prevention of disease transmission in health care settings. The goal of infection control is to break the chain of infection and prevent disease from traveling from one person to another. Different levels of infection control are appropriate for different health care settings. In general, the removal of infectious agents can occur at three levels:

- **Cleaning** removes dirt and some infectious agents.
- **Disinfection** kills all pathogens except bacterial spores. Most surfaces in health care settings are disinfected using chemical agents, such as alcohol or chlorine bleach.
- **Sterilization** kills all infectious agents, including bacterial spores. Medical equipment is sterilized using heat or chemicals (e.g., ethylene oxide).

Asepsis is the absence of infectious organisms, and **medical asepsis** is the practice of destroying infectious agents outside the body to prevent the spread of disease. Aseptic technique requires the use of sterile personal protective equipment (PPE) and sterile instruments. In pharmacies, aseptic techniques are used during sterile compounding to prevent contamination of medications. Sterile compounding is required for medications administered intravenously, with an injection, or in the eye.

Medical asepsis is different from **clean technique**, which also aims to minimize the spread of infectious agents but does not require sterilization. Wearing gloves is an example of clean technique: the gloves are not sterile, but they provide a barrier that prevents the spread of infection. Pharmacy technicians should use clean technique when preparing nonsterile medications to prevent the spread of infection.

Pharmacy technicians are responsible for infection control during all aspects of their work, including hand hygiene, disinfection of surfaces and equipment, and proper use of PPE. Guidelines for proper **hand hygiene** include the following:

- handwashing
    - Use soap and water when hands are visibly soiled and wash for at least 15 seconds.
    - Use antimicrobial foam or gel if hands are not visibly soiled.
    - Wash hands after eating and using the bathroom.
    - Use aseptic handwashing techniques for sterile compounding.
- gloves
    - Wear gloves when handling medications, including nonsterile compounds.

> **HELPFUL HINT:**
>
> Clean or sterile surfaces become **contaminated** when they come in contact with pathogens.

- Discard gloves when soiled and apply a new pair.
- Practice hand hygiene after removing gloves.
- nails and jewelry
  - Keep nails short to prevent harboring bacteria.
  - Minimize jewelry use and remove before performing hand hygiene.

Pharmacy surfaces, including equipment, carts, and shelves, must be disinfected regularly using a disinfectant approved by the Environmental Protection Agency (EPA). The EPA defines three levels of disinfecting and sterilizing agents based on the substance's ability to kill microorganisms:

- **Low-level disinfectants** kill most microorganisms but are not tuberculocidal or sporicidal. Most health care facilities use low-level disinfectants to clean floors, walls, and surfaces not directly involved in clinical care.
- **Intermediate-level disinfectants** do not kill bacterial spores but do kill most microorganisms, including bacteria, fungi, and viruses; they are also tuberculocidal. In health care settings, these disinfectants are used to clean clinical contact surfaces.
- **High-level disinfectants** kill viable microorganisms like bacteria, fungi, viruses, and low numbers of bacterial spores. These are immersion-only products used to disinfect reusable items.
- **Sterilants** destroy all microorganisms and high numbers of spores. These are immersion-only products used to disinfect reusable items.

To clean surfaces and equipment, obvious soiling or visible dirt must be removed first (usually with soap and water). The surface can then be disinfected (usually with 70% isopropyl alcohol [IPA]). Paper towels, sponges, or mops can be used to clean, but they must be made of a non-shedding material. The schedule for cleaning surfaces is guided by the minimum cleaning frequency table displayed in USP <797>.

Personal protective equipment (PPE) is any item necessary for the prevention of microorganism transmission. PPE includes gloves, gowns, goggles, eye shields, shoe covers, and masks.

In the pharmacy, PPE should be used
- in all sterile environments,
- when handling hazardous materials,
- during routine cleaning,
- during possible exposure to bloodborne pathogens, and
- around toxic spills.

HELPFUL HINT:

USP <800> specifies the items that must be worn when working with hazardous materials, including chemotherapy drugs and other types of compounded sterile products.

 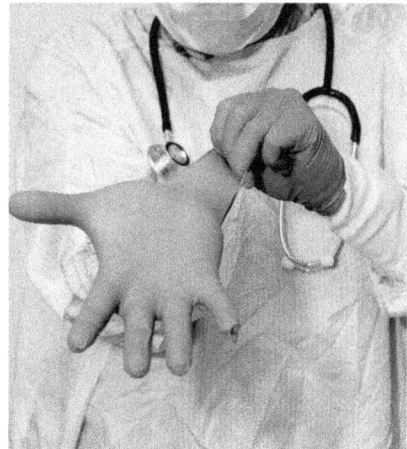

Figure 6.2. Personal Protective Equipment

PRACTICE QUESTIONS

4. A surface is disinfected after it has been
   A) cleaned with chlorine bleach.
   B) washed with soap and water.
   C) covered with a drape sheet.
   D) allowed to sit unused for 24 hours.
5. The pharmacy technician MUST wear PPE when
   A) stocking inventory in a non-compounding area.
   B) compounding sterile products.
   C) handling cash from customers.
   D) dispensing controlled substances.

STANDARD PRECAUTIONS

Standard precautions (also called "universal precautions") are based on the assumption that all patients are infected with microorganisms, whether or not there are symptoms or a diagnosis. The standards apply to contact with blood, all bodily fluids, secretions, and excretions (except sweat), non-intact skin, and mucous membranes.

This set of principles is used by all health care workers who have direct or indirect contact with patients. When working with patients and specimens, the technician should always follow these standard precautions:

- Assume that all patients are carrying microorganisms.
- Use appropriate PPE.
- Practice hand hygiene.
- Follow needle-stick prevention policies.
- Clean and disinfect surfaces after each patient.

- Use disposable barriers to protect surfaces that are hard to disinfect.

Additional precautions, such as N-95 masks or face shields, may be needed when interacting with patients with known infections. These precautions are based on the transmission route for the infection.

> **PRACTICE QUESTION**
>
> 6. The use of standard precautions is NOT required for contact with which substance?
>   A) blood
>   B) urine
>   C) sweat
>   D) vomit

BLOODBORNE PATHOGENS STANDARDS

Bloodborne pathogens are microorganisms found in human blood and tissue. Common bloodborne pathogens that present a risk to health care providers include

- human immunodeficiency virus (HIV), a virus that attacks the immune system;
- hepatitis B (HBV), hepatitis C (HCV), and hepatitis D (HDV), viruses that attack the liver; and
- cytomegalovirus, a common virus that usually has no symptoms but may lead to more serious disorders in people with compromised immune systems.

OSHA's **Bloodborne Pathogens Standards** require precautions to protect against bloodborne pathogens. Employers may face penalties if these protocols are not followed. According to the standards, employers must provide

- all necessary PPE;
- environmental control methods, including access to clean air and water and appropriate processes for waste disposal;
- training on bloodborne pathogens for employees; and
- an exposure control plan that explains steps to be taken by employees exposed to bloodborne pathogens.

The **exposure control plan** outlines how the pharmacy must handle exposure to blood, bodily fluids, or other infectious agents. The plan is updated annually with employee input. Employees must be regularly trained on the plan. The plan must also be posted in a visible area and available at all times to employees.

Exposure controls defined by OSHA include engineering and work practice controls. **Engineering controls** refer to devices such as eyewash stations, biohazard symbols, needle-less systems, and proper handwashing facilities that reduce exposure to microorganisms. **Work practice controls** are defined by OSHA as the use of universal precautions for infection control, proper disinfection procedures, and proper handling of spills.

PRACTICE QUESTION

7. Which of the following is a common bloodborne pathogen that may be transmitted in a health care setting?

    A) tuberculosis
    B) influenza
    C) hepatitis B
    D) varicella zoster virus

Hazardous Materials
Classifying Hazardous Materials and Waste

Hazardous materials are any substances or chemicals that can harm humans or the environment. Hazardous materials that need to be disposed of are called **hazardous waste**. The EPA regulates the disposal of hazardous waste through the Resource Conservation and Recovery Act (RCRA). It maintains lists of substances that are considered hazardous and must be disposed of using EPA regulations:

- **P-list** wastes are acutely hazardous chemicals sold as commercial formulations (e.g., nicotine, epinephrine, and warfarin).
- **U-list** wastes are hazardous chemicals sold as commercial formulations (e.g., lindane and many chemotherapy agents).
- The **F-** and **K-lists** include hazardous waste generated by manufacturing and industrial processes.

The EPA also considers materials to be hazardous if they have any of the following characteristics:

- ignitable (substances that catch fire easily)
- corrosive (strong acids or bases)
- reactive (release toxic fumes or cause explosions)
- toxic (harmful when ingested or absorbed)

HELPFUL HINT:

Drugs on the P- and U-lists are assigned a hazardous waste number (e.g., warfarin >3% is P001).

HELPFUL HINT:

The EPA no longer considers specific nicotine replacement therapies, such as nicotine patches, gums, and lozenges, as hazardous waste.

PRACTICE QUESTION

8. Which of these is an example of a U-list compound?

    A) nicotine
    B) levothyroxine
    C) lindane
    D) warfarin

Hazard Communication Programs

OSHA requires all businesses that handle hazardous materials to have a **hazard communication program**. The key elements of this program are

- properly labeling hazardous materials;
- maintaining an up-to-date safety data sheet (SDS) for all hazardous material on site; and
- training workers to properly handle hazardous materials.

OSHA requires special labeling that includes visual notation for hazardous materials in order to quickly warn users of hazardous products and provide instructions for proper handling. The label must also include

- relevant pictograms;
- signal words ("danger" or "warning");
- a hazard statement (describes nature of hazard);
- a precautionary statement (describes recommended measures for prevention, exposure, storage, and disposal);
- a product identifier;
- supplier identification; and
- the manufacturer's name, address, and phone number.

Figure 6.3. OSHA Pictograms

The **safety data sheet (SDS)** is provided by the manufacturer and lists the properties, hazards, and safe handling protocols for a specific substance. The SDSs should be stored together (usually in a binder) in the pharmacy so they can be easily accessed when needed.

Hazardous material training should include a review of the hazards that exist in the workplace as well as the location of SDSs and all other hazard-related information. Employees should review how to read and understand chemical labels and hazard signs. They must also be told when and how PPE is used and the location of equipment, including cleaning supplies. Finally, training should describe management of chemical spills and decontamination procedures.

HELPFUL HINT:
All cleaning must start at the edge of the spill, gradually working to the center.

PRACTICE QUESTION

9. Which is NOT included in the hazard communication program?
   A) location of SDSs
   B) location of hazard-related information
   C) location of cleaning equipment
   D) instructions on how to fill out a workers' compensation claim

Waste Disposal

All waste generated in the pharmacy must be handled and disposed of properly. Everyday waste, such as paper and stock bottles, can be recycled or thrown out with general waste; however, many types of pharmacy waste must meet special disposal guidelines. These types include

- nonhazardous pharmaceutical waste,
- hazardous waste, and
- biohazardous waste.

Nonhazardous pharmaceutical waste includes unused drugs not listed by the EPA on the P- or U-lists. This type of waste is disposed of in designated containers labeled "for incineration." These containers are typically blue or white with a blue lid. The collected waste can then be gathered and properly disposed.

Hazardous pharmaceutical waste (also called RCRA waste) includes drugs on the P- and U-lists. Hazardous pharmaceutical waste is collected in appropriately labeled black waste containers. Pharmacies can store hazardous waste that is not eligible for reverse distribution for up to 1 year before shipping it to waste treatment facilities.

HELPFUL HINT:
It is a violation of EPA guidelines to dispose of hazardous pharmaceutical waste in a sewer (i.e., in a sink or toilet).

Hazardous pharmaceutical waste is collected and sent to EPA-approved facilities for destruction. The EPA requires a **hazardous waste manifest** when pharmaceutical waste is removed from pharmacies and sent to a licensed waste treatment facility. The manifest contains information on the pharmacy, disposal facility, and transportation.

Regulated medical waste (RMW) (also called **biohazardous waste**) is any waste that is or may be contaminated with infectious materials, including blood, secretions, and excretions. To prevent exposure, RMW must be handled carefully. The disposal of RMW is governed by federal, state, and local regulations that vary by location. Some general waste disposal guidelines include the following:

- Bandages, dressing gauzes, and gloves with small amounts of RMW can be put in regular garbage disposal cans.
- Items soiled by blood or infectious material should be placed in a red biohazard waste bag or container.
- Blood and bodily fluids, such as urine and sputum, can be disposed of in a drain, toilet, or utility sink. (State and local regulations may limit the amount of fluid that can be disposed of into the sewage system.) Feces should be flushed in a toilet.

Sharps should be disposed of in a **biohazard sharps container**. The term *sharps* refers to needles, lancets, blood tubes, capillary tubes, razor blades, suturing needles, hypodermic needles, and microscope slides and coverslips.

Figure 6.4. Sharps Container

PRACTICE QUESTION

10. Hazardous pharmaceutical waste should be collected in a properly labeled container that is which color?

    A) blue

    B) black

    C) red

    D) green

SPILLS AND CLEANUPS

A pharmacy's health and safety program should include procedures for dealing with hazardous and nonhazardous drug spills. All employees should be educated on these procedures. Every facility has its own policies, but some general guidelines for handling spills are as follows:

- Spills and breaks should be cleaned up immediately.
- The person cleaning the spill should wear appropriate PPE.
- A warning sign should be placed by spills of hazardous materials to limit access.
- Anyone who comes in contact with a spilled substance should decontaminate appropriately (e.g., washing hands, brushing off dry powders, removing contaminated clothing, washing eyes).

An **incident report** documenting the spill and the exposed people should be completed to track exposures.

Spill kits containing all the required materials to clean up hazardous spills must be available. These kits should be labeled and placed in areas where hazardous materials are handled. Kits should include

- sufficient supplies to absorb approximately 1,000 mL of spilled liquid;
- appropriate personal protective equipment;
- absorbent sheets with a plastic backing or spill pads;
- disposable paper towels;
- at least two sealable, thick plastic hazardous waste disposal bags (prelabeled with an appropriate warning label);
- one disposable scoop for gathering glass fragments;
- one puncture-resistant container for glass pieces; and
- a National Institute for Occupational Safety and Health (NIOSH)-approved respirator.

PRACTICE QUESTION

11. Spill kits should contain sufficient supplies to absorb approximately how much spilled liquid?

    A) 1 mL
    B) 10 mL
    C) 100 mL
    D) 1,000 mL

ANSWER KEY

1. **C)** Before gloving, workers must bandage any breaks in skin or lesions on hands.

2. **C)** Viruses are responsible for the common cold, influenza, and HIV (human immunodeficiency virus).

3. **D)** Vector-borne diseases are carried by other organisms (called vectors) between hosts.

4. **A)** Chlorine bleach is a disinfectant that kills most pathogens.

5. **B)** Compounding sterile products requires the use of personal protective equipment (PPE), including gloves and masks.

6. **C)** Standard precautions are recommended whenever a worker comes in contact with blood or bodily fluids that could transmit bloodborne pathogens. Bloodborne pathogens cannot be transmitted via sweat.

7. **C)** Hepatitis B (HBV) is a common bloodborne pathogen that presents a risk to health care providers.

8. **C)** Lindane is considered a hazardous chemical that is sold as a commercial formulation.

9. **D)** The hazard communication program does not need to discuss workers' compensation claims.

10. **B)** Hazardous pharmaceutical waste is collected in black waste containers labeled "hazardous pharmaceutical waste."

11. **D)** Spill kits should contain sufficient supplies to absorb approximately 1,000 mL of spilled liquid.

PART IV

ORDER ENTRY AND PROCESSING

7 ORDER PROCESSING

Prescription Processing

Prescription Review and Data Entry

Pharmacy technicians may receive either handwritten or printed **hard-copy** prescription orders from patients. All hard-copy prescriptions are required by federal law to include specific information:

```
                        PRACTICE NAME
                        Practitioner Name
                         1234 Main St.
                         City, State Zip
                Tel: (000) 555 1234   Fax: (000) 555 2345

    Name     John Doe                          DOB   10/14/1963
    Address  1234 Second St. Chicago, Ill      Date  8/19/2016

    R   no dng allergies

        metFORmin (Glucophage) 500 mg tablets
        #100
        take 1 daily for control of diabetes


      Label  ☐

      Refill_____3_____times

                                       Barbara N. Clay   MD

                                                                 Script 1000
```

Figure 7.1. Hard-Copy Prescription

→ **CONTINUE**

- patient name: required for verification
- patient phone number: required for verification and to notify the patient when the prescription is ready or for any issues with the filling process
- patient date of birth (DOB): used for verification
- prescriber's office name, address, and phone number: required to contact prescribers' offices with questions or requests for refills
- prescriber's signature (copied or handwritten)
- date the prescription was written
- medication, strength, quantity, dose, and dosage form of the medication
- administration route
- signa (directions for use)
- refill information: how many refills the prescriber authorized

HELPFUL HINT:

Most prescriptions for noncontrolled substances expire one year after the prescription was written.

The pharmacy technician must carefully check all information when processing a hard-copy prescription. Verifying these details before the customer leaves the counter improves accuracy and prevents delays.

The pharmacy technician must first ensure the patient's name and DOB are legible on the prescription. If the physician wrote the prescription, verify the spelling. Ask for the patient's date of birth and write it on the prescription, even if the physician already added it.

Next, the technician should ask whether the patient has filled prescriptions at the pharmacy before. If she already has a patient profile, make any necessary updates. Check the status of her insurance and, if it has changed, enter the correct information into her profile before she leaves the counter. If the patient is new to the pharmacy, the technician will need to create a new profile.

The technician should also ask if the patient has any drug allergies. Write these on the prescription or confirm the information in the patient's profile. If the patient has no allergies, write the abbreviation **NKA** (no known allergies) in the profile and on the prescription.

Next, the technician should review the prescription details, including

- drug name,
- dosage,
- dose form,
- directions, and
- quantity.

Although the prescriber usually checks for accuracy, mistakes can happen, which can delay the processing of the prescription. If the prescriber needs to be contacted, notify the patient of the delay to prevent customer frustration.

After the technician has reviewed the prescription, it can be entered into the pharmacy's software program. The software program will prompt the technician to add the information into specific fields that include

- name of the drug,
- strength,
- dose,
- number of refills available,
- physician's information, and
- sig codes.

Electronic prescriptions (e-prescriptions) are sent directly from the point of care to the pharmacy to ensure accurate and comprehensible prescriptions. State and federal guidelines for e-prescribing continue to evolve, with some states mandating e-prescribing in certain scenarios. The federal government promotes the use of e-prescriptions to create a nationwide electronic health information infrastructure.

E-prescriptions are received by the pharmacy's prescription tracking program and are automatically placed in a queue. The program provides a notification that a new prescription has arrived.

Technicians process e-prescriptions similarly to hard-copy prescriptions. First, the information in the prescription is reviewed for errors. (A hard copy may be printed to make this process easier.) Next, the prescription information is entered. This information may auto-populate in the patient's profile, or the technician may need to enter it manually.

HELPFUL HINT:

Electronic prescriptions must be transmitted using software that complies with HIPAA and DEA regulations.

PRACTICE QUESTION

1. What is the signa on a prescription?
   A) physician's signature
   B) patient's social security number
   C) physician's medical license number
   D) directions for taking the medication

THE PATIENT PROFILE

The **patient profile** holds important demographic and medical information about the patient. Keeping the profile updated is vital to dispensing medications correctly and preventing medication errors.

The profile contains the patient's name, telephone number, and date of birth. These identifiers can be used to ensure that the patient is matched with the correct profile in the computer. The patient should confirm personal information at each pharmacy visit. If the patient has moved or changed numbers, the profile must be updated.

The patient profile also contains the patient's allergies, medical history, and a list of current medications. All of these sections must be kept up to date to ensure that the drug utilization review (DUR) is accurate. The profile may also contain information related to a patient's history of substance use.

Any special considerations made by the pharmacist, physician, or patient should be added to the patient's profile. Special considerations are anything that restricts the patient, including

- vision problems;
- difficulty opening bottles (e.g., due to arthritis);
- mobility restrictions necessitating delivery or an authorized representative to pick up a patient's medication; and
- language barriers (e.g., medication directions to be written in a language other than English).

The patient profile includes payment information and details of the patient's insurance plan:

- Cardholder's name and **insurance ID number**: This is the name of the person, or beneficiary, who receives the health insurance; it may differ from that of the patient who brought in the prescription to be filled.
- **Dependent relationship code**: If the patient is not the cardholder, she is considered a dependent of the cardholder and will have a specific code.
- **Prescription group number**: The group number directs the claim to the specific insurance benefits for that group. The groups are a collection of people who have similar benefits packages, such as employee groups.
- **Processor control number (PCN)**: This number is used by pharmacy benefit managers for network benefit routing and may change depending on which benefit is being billed.
- Pharmacy **benefit international identification number (BIN)** or **issuer identification number (IIN)**: This number directs the claim to the correct third-party provider. All pharmacy third-party payers have BIN numbers.
- **Date of birth**: The patient's date of birth is used as an identification tool; the date of birth for each person covered is located next to the person's name on the card.

Finally, the patient's profile will have up-to-date information on current prescriptions filled and refills available. In this section, information such as date of last refill and copay price at the time of service is provided. This information changes with each new fill.

HELPFUL HINT:

Certain drugs derived from food products can cause severe allergic reactions. Drug companies use dyes for color identification of pills.

PRACTICE QUESTIONS

2. What is the FIRST and most important step when inputting new prescriptions for patients?

- **A)** correctly translating sig codes
- **B)** inputting third-party payer information
- **C)** adding override codes
- **D)** using identifiers to find the correct patient profile

3. Which number is necessary to ensure that claims are sent to the correct third-party payer?

- **A)** prescription group number
- **B)** processor control number
- **C)** issuer identification number
- **D)** insurance ID number

HELPFUL HINT:

The pharmacy label attached to the patient's prescription will translate the sig code directions from the original prescription into easily understandable directions for the patient.

SIG CODES AND ABBREVIATIONS

Pharmacy abbreviations—also called **sig codes**—are used by health care providers when writing prescriptions. They encode medication dosage and instructions for administration. The pharmacy technician MUST know these codes to accurately process prescriptions.

TABLE 7.1. Common Sig Codes

Abbreviation	Meaning
Drug Form	
aq, aqua	water
cap or caps	capsules
comp.	compound
cr., crm.	cream
D.W.	distilled water
elix.	elixir
emuls.	emulsion
fl., fld.	fluid
LCD	coal tar solution
lin.	liniment
liq.	liquid
lot.	lotion
mist.	mixture
NS	normal saline, sodium chloride

continued on next page

TABLE 7.1. Common Sig Codes (continued)

Abbreviation	Meaning
Drug Form	
½NS	half-strength normal saline
RL, R/L	Ringer's lactate solution (or lactated Ringer's solution)
sol.	solution
SR, XL, XR	slow release/extended release
sup.	suppository
susp.	suspension
syr.	syrup
tab.	tablet
talc.	talcum
troche	lozenge
ung., oint.	ointment
Measurement	
ī	1
ss ; ss	one-half
a.a., aa	of each
ad	to, up to
aq. ad	add water up to
B.S.A.	body surface area
cc	cubic centimeter
dil.	dilute
div.	divide
fl. oz.	fluid ounce
g, G, gm	gram
gtt(s)	drop(s)
l., L.	liter
mcg	microgram
mEq	milliequivalent
mg	milligram
mL	milliliter
oz	ounce
q.s.	a sufficient quantity

Abbreviation	Meaning
Measurement	
tbsp	tablespoonful
tsp	teaspoonful
Route of Administration	
a.d.	right ear
app.	apply
a.s., a.l.	left ear
a.u.	both ears
i.m., IM	intramuscularly
inj.	inject
i.v., IV	intravenously
IVP	IV push
IVPB	IV piggyback
NAS	intranasal
o.d.	right eye
o.s., o.l.	left eye
o.u.	both eyes
p.o.	by mouth
p.r., PR	rectally
prn	as needed
SC, subc, subQ, subcut	subcutaneous
SL	sublingual
TOP, top.	topically
PV, vag.	vaginally
Time	
a.c.	before meals
ad lib	at one's pleasure
alt. h.	every other hour
a.m.	morning
A.T.C.	around the clock
b.i.d., b.d.	twice daily
e.t.	expired time
h, hr.	hour
h.s.	at bedtime

continued on next page

TABLE 7.1. Common Sig Codes (continued)

Abbreviation	Meaning
Time	
min.	minute
noct.	at night
non rep.	do not repeat
p.c.	after food, after meals
p.m.	afternoon, evening
q	each, every
q.a.m.	every morning
q.d.	every day
q.h.	every hour
q.h.s.	every night at bedtime
q.i.d.	4 times daily
q.o.d.	every other day
stat.	immediately
t.i.d., tid	3 times daily
t.i.w.	3 times a week
Other	
s	without
agit.	shake, stir
amp.	ampule
b.m.	bowel movement
bol.	bolus
B.S.	blood sugar
c	with
D.A.W.	dispense as written
dc, D/C, disc.	discontinue
disp.	dispense
d.t.d.	dispense such doses
ex aq.	in water
i.d.	intradermal
neb., nebul.	nebulizer
NMT	not more than
NR	no refill

Abbreviation	Meaning
Other	
NTE	not to exceed
per	by
pulv.	pulverized
R	rub
rep., rept.	repeat
sig	write on label
ss	one-half
TPN	total parenteral nutrition
u.d., utd., ut. dict.	as directed
USP	United States Pharmacopeia
w	with
w/o, wo	without
X	times
y.o., Y.O.	years old

PRACTICE QUESTIONS

4. What does "Take 1 tab. q.i.d. prn pain" mean?
    A) Take 1 teaspoonful every 4 hours as needed for pain.
    B) Take 1 tablet every day as needed for pain.
    C) Take 1 tablet 4 times daily as needed for pain.
    D) Take 1 tablespoonful every day as needed for pain.
5. What does "Instill 1 gtt in o.u. b.d." mean?
    A) Instill 1 drop in the left ear twice daily.
    B) Instill 1 drop in both eyes twice daily.
    C) Instill 1 drop in the left eye twice daily.
    D) Instill 1 drop in both ears twice daily.

NATIONAL DRUG CODE NUMBERS AND LOT NUMBERS

In 1972, the **Drug Listing Act** implemented the use of **national drug codes (NDCs)**. Every drug has a 10-digit NDC divided into three sections:

- The first section, which consists of 5 numbers, is the labeler or manufacturer's code and is provided by the FDA.
- The second is the product code, which specifies the product or drug.

▫ The third is the package code, which represents the size and type of the product.

If the NDC has two asterisks (**) at the end of the package number, it means that the product is a bulk, raw, or non-formulated controlled substance.

> **HELPFUL HINT:**
>
> Each NDC is also assigned a **barcode** that is included on the drug label for easy scanning and verification.

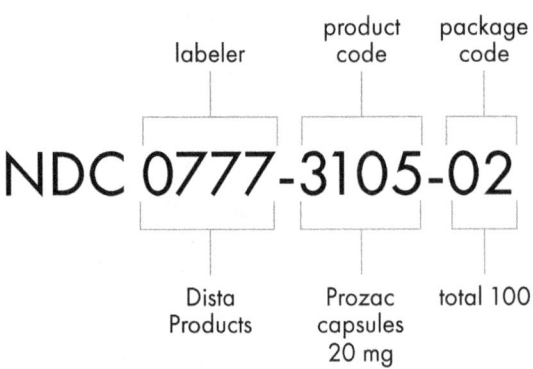

Figure 7.2. NDC Number

Federal regulations state that all manufactured drugs must have **lot numbers**, which are assigned by the manufacturer. Batches of drugs that are manufactured together have the same lot numbers. This allows manufacturers to easily recall specific batches of drugs—when a drug is recalled, the pharmacy is given a lot number to be pulled from shelves.

> **PRACTICE QUESTION**
>
> 6. What does the third section of an NDC number represent?
>   A) package size and type
>   B) manufacturer
>   C) dosage form
>   D) strength of the medication

Prescription Adjudication

After the prescription is entered into the pharmacy software, a **claim** can be filed with the patient's insurer. This process—called **prescription adjudication**—lets the pharmacy know whether the patient's insurance will reimburse the pharmacy for the cost of the medication. This process is done quickly through the pharmacy's software program.

Pharmacy technicians are responsible for submitting insurance claims and collecting payments from customers. They may also work with the pharmacist to help resolve disputes with insurers or manage rejected claims.

Private Health Insurance

Health insurance companies act as the financial "middleman" between patients and medical providers. The consumer pays the insurance company a **premium**—a regular, predetermined amount of money. In return, the insurer covers some amount of the financial costs of the consumer's medical care. The types of services covered and the amount the insurance company will pay are determined by each person's individual health insurance plan.

Most health care in the United States is provided through **managed care organizations (MCOs)**, which seek to control quality and costs by managing patients' use of medical services. They may require patients to use specific providers or to obtain referrals or preapproval for specialized medical care. They may also limit the amount paid for specific services that they believe are not medically necessary. There are three main types of MCOs available to patients:

- **Preferred provider organizations (PPOs)** allow patients to see any in-network physician or specialist without needing prior authorization; benefits are reduced if the patient sees an out-of-network physician.
- **Health maintenance organizations (HMOs)** require patients to get referrals for specialist care from their primary care physician.
- **Point-of-service plans (POSs)** combine a PPO and an HMO: the plan requires an in-network primary care physician, but a patient can get out-of-network services at a higher cost.

MCOs also minimize the money they pay out for a patient's medical care by sharing the cost of care with the patient. In addition to the cost of their premium, patients also share the cost of their medical expenses through payments referred to as copays, deductibles, and coinsurance:

- **Copays** are set payments that patients pay each time they seek medical care. For example, their insurance requires them to pay a $15 copay every time they see their medical provider.
- A **deductible** is a set amount that patients must pay before the insurance company will cover any of their medical care.
- **Coinsurance** is the total percentage an insurance company will pay for a patient's medical care.

> **HELPFUL HINT:**
>
> Pharmacies are required to have a **National Association of Boards of Pharmacy (NABP)** number in order to practice. For Medicare, pharmacies must also apply for a **National Provider Identifier (NPI)** number through the Centers for Medicare & Medicaid Services. The NPI is used for electronic billing and can be given to a pharmacy as a whole or to the individual pharmacists.

PRACTICE QUESTION

7. A pharmacy customer has a $10 copay for generic drug prescriptions. This amount will be paid by
    - **A)** the patient at her physician's office.
    - **B)** the patient at the time of prescription pickup.
    - **C)** the insurance company when the claim is filled.
    - **D)** the insurance company after the prescription has been dispensed.

Government Health Insurance Plans

Medicare is a nationwide federal health insurance program administered by the **Centers for Medicare & Medicaid Services (CMS)**. It is the largest medical benefits program in the United States. People eligible for Medicare include those who

- are 65 or older and have paid payroll taxes;
- are younger than 65 and have a disability;
- have end-stage renal failure;
- have amyotrophic lateral sclerosis (ALS).

Medicare includes four parts, each of which covers different medical services:

- **Medicare Part A** covers hospital services. These services include in-hospital stays, hospice care, long-term care, and some home health care.
- **Medicare Part B** helps to cover physicians' appointments and services, outpatient care, medical services, and preventive care.
- **Medicare Part C (Medicare Advantage plans)** is administered through a private insurer that contracts with the government. These plans must offer coverage for all services included in Medicare Parts A and B. They are usually HMO-style plans with a network and a PCP who acts as a gatekeeper; however, a small number are PPOs.
- **Medicare Part D** (prescription drug plans) is administered by private insurers or pharmacy benefit managers who provide prescription drug coverage. The insurer may choose which drugs to cover, but the CMS requires that insurers cover drugs from specific classes. In addition, the CMS also provides a list of drugs that it does not allow Part D plans to cover. Part D plans can be stand-alone prescription drug plans (PDPs) or bundled with Medicare Advantage (Part C) plans.

Medicaid is a joint federal-state program that provides health coverage for individuals with low incomes. Because Medicaid is partially funded and regulated by states, eligibility and coverage vary widely. Generally, Medicaid will cover individuals with low incomes and has special provisions for coverage of pregnant people, children, people over 65, and people with disabilities.

TRICARE is a health care program for military personnel, including active-duty US armed forces, those in the National Guard or military reserve, and military family members. Dependents and surviving spouses are also covered if the veteran was killed in active duty. The Defense Health Agency manages the program, but health benefits are provided by a civilian provider network.

> **HELPFUL HINT:**
>
> If patients do not have insurance that covers their prescriptions, they must pay the **usual, customary, and reasonable (UCR)** amount or the **cash price**.

TRICARE offers many different options. Costs vary and are based on the plan selected, whether the service member enlisted before or after January 1, 2018, and whether the member is currently on active duty, retired, or medically retired. Survivors are also eligible to enroll and pay the same rates as medically retired members. Premiums for TRICARE are referred to as **enrollment fees** and can be a one-time fee or a monthly fee, depending on the plan.

Workers' compensation (also known as workman's compensation) is an insurance benefit that most employers are required to carry in the United States (except for Texas). Workers' compensation provides medical benefits and a replacement income while an employee recovers from a work-related injury. If the injury results in a permanent disability, workers' compensation benefits would provide the employee with an income for a predetermined length of time or a lump-sum compensation payment, medical benefits, and job retraining.

PRACTICE QUESTION

8. All of the following patients are eligible for Medicaid EXCEPT
   A) patients who are blind.
   B) patients who are disabled.
   C) patients whose incomes are below the poverty level.
   D) patients above the poverty level who cannot find work.

Pharmacy Benefit Managers

Health insurance plans use a **pharmacy benefit manager (PBM)** or **third-party administrators (TPAs)** to manage prescription drug benefits. The PBM is an outsourced company and is not the insurance plan itself. Some common PBMs include Diversified Pharmaceutical Services (DPS), WellPoint Pharmacy Management, and Express Scripts.

PBMs compile a **formulary**, a list of drugs for which the insurance provider has agreed to cover all or part of the cost. The drugs in the formulary are **tiered**, with different co-payments required for each tier:

- **Tier 1 drugs**: generic drugs with the lowest copay
- **Tier 2 drugs**: preferred brand-name drugs
- **Tier 3 drugs**: non-preferred or non-formulary drugs with the highest copay

Many third-party payers have DURs that are sent electronically when the pharmacy submits the claim to the third-party payer. DUR notifications have different levels of severity and are resolved in order, based on whether the contraindication is high, moderate, or low. Depending on the DUR, the prescription may not be accepted as a claim by the third-party payer until the pharmacist or prescriber fixes or overrides the issue.

> **HELPFUL HINT:**
> When the patient receives a prescription drug benefit card, the PBM is listed under the drug benefit section of the card along with information the pharmacy technician needs to process the claim.

PRACTICE QUESTION

9. Which drug tier is for preferred brand names?
   A) Tier 1
   B) Tier 2
   C) Tier 3
   D) Tier 4

Rejected Claims

When a claim is **rejected** by the third-party payer, an error code and explanation appear on the submission screen. Common rejection scenarios are described below.

HELPFUL HINT:

The insurance company may require **step therapy** before authorizing a prescription. In step therapy, the insurance company requires using a first-line drug, which is a preferred drug, before covering a more expensive alternative.

- **Expired coverage:** A claim may be rejected if a patient is no longer covered under a certain health plan or if the plan has changed. Resolve this problem by asking the patient for the new insurance information and updating the patient's profile.

- **Invalid patient, date of birth, person code, or gender:** This rejection is frequently due to technician or insurance company error. Check the patient's profile to see if the information is correct. If it is not, update the profile with the correct information and resend the claim. In case of further problems, the insurance company may need to be contacted.

- **Prescribed quantity exceeds limit:** This rejection may occur if, for example, the physician writes a prescription for 100 pills for a 100-day supply when the insurance company will only cover a 30-day supply. This error can be resolved by reducing the quantity written to a 30-day supply.

- **Refill too soon:** This rejection occurs when the prescription is submitted too early for refill; for example, if a patient requests a refill of a 30-day supply of a medication only 15 days after it was filled, the claim will be rejected. Most insurance companies allow a grace period of 5 to 7 days to refill a prescription before it is due. If a patient tries to refill earlier, this rejection will come up, usually with a date indicating when the prescription can be filled. It is important to find out why the patient is trying to refill early. If the medication is being taken incorrectly, refer the patient to the pharmacist for counseling.

- **Prescriber not covered:** If a physician is not part of an insurance company's in-network group, a "prescriber not covered" rejection message may appear on the computer screen. In this case, the patient will have to pay the out-of-pocket cost for the medication.

- **NDC, or drug not covered**: A rejection of "NDC not covered" usually means that the insurance company will not cover the drug, either because it is the brand-name version or because the drug itself is not covered. Brand-name prescriptions may need to be replaced with their generic versions. In other cases, the patient may need to pay cash for the prescription, or the pharmacy may need to call the physician to see if the drug can be changed to a therapeutically equivalent drug that the company will cover.
- **Prior authorization required**: Insurance companies require prior authorization for some medications. In this case, the pharmacy asks the physician to send prior authorization forms to the insurance company. Once authorization is approved, the company removes the rejection so that the claim can be submitted.

If a drug is not covered under a patient's drug plan or the patient is uninsured, many drug companies will offer **patient assistance programs (PAPs)**, provided the patient meets certain criteria. These criteria can vary and are set by the pharmaceutical drug companies. Patients fill out an application to the drug company that determines eligibility. If the patient is accepted, the company will send a 30- or 90-day supply of the drug to the pharmacy, and the pharmacist can dispense the medication to the patient for free or at a reduced price designated by the drug company.

PRACTICE QUESTION

10. Which of the following reasons for a rejected claim can usually be resolved by speaking with the patient's physician?

    A) expired coverage

    B) prior authorization required

    C) refill too soon

    D) invalid date of birth

Filling, Packaging, and Labeling the Prescription Order

Pharmacy Labels

A **pharmacy label** is generated once the prescription is entered in the computer and the claim is accepted. The **pharmacy label** explains how to correctly take the medication and provides information for refilling and contacting the pharmacy. Information found on the label includes

- patient's name and address;
- pharmacy's name, address, and phone number;
- prescriber's name;

- prescription number;
- name, dose, and strength of the drug;
- drug quantity;
- description of the drug;
- original prescription date (when the prescription was first filled);
- beyond-use date or expiration date (usually a year after the prescription was last filled);
- directions for use;
- federal caution statement for controlled substances ("CAUTION: Federal law prohibits the transfer of this drug to any person other than the patient for whom it was prescribed.");
- date of prescription refill, date of the most recent refill, and/or number of refills available;
- drug manufacturer and NDC number/barcode;
- initials of the pharmacist who will be verifying the prescription; and
- initials of the pharmacy technician who entered the prescription in the system.

HELPFUL HINT:

Pharmacy technicians use the NDC number to be sure they are filling the prescription with the correct drug by matching the NDC on the label with the NDC on the manufacturer's bottle.

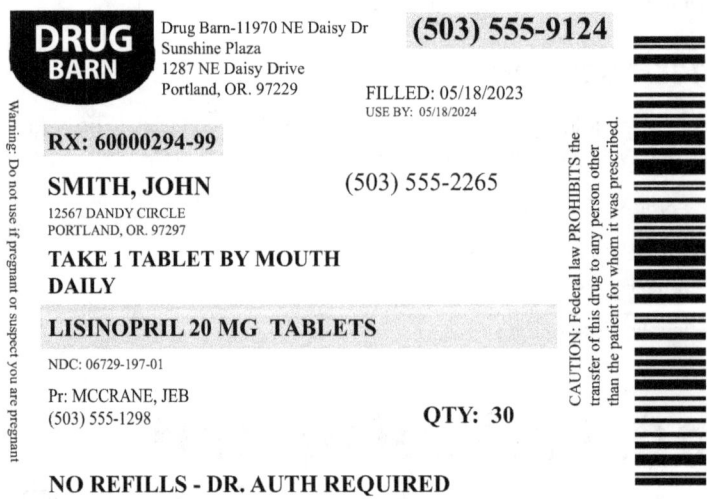

Figure 7.3. Pharmacy Label

PRACTICE QUESTION

11. Which is NOT required to be on a prescription label?

    A) picture of the drug
    B) order number
    C) directions for use
    D) patient's name

Packaging the Order

The technician must verify the information on the label against the information on the prescription. If any information is missing or unclear, the technician should check with the pharmacist before filling the prescription.

Next, the technician must find the correct medication on the shelf and match the NDC number on the bottle to the NDC number on the label to ensure the correct drug is dispensed. Some pharmacies also provide a picture of the drug on the label or on the paperwork that accompanies the prescription.

After finding the medication, the pharmacy technician checks the quantity to be filled as indicated on the label. Some medications may come prepackaged (e.g., Z-Pak). The label can be attached directly to these packages.

Many medications will be dispensed from **stock bottles** (containers that hold large volumes of a drug). These will need to be counted or measured, then placed in the appropriate container. A **counting tray** helps ensure accuracy if pills or tablets must be counted.

HELPFUL HINT:

If the generic manufacturer that the pharmacy normally uses is unavailable, a different generic manufacturer must be used. In such cases, the label must be changed to reflect the drug and NDC number used.

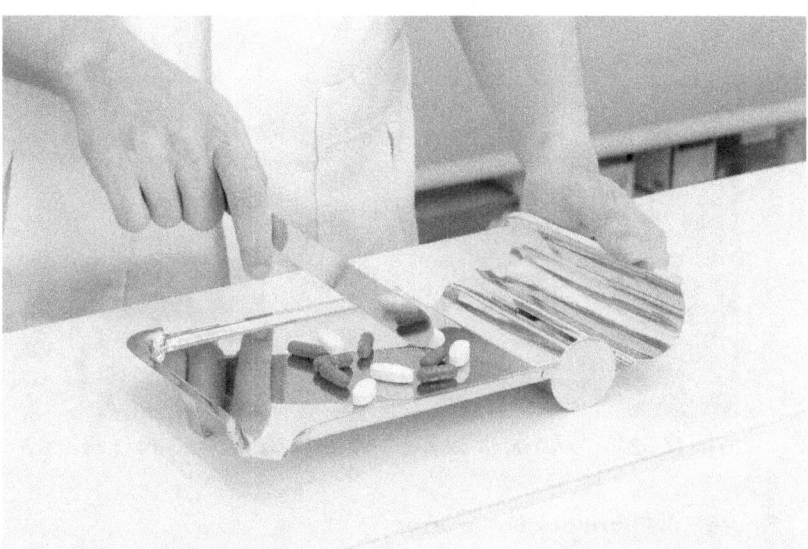

Figure 7.4. Counting Tray

Some pharmacies have **automated counting machines** for common medications. When a label is generated, the machine counts out the correct number of pills. However, automated counting systems can miscount due to technical problems or if they need maintenance, so it is important to make sure equipment is working properly. Once the pills have been counted out to dispense, the technician chooses the correct dram vial or bottle:

- **Dram vials** are used for pills and tablets and are usually amber-colored to protect the medication from light degradation.

(A **dram** is a unit of measurement in the British imperial system. One dram equals one-eighth of a liquid ounce.)
- **Bottles** are used for liquids. They are measured in liquid ounces and milliliters (1 oz = 30 mL).

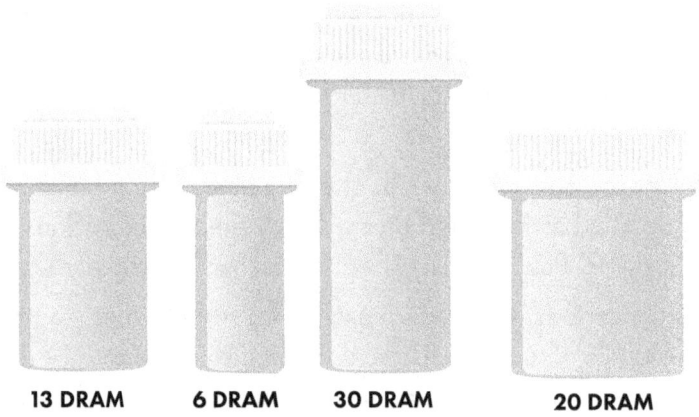

Figure 7.5. Dram Vial Sizes

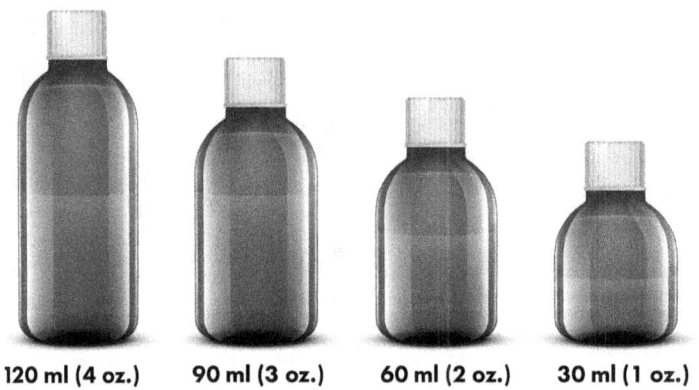

Figure 7.6. Pharmacy Bottle Sizes

Some ambulatory pharmacies use blister packaging for patients. **Blister packaging** helps improve compliance and is common in nursing homes and long-term care facilities:
- Each dose is marked by date and time.
- The medications are easily popped out of the package when the dose is due.
- Blister packaging helps the patient and health care professionals keep track of doses.

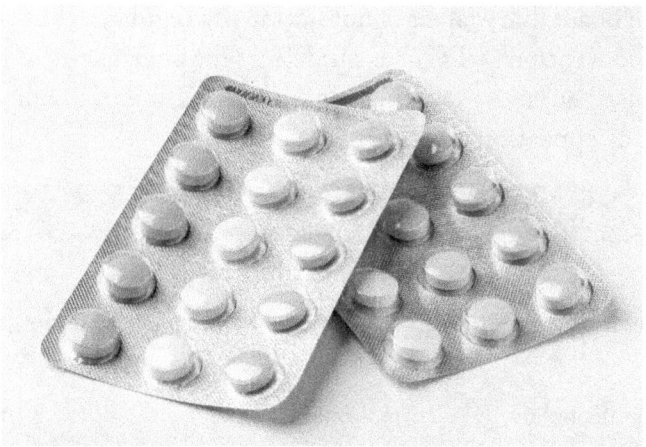

Figure 7.7. Blister Packages

Finally, the container is labeled with both the prescription label and any auxiliary labels (discussed in the next section). Work should always be checked for accuracy. When packaging is complete, the container should be sent to the pharmacist along with the manufacturer's bottle for verification.

PRACTICE QUESTION

12. Which must be verified FIRST upon removing the bottle from the shelf when filling a prescription?

- **A)** size of the dram vial
- **B)** how many pills to count
- **C)** NDC number
- **D)** patient's name on the label

AUXILIARY LABELS

Auxiliary labels are attached to medication bottles to inform patients how to take or store medications. These labels are not meant to replace counseling from the pharmacist but rather should reinforce the pharmacist's instructions, which are included in patient handouts or written on the product label. Auxiliary labels usually address one of the following concerns:

- administration (e.g., for topical use; take with food)
- interactions (e.g., do not take with grapefruit)
- storage requirements (e.g., keep in refrigerator)

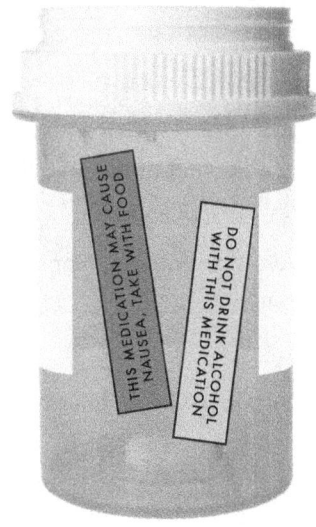

Figure 7.8. Auxiliary Labels

The use of auxiliary labels is not nationally regulated, but the US Pharmacopeial Convention (UPC) has guidelines for pharmacies to follow. Some commonly used auxiliary labels are included in Table 7.2., but many others exist (and may appear on the exam).

TABLE 7.2. Common Auxiliary Labels

Label	Drug Examples
Chew tablets before swallowing.	methylphenidate (chewable tablets) Vyvanse (chewable tablets)
Do not drink alcoholic beverages when taking this medication.	metronidazole CNS depressants insulin antidiabetics
Do not eat grapefruit or drink grapefruit juice while taking this medication.	statins calcium channel blockers
Do not take dairy products, antacids, or iron preparations within 1 hour of taking this medication.	alendronate tetracyclines fluoroquinolones
Do not take this drug if you become pregnant.	ACE inhibitors ARBs statins warfarin NSAIDs carbamazepine
Medication may cause drowsiness/dizziness.	opioids benzodiazepines Note: usually not added for drugs whose main effect is drowsiness
Medication should be taken with plenty of water.	sulfonamide antibiotics Bactrim
Avoid prolonged exposure to sunlight.	sulfonamide antibiotics metronidazole tetracyclines
Swallow whole; do not crush/chew.	all extended-release (ER) tablets and capsules benzonatate

Label	Drug Examples
Take medication on empty stomach.	macrolide antibiotics levothyroxine sildenafil tadalafil
Take medication with food.	NSAIDs metformin carvedilol lovastatin

PRACTICE QUESTION

13. The auxiliary label "Take medication with food" would be attached to which of the following medications?
    - **A)** sildenafil
    - **B)** lorazepam
    - **C)** metformin
    - **D)** carbamazepine

Pharmacist Verification

Once the prescription is prepared, the pharmacy technician gives it to the pharmacist for **verification**. During the verification process, the pharmacist

- compares the original hard copy against the bottle label to make sure the information is entered correctly;
- opens the bottle to check the pills for the correct color, imprints, and shape;
- inspects the drug by checking the NDC number on the stock bottle against the NDC number on the label;
- visually checks the prescription for accuracy; and
- pulls up the patient's profile to run a DUR.
- The pharmacist should not be interrupted during this process.

Some prescriptions cannot be filled, usually due to problems with insurance or prescription issues that must be resolved by the prescriber. In these cases, the pharmacist puts the information aside until the issue is resolved and/or the patient can be contacted. The patient can often provide information to help solve the problem.

Once any issues have been resolved and the pharmacist is sure the prescription is filled accurately, the medication is placed in a bag with the

HELPFUL HINT:

It is crucial to bring any concerns about the prescription to the pharmacist *before* verification so that they can be investigated and resolved before the patient arrives for pickup.

necessary paperwork. Information that may need to be handed out with a drug includes the following:

- **Patient package inserts (PPIs)** are developed by the manufacturer using FDA guidelines. They include information on the pharmacology, indications, administration, dosage, adverse effects, and warnings/precautions/contraindications for a drug.
- **Medication guides (MGs)** are mandated by the FDA for certain drugs. The guides help patients avoid potentially serious side effects and/or properly use medications with complicated dosage regimens.
- **Instructions for use (IFU)** are mandated by the FDA for drugs with complicated directions for preparation, administration, or storage.

PRACTICE QUESTION

14. What is the purpose of a medication guide?
    A) It helps patients avoid serious adverse effects.
    B) It explains the pharmacology of the drug.
    C) It directs the customer to patient assistance programs.
    D) It gives directions on how to store the drug.

Dispensing Medication to Patients

THE DISPENSING PROCESS

The most important step when dispensing medication is verifying patient identity. To comply with HIPAA, patient identity must be confirmed as inconspicuously as possible to protect privacy. Pharmacy technicians follow these steps when dispensing medication:

1. When greeting the patient, ensure other customers are at a distance away to safeguard the patient's privacy. (Most pharmacies ask other patients to stay a certain distance from the pickup window for this purpose.)
2. Verify the patient's identity using name, date of birth, or other identifiers.
3. Determine the type of medication the patient is picking up and collect it. (New medications, refills, opioids, and refrigerated drugs may be stored in different areas.)
4. Verify the patient's address or phone number after collecting the medication.

5. Verify the drug(s) and price, and determine if the patient has any other prescriptions to pick up.
6. Reconstitute medications as needed.
7. Scan or ring up the order and advise the patient of the total price.
8. Special procedures are required for controlled substances:
    - Pharmacy technicians must check a valid picture ID.
    - The patient must sign for the medication.
    - Patients may authorize representatives to pick up controlled medications. The representatives must bring both the patient's photo ID and their own.
9. Ask if the patient has questions about the medication(s). Pharmacist consultation may be required for new or updated prescriptions.
10. Collect payment.

When greeting patients, pharmacy technicians represent the pharmacy and the store. Pharmacy staff should be professional and courteous. Patients with disabilities may need special assistance, but staff should first ask patients if they need help.

> **PRACTICE QUESTION**
>
> 15. The line at a pharmacy is placed 6 feet from the prescription pickup counter. This setup prevents violations of which federal act?
>   A) Americans with Disabilities Act
>   B) Health Insurance Portability and Accountability Act
>   C) FDA Modernization Act
>   D) SUPPORT Act

Drug Administration Equipment

After the completion of drug preparation, it is critical to make sure the patient understands how to administer or self-administer the medication correctly. The technician may need to provide **administration equipment** appropriate to the specific patient and medication form. Some common examples of this equipment include the following:

- **Oral syringes** are used to measure and dispense oral liquids to children or adults who cannot swallow solid drug forms. They are also used for liquid measurements in small doses (under a teaspoon).
- **Droppers** are used to administer smaller volumes of liquid to infants and children.
- **Medication cups** are used to measure larger liquid dosages.

> **HELPFUL HINT:**
>
> **Scored** tablets are marked with lines that equally divide the tablet into 2 or 4 parts.

- **Pill splitters** are devices used to cut solid forms, like tablets, into pieces.
- **Spacers** are tubes attached to inhalers that ensure the patient receives an accurate dose of a medication. They are usually given to children, older adults, or anyone who cannot use an inhaler properly.
- **Unit dose drug packages** are prepackaged with a single dose of a drug.
- **Syringes and needles** are used to measure and dispense drug medications given parenterally, including IM, IV, ID, and SubQ. Types of syringes include standard (for volumes over 1 mL), tuberculin syringes (for volumes less than 1 mL), and insulin syringes (which have measurements marked in units).

> **HELPFUL HINT:**
>
> Spacers may be covered under some insurance plans, but a provider will need to prescribe them.

PRACTICE QUESTION

16. A pharmacy technician is dispensing an antibiotic oral suspension for an infant. If the dosage is 10 mL, what administration equipment should the technician include?
    A) oral syringe
    B) medication cup
    C) syringe
    D) unit dose packaging

Refills and Prescription Transfers

The technician can **transfer** a refill to any store provided the pharmacy is the same; however, if the prescription is from a different pharmacy, the pharmacist must order the refill.

Refilling Prescriptions

Patients have several options to refill prescriptions, including dropping off a prescription bottle and asking for a **refill**. If there are refills left, the technician will enter the order number on the bottle to refill.

Most refill requests are for **maintenance medications** that must be taken by the patient every day. Pharmacies can automatically refill maintenance medications, and the automated system will call the patient when it is available for pickup.

Pharmacies also have automated phone systems and online refills. Patients can enter the prescription information through a phone call or online portal to request a refill.

Most refill requests are entered in the computer automatically (either auto-refills or through phone/online requests). On the pharmacy software system, a file—called a **queue**—holds the refill request and helps keep an organized workflow. This allows pharmacy staff to distinguish among prescriptions for patients who are waiting, patients who will be picking up a prescription soon, and patients who will pick up refills later.

Pharmacy technicians who receive a refill request by phone or in person will enter the order number into the system, either by manually typing it into the appropriate field or by directly scanning the label. When the refill request appears on the computer screen, the pharmacy technician can review the information and, if everything is correct, process the refill request and print the refill label. Patients may request refills that cannot be dispensed. A refill may be denied because the

- prescription is out of refills;
- prescription has expired;
- prescription is for a controlled substance;
- medication is for a temporary ailment (e.g., antibiotic), so no refills were included in the prescription;
- patient has changed prescribers; and/or
- patient requests more than a 30-day supply.

The pharmacy can offer to contact the physician's office to make a **refill request**, which can be faxed to the physician's office, called to the office over the phone, emailed, or submitted through compliant software. In a **refill authorization**, the prescriber's office sends the request back to the pharmacy with the number of refills authorized.

> **HELPFUL HINT:**
> Some pharmacies have programs that allow patients to use smartphones to photograph the order number on their refill bottles and text the refill request to the pharmacy.

PRACTICE QUESTION

17. Which of the following describes when a prescription has no refills left and the prescriber's office authorizes more refills on the prescription?

    A) refill request
    B) prescription transfer
    C) refill authorization
    D) maintenance medication

Transferring a Prescription

When transferring prescriptions, pharmacists and technicians must follow specific federal and state laws. (This section covers noncontrolled substances. See Chapter 4 for discussion of transferring prescriptions for controlled substances.) Pharmacy technicians can only transfer prescriptions if

- the medication is not a controlled substance; AND
- it was filled at a different location of the same pharmacy.

Chain pharmacy software programs link all the stores in the pharmacy chain. The technician can input the order number and store number into the refill field on the computer screen and bring up the refill. If refills are available, the technician can refill on the spot for the patient.

If the prescription is currently at another pharmacy, the pharmacist transfers it. The pharmacy technician should get the patient's demographic information and the phone number of the previous pharmacy. The pharmacist can then call the pharmacy and retrieve the rest of the prescription information.

> **HELPFUL HINT:**
> To comply with HIPAA, pharmacy technicians must verify the identity of customers on the phone. They should confirm that they are speaking directly with the patient or authorized representative.

PRACTICE QUESTION

18. When transferring a prescription from one pharmacy to another, pharmacy technicians can get all the information from the patient and/or patient's prescription bottle for the pharmacist (who then calls for the transfer) EXCEPT for which of the following?

    A) patient's name
    B) amount of refills left on prescription
    C) name of drug
    D) pharmacy name

Inventory

INVENTORY MANAGEMENT AND STOCKING

Proper **inventory management** ensures that needed medications and supplies are always available. It also helps minimize cost and increase profits.

Pharmacies develop a **periodic automatic replenishment (PAR) level** for each drug. The PAR level defines the minimum and maximum levels of the drug available. PAR levels are maintained in the pharmacy by inventory systems. When the available stock falls below the PAR level, it is reordered.

Barcode technology refers to handheld systems that scan the barcode and NDC number on the stock bottle. The scanning system is used to scan inventory and calculate the estimated quantity of the drug available in the pharmacy. These systems are connected to the pharmacy software system, and a report is generated for ordering when stock is low.

Pareto ABC Systems classify drugs based on their use and profitability. The inventory of drugs that are commonly used and have high unit value is tightly controlled. The inventory of slow-moving items with low unit value is less securely controlled.

Pharmacies that use **just-in-time inventory systems** only order a drug as demand requires. These systems are designed to control costs by avoiding excessive inventory. However, unexpected events (e.g., delivery issues) can cause stock shortages.

Pharmacy technicians must store medication in the proper areas. Proper storage means adhering to the manufacturer's recommendations on proper lighting, temperature, and exposure.

When shelf stocking, technicians must be knowledgeable about the arrangement of the drug supply. For safety purposes, drugs are first separated by their routes of administration and then arranged alphabetically. (Retail pharmacies normally organize medications by brand name, while institutional pharmacies arrange them by generic name.) Some drugs must be stored in more specific locations to keep them secure or to prevent errors:

- Controlled substances are stored in locked areas away from noncontrolled drugs.
- Sound alike/look alike drugs (SALAD) are separated from drugs they may be confused with.
- Cytotoxic drugs are stored in a biological safety cabinet or isolator to prevent them from contaminating other drugs.

Drug stock should be **rotated** while stocking. Opened bottles and bottles with earlier expiration dates should be placed in the front; those with later expiration dates should be placed in the back. Open bottles must be marked to prevent staff from opening new bottles before the currently open bottles are empty.

HELPFUL HINT:

Any refrigerated items received by the pharmacy should be stocked in the refrigerator as soon as possible to avoid damaging the product.

PRACTICE QUESTION

19. A technician has opened a stock bottle of atorvastatin 20 mg tablets. Where should the bottle be placed after the prescription is filled?

  A) in a refrigerated area
  B) in a secure, locked cabinet
  C) behind bottles with earlier expiration dates
  D) on the shelf in front of unopened bottles

Disposing of Medications

To effectively manage the drug inventory inside of a pharmacy, a technician will check for expired drugs, prescriptions not picked up by patients, or drugs that have not been prescribed. These drugs must be properly disposed of.

The technician must maintain the inventory of stocked drugs on the shelf by consistently checking for **expired medications** to ensure that patients are receiving quality products. Three months before the drug is due to expire, the pharmacy technician marks the stock bottle to alert the staff that the drug will be expiring soon. (Many pharmacies use a brightly colored sticker with the date of expiration.) Medications must be completely removed from the shelf at least 1 month before the expiration date.

HELPFUL HINT:

If the expiration date on the stock bottle states 9/25, the medication will expire on the last day of September in the year 2025. If the expiration date states 9/15/25, the medication will expire on September 15, 2025.

Once expired drugs are pulled from the shelves, they are stored separately from other active drugs in the pharmacy to prevent the staff from accidentally dispensing them. The drugs are then disposed of based on the pharmacy's policy.

If patients do not pick up their medication within 7 days of the original fill, the pharmacy should contact them about the filled medication. If all communication attempts are unsuccessful, the pharmacy can categorize the order as a **patient decline**, and the technician can return the drug item to stock. Special-order items can be returned to the manufacturer for credit, and the medication claim is canceled for third-party billing purposes.

Excess stock should be returned to the manufacturer, often for full or partial credit. This return is usually done through a **reverse distributor**, an independent company that manages drug returns. (These companies are regulated by the DEA.) Excess, expired, or damaged stock is sent to the reverse distributor, which manages the return to the manufacturer and attempts to recoup the pharmacy's cost.

Controlled substances have specific disposal procedures that require a pharmacist. (For information on disposing of controlled substances, see Chapter 4.)

> **PRACTICE QUESTION**
>
> **20.** When should stock bottles be removed from the shelf?
>
> **A)** at least 1 month before expiring
>
> **B)** on their expiration date
>
> **C)** 30 days after their expiration date
>
> **D)** 6 months before their expiration date

Compounding

Compounding is the personalized preparation made from one or more ingredients of a prescribed medication that is not commercially available. There is a wide range of medications that can be compounded. Some methods of compounding can be as simple as adding flavoring to a child's antibiotic to improve taste, while other product formulations must be precisely calculated into patient-specific customized dosage forms.

Nonsterile Compounding

Nonsterile compounding (also called **extemporaneous compounding**) refers to the compounding of two or more ingredients that a patient can swallow, drink, insert, or apply topically. Some of the following circumstances require compounding:

- Commercially unavailable products: Topical hormonal therapies, veterinary preparations, specialty dermatologic products that are applied topically, and patient-specific rectal or vaginal compounds all may require compounding.
- Specialized dosage strengths: If a patient-specific dosage or strength of a preparation is not commercially available, the pharmacy technician may need to compound it.
- Product flavoring: If the taste of a medication affects compliance, compounding may be necessary.
- A different dosage form is needed: If a patient cannot take capsules or tablets, then a liquid formulation may be compounded.

According to USP 795, any equipment or supplies used to compound MUST

- reduce ingredients to the smallest particle size;
- ensure the solution has no visible undissolved matter when dispensed; and
- make sure preparations are similarly structured to ensure uniform final distribution.

Some preparations are made to the patient's order, while others may be prescribed by a physician. In the latter case, the pharmacy has a **master formula record**, or recipes of frequently used compounding formulas and record keeping. Some frequently prescribed formulations may be made in bulk so the product can be dispensed to the patient promptly.

Whenever a compounded medication is prepared, it must be verified by a pharmacist. It also must be recorded in a **compounding log** with the name of products used, lot numbers, expiration and beyond-use dates, quantity made, and amount of ingredients used (lot numbers and expiration dates on packaging are always grouped together). The initials of the technician who prepared the medication and the pharmacist who verified it are required as well. It is then filed as a permanent record.

> **HELPFUL HINT:**
>
> The FDA requires that nonsterile compounding must adhere to the standards of **USP Chapter 795** and follow DEA guidelines. The DEA requires specific compounding record logs for opioids, a recording of inventory after each batch, and a record kept by the pharmacist regarding any waste.

PRACTICE QUESTION

21. Which of the following situations would NOT require nonsterile compounding?

    A) A patient is allergic to an inactive ingredient in a commercially made topical cream.

    B) A patient has a prescription for an enteric-coated tablet that is small and easy to swallow.

    C) A child refuses to take an antibiotic because of its bad taste.

    D) A physician prescribes a drug for which a dosage form is not currently manufactured.

Tools for Compounding

Technicians use different tools for measuring and weighing. **Class III** (also called **Class A**) **balances** are required in all pharmacies and must be inspected and meet the requirements of the National Bureau of Standards (NBS). A Class A balance is a two-pan torsion type with internal and external weights. It has a capacity of 120 mg and a sensitivity of 6 mg. **Counterbalances** are less accurate than Class A balances. They have a limit of 5 kg and a sensitivity of 100 mg.

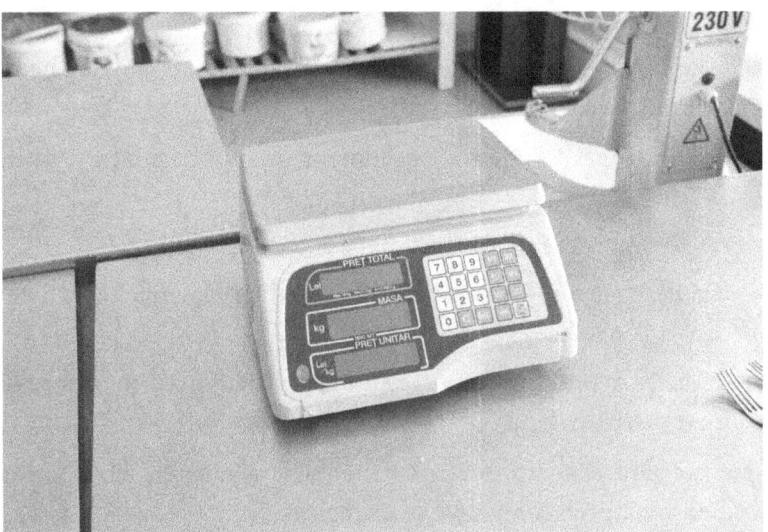

Figure 7.9. Counterbalance

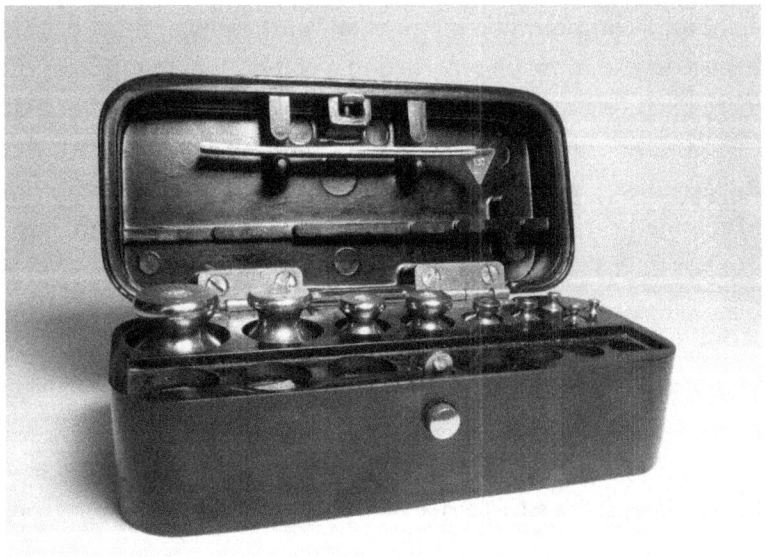

Figure 7.10. Class III Balance

Weighing boats and **glassine paper** are flexible containers used for holding liquids and solids that are weighed on the balances.

Weights are usually made of brass or polished metal and must be maintained and handled properly. Sets generally contain cylindrical weights ranging from 1 – 50 g and fractional weights of 10 – 500 mg. The weights should be calibrated annually to ensure accuracy; **forceps** should be used to prevent damage when picking up weights.

Figure 7.11. Weights

Figure 7.12. Forceps

Conical graduated cylinders are used for measuring liquids and allow for easy pouring due to their circular design. **Cylindrical graduated cylinders** are also used for measuring liquids but have a narrow design. The **meniscus** is the curved upper surface of a liquid in a container: it is curved in if the liquid wets the walls and curved out if it does not.

Some other common tools and equipment used for extemporaneous compounding include the following:

- **Suppository molds**: Plastic or metal, these molds are used to form the suppository after it has been prepared.
- **Capsule-filling equipment**: This mechanical device fills the gelatin capsules with powder.
- **Tablet mold**: Tablet molds are small, usually cylindrical, molded, or compressed disks of different sizes. They contain a diluent—usually made of dextrose or a mixture of lactose and powdered sucrose—and a moistening agent or diluted alcohol.
- **Compounding or ointment slab**: This slab is a glass or porcelain plate used for geometric dilution and mixing. It can be easily cleaned.

Figure 7.13. Cylindrical Graduated Cylinder

HELPFUL HINT:

Measurement should be taken at the bottom of the meniscus.

- **Compounding spatula:** This tool is made of flexible rubber or metal and is used to mix and shear ointments and creams.
- **Blenders and mixers:** These common devices can be used for mixing as well.
- A **mortar and pestle** is a tool that has been used for centuries in pharmacy compounding. It is used to grind and crush, or **levigate**, ingredients into a fine paste. These tools are usually made of wood, ceramic, or stone.

Figure 7.14. Mortar and Pestle (ceramic)

PRACTICE QUESTION

22. Which compound can be made using a mold?
    A) capsule
    B) tablet
    C) solution
    D) lotion

COMPOUNDING PROCEDURES

Common preparations that can be made by extemporaneous compounding include the following:

- **ointment:** an oily preparation that is normally medicated and applied topically
- **cream:** a thick or semisolid preparation applied topically
- **paste:** a thick, soft, and moist substance usually produced by mixing dry ingredients with a liquid

- **oil-in-water emulsion**: a diffusion (droplets) of one liquid in another, impassible liquid
- **solution**: a liquid preparation of one or more soluble chemical substances that are usually dissolved in water
- **suspension**: a preparation of finely divided, undissolved drugs or powders distributed in a liquid medium
- **capsule**: a solid encapsulated in gelatin
- **tablet**: a compressed solid dosage unit
- **troche** (lozenge): a molded solid meant to dissolve in the mouth
- **suppository**: a solid preparation in a conical or cylindrical shape that is inserted into the rectum or vagina to dissolve

Compounding requires precision and attention to detail. Mistakes can result in medications that are ineffective or even harmful to the patient. Each pharmacy will have its own policies and procedures for compounding, so only general guidelines are discussed here.

Solutions and suspensions are some of the most commonly compounded medications. In a solution, a **solute** is dissolved in a **solvent**. Solutions should always be mixed thoroughly to ensure that all of the solute has been dissolved. **Precipitation**—solids falling out of a solution—is usually a sign that the solution has not been mixed completely or has been compounded incorrectly. Unexpected discoloration can be another sign that a medication has been compounded incorrectly.

Reconstitution is the process of adding a precise amount of sterile water to the powdered form of a drug to form a suspension. Reconstituted suspensions must be shaken thoroughly by the patient before use to ensure that the drug has been distributed evenly throughout the water.

Tablets are made by mixing the active drug with a **base** (usually a sugar, like dextrose) and other additives. The mixture is pressed into tablets using a mold. Capsules are made similarly by measuring the appropriate amount of a powdered mixture and using a capsule-filling machine. USP 795 states that both tablets and capsules cannot weigh less than 90% or more than 110% of the calculated unit weight.

HELPFUL HINT:

Compounded sterile preparations (CSPs), such as IV admixtures, are compounded in a sterile room. Sterile compounded techniques are not covered on the current version of the PTCE.

PRACTICE QUESTION

23. A formulation in which an undissolved drug or powder is distributed in a liquid medium is called what?

    A) cream
    B) suppository
    C) suspension
    D) ointment

Institutional (Hospital) Pharmacies

An **institutional** (hospital) **pharmacy** provides medications for patients in large health systems. Pharmacy technicians in an institutional setting do not work directly with patients; instead, they process orders in the pharmacy, make IV admixtures, deliver medications, and stock dispensing machines, among other tasks.

The **medication order** in an institutional pharmacy is equivalent to the prescription in an ambulatory pharmacy. All of a patient's medications, including OTC drugs, are written as a medication order by the prescriber and filled in by the institutional pharmacy. Medication orders must contain specific information:

- patient's name, date of birth, weight, height, and allergies
- patient's medical condition (in case of therapeutic contraindications)
- patient's medical record number (for accurate billing and documentation)
- patient's hospital room number and nursing unit floor (indicate where the order will be sent)
- dosage form (e.g., solutions, IV admixtures, tablet), strength, and schedule
- drug preparation instructions (including IV concentration and volume)
- route of administration (e.g., oral, IV) and directions for use

The pharmacy technician will also encounter different types of medication orders in hospital settings.

> **HELPFUL HINT:**
> Pharmacy technicians prepare enough of a scheduled order to last for a 24-hour period.

> **HELPFUL HINT:**
> Medications in the hospital can be more patient specific, especially IV admixtures. Height, weight, and age are used for formulating dosages.

TABLE 7.3. Medication Orders in the Hospital Setting

Type of Medication Order	Purpose
Scheduled medication orders	medications that are given on a continuous, around-the-clock schedule
Scheduled intravenous (IV) or total parenteral nutrition (TPN) orders	injectable medications that are prepared and taken on an around-the-clock schedule
As-needed (PRN) orders	medication that is used only in response to a specific parameter or condition
Controlled substance medication orders	an opioid medication that requires proper documentation of dispensing and administration

Medication orders are processed in the **central pharmacy** and then delivered to the nursing unit medication room. Drugs may also be stored in **automated dispensing machines (ADMs)** located in medication rooms. This **decentralized** approach allows faster access to medications and more secure storage of controlled substances.

Commonly prescribed drugs are kept stocked in ADMs. The hospital pharmacy also prepares patient-specific medications when the order calls for a medication that is not already available in the nursing unit medication room in an ADM.

The fill process begins in the central pharmacy when a copy of the medication order is received. Medication orders are entered electronically by the provider and put in the queue for pharmacists to verify. The central pharmacy may also receive orders to replenish stocks in ADMs. The technician fills these orders as instructed by the pharmacist.

In a hospital pharmacy, all medications distributed to the patient are **unit-dosed**. Pharmacies usually order drugs from the manufacturer that are already unit-dosed. This means they are already placed in blister packages where the unit of medication is put in its own package labeled with the lot number, expiration date, NDC number, and the name of the drug. When a medication is only available in a stock bottle, the pharmacy must use a unit-dose drug distribution system to make its own unit doses.

After the order has been verified by the pharmacist, the technician must deliver it to the decentralized pharmacy. Once the medication order has been entered in the pharmacy system, nurses can access it on the **medication administration record (MAR)**. The MAR alerts nurses when the medication needs to be administered.

A **census** shows a count of patients and which ones are still in the hospital. While delivering medications, technicians carry out a census to check if a patient has been discharged or is still in the hospital. When a patient is discharged, the technician will send unused medications back to the central pharmacy.

HELPFUL HINT:

STAT drugs are needed as soon as possible. Filling and delivering these orders is prioritized over other orders.

HELPFUL HINT:

Hospital pharmacy technicians must return unused medications to the central pharmacy. Hospital rooms may quickly turn over; ignoring unused medications could cause confusion and billing errors.

PRACTICE QUESTION

24. Which patient information is NOT needed on a medication order?
    A) first name
    B) medical record number
    C) date of birth
    D) home address

Medical Terminology

Pharmacy technicians should be familiar with common medical terminology. Part of this knowledge is simply built through memorizing. Technicians can also use roots and affixes to help them figure out the meaning of unfamiliar words:

- Roots give words meaning. Words are formed from roots or are roots themselves. In English, many roots come from Latin or Greek words.
- Affixes are added to a root word to modify its meaning:
  - **Prefixes** are added to the beginning of a root word.
  - **Suffixes** are added to the end of a root word.

Many words in medicine and health care can be understood by analyzing their roots, prefixes, and suffixes. For instance, in Greek, *hepar* means "liver"; the Latin-based suffix *–itis* means "inflammation." Thus, *hepatitis* means "inflammation of the liver."

TABLE 7.4. Common Roots

Root	Definition	Example
aud, audi	hear	audible
auto	self	automatic, automobile
bene	good	benign
bio	life	biology
card, cardio	heart	cardiac
chrono	time	chronology
corp	body	corpse
derm, dermis	skin	dermatitis
dict	say	dictionary
duc	lead	abduct, deduce
gast, gastro	stomach	gastritis, gastroenterology
gen	birth	gene, generate
graph	write	graphics
hema, hemato	blood	hemophilia, hematology
hepa	liver	hepatology, hepatitis
ject	throw	reject
man	hand	manual
mand	order	mandate
mis, mit	send	transmit
mor, mort	death	morgue, mortality
omni	all	omnivorous

Root	Definition	Example
path	feel	empath, pathology
phil	love	philosophy
phon	sound	telephone
port	carry	portable
ren	kidneys	renal
scrib, script	write	scribble
sect	cut	dissection
sens, sent	feel	sensical, sentimental
tele	far	television
uni	single	unisex
vac	empty	vacuum
vid, vis	see	video, visual

TABLE 7.5. Common Prefixes

Prefix	Definition	Example
a–, an–	to, toward, of, not, without	asymmetric, anorexic
ab–	away	abduct
ad–	toward	addition
ante–	before	anterior, antenatal
anti–	against	antibiotic, anti-inflammatory
co–, col–, com–, con–, cor–	with	cooperate, collaborate, communicate, connect, corroborate
de–	negation	dehydrate
di–, dis–	negation or duality	divide, disconnect
em–, en–	put into or on	embalm, encircle
hyper–	above, more	hypertensive
hypo–	below, less	hypothermic, hypodermic
il–, im–, in–, ir–	not, without	illegal, imperfect, inaccessible, irregular
intra–	within	intraosseous, intravenous
myo–	muscle	myocardial

continued on next page

TABLE 7.5. Common Prefixes (continued)

Prefix	Definition	Example
out–	more than, away from, beyond	outweigh, outperform
over–	too much, above	overstimulated, overweight
pre–	before	premature, prevent
re–	again, in addition, back	recall, remind
semi–	half	semiconscious, semipermeable
sub–	under	submerge, submit
super–	above	superior, supervisor
sym–, syn–	together	symbiotic, synthesize
trans–	across, into	transdermal
under–	below, not enough	underneath, underweight

TABLE 7.6. Common Suffixes

Suffix	Definition	Example
–algia	pain	fibromyalgia
–ectomy	removal surgery	appendectomy, splenectomy
–emia	in the blood	anemia
–genic	causing	carcinogenic
–itis	inflammation	diverticulitis, dermatitis
–metry	measurement	telemetry
–otomy	surgical incision	tracheotomy
–paresis	paralysis	gastroparesis
–pathy	disease	nephropathy, retinopathy

PRACTICE QUESTION

25. Select the meaning of the underlined word in the sentence.
    The surgeon had to resect a portion of the intestine due to a diagnosis of volvulus.

    A) remove
    B) repair
    C) replace
    D) relocate

ANSWER KEY

1. **D)** The signa on a prescription is the directions for use.

2. **D)** The first and most important step when inputting new prescriptions for patients is verifying the accuracy of the information in the patient profile.

3. **C)** The issuer identification number (IIN) directs claims to the appropriate third-party payment provider.

4. **C)** tab. = tablet
   q.i.d. = 4 times a day
   prn = as needed

5. **B)** gtt (gutta) = drop
   o.u. (oculus uterque) = both eyes
   b.d. or b.i.d. (bis in die) = twice daily

6. **A)** The third part of a national drug code (NDC) describes the package size and type.

7. **B)** A prescription copay is paid by customers when they pick up their prescriptions.

8. **D)** Patients who do not work and who live above the poverty level do not qualify for Medicaid.

9. **B)** Tier 2 is for preferred brand-name drugs.

10. **B)** If prior authorization is required, the pharmacist should alert the physician's office so that the appropriate forms can be filed.

11. **A)** A description of the drug is required to be on the label, but a picture is not.

12. **C)** The NDC number must be checked immediately upon removing the bottle from the shelf.

13. **C)** Metformin is an antidiabetic that should be taken with food.

14. **A)** Medication guides are mandated by the FDA for certain drugs to help patients avoid potentially serious side effects.

15. **B)** The Health Insurance Portability and Accountability Act of 1996 (HIPAA) requires patient health information to be confirmed at a distance from other people to avoid accidentally disclosing sensitive information.

16. **A)** An oral syringe is used to measure and administer small amounts of an oral suspension to infants.

17. **C)** When the physician approves refills for a patient on a prescription that has none left, it is called a refill authorization.

18. **B)** Pharmacy technicians confirm the number of refills left when they call the other pharmacy.

19. **D)** Open bottles should be stored on the shelf in front of unopened bottles.

20. **A)** Expiring medications should be removed from the shelf 1 month before the expiration date.

21. **B)** A coated tablet would not be made using nonsterile compounding techniques.

22. **B)** A tablet can be made using a mold.

23. **C)** A suspension is a preparation of undissolved drugs or powders distributed in a liquid medium.

24. **D)** A medication order is used to request drugs for patients in a hospital or other inpatient setting, so their home address is not required.

25. **A)** *Resect* means "to remove or cut back organs or tissue."

PHARMACY MATH

Measurement Systems

METRIC AND US CUSTOMARY UNITS

The numeric systems used in pharmacy include the US customary (or American) system and the metric (International System of Units, or SI) system. The **US customary system** includes many of the units used in day-to-day activities, including teaspoon, pound, and cup. The **metric system** is used throughout most of the rest of the world and is the main system used in science and medicine. Common units for the US and metric systems are shown in Table 8.1.

TABLE 8.1. Units		
Dimension	**US Customary**	**Metric/SI**
Volume	teaspoon/tablespoon/fluid ounce/cup/pint/quart/gallon (tsp/tbsp/fl oz/c/pt/qt/gal)	liter (L)
Mass	ounce/pound/ton (oz/lb/t)	gram (g)
Temperature	Fahrenheit (F)	kelvin, Celsius (C)
Length	inch/foot/yard/mile (in/ft/yd/mi)	meter (m)

HELPFUL HINT:

When providing dosing instructions in US customary units, patients should be advised to use a standardized measuring instrument, often provided with the medication.

The metric system uses prefixes to simplify large and small numbers. These prefixes are added to base units. For example, the measurement "1000 meters" can be written using the prefix *kilo–* as "one kilometer." The most commonly used metric prefixes are given in Table 8.2.

TABLE 8.2. Metric Prefixes

Prefix	Symbol	Multiplication Factor
kilo	k	1000
hecto	h	100
deca	da	10
base unit	--	--
deci	d	0.1
centi	c	0.01
milli	m	0.001

Conversion factors can be used to convert between units both within a single system and between the US and metric systems. Some common conversion factors are given in Table 8.3.

TABLE 8.3. Conversion Factors

Volume	Mass	Temperature	Length
1 gal (US) = 3.79 L 1 cm³ (SI) = 1 mL 1 tsp (US) = 5 mL 1 tbsp (US) = 3 tsp (US) = 15 mL 1 fl oz (US) = 30 mL 1 c = 8 fl oz (US) = 237 mL 1 pt (US) = 2 c (US) = 473 mL 1 qt (US) = 2 pt (US) = 946 mL 1 gal = 4 qt (US) = 3785 mL	1 oz (US) = 28 g 2.2 lb (US) = 1 kg	$°C = \frac{5}{9}(°F - 32)$ $°F = (°C \times \frac{9}{5}) + 32$	1 in (US) = 2.54 cm 1 yd (US) = 0.914 m 1 mi (US) = 1.61 km

To perform unit conversion, start with the initial value and multiply by a conversion factor to reach the final unit, as described in Figure 8.1.

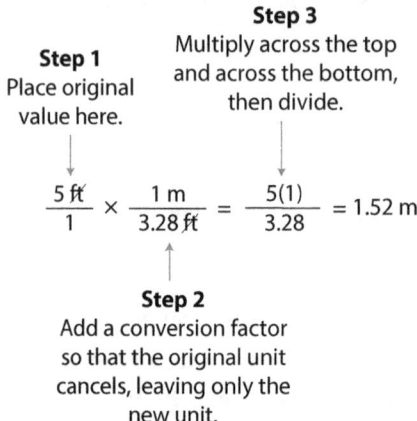

Figure 8.1. Unit Conversion

PRACTICE QUESTIONS

1. Convert 3 tablespoons to milliliters.

    A) 5 mL

    B) 30 mL

    C) 45 mL

    D) 60 mL

2. Convert 4 ounces to grams.

    A) 0.25 g

    B) 7.5 g

    C) 113 g

    D) 240 g

Other Units

The **international unit (IU)** quantifies the biological activity of a drug instead of its volume or mass. It is used for drugs such as insulin, hormones, and vitamins. International units allow patients to know they are taking the same amount of a drug regardless of the dosage form. For example, a person who takes insulin can be sure that one unit of insulin will have the same effect no matter the route of administration (ROA). Conversions from international units to metric units are specific to each drug and provided by the manufacturer.

Milliequivalents per liter (mEq/L) describe electrolyte concentration—the number of charged ions per liter; it is used for IV fluids.

The **grain (gr)** is a unit from the outdated apothecary system of measurement. One grain is equivalent to 60 – 65 milligrams (mg), depending on the drug or manufacturer. Grains are not used in pharmacy anymore but may appear in labeling for older drugs. For example, a 325 mg aspirin tablet is equivalent to 5 grains.

PRACTICE QUESTION

3. A U-100 insulin pen has a concentration of 100 units per milliliter. If a patient needs to take a dose of 10 units, how many milliliters should be administered?

    A) 0.1 mL

    B) 1.0 mL

    C) 10 mL

    D) 100 mL

Roman Numerals

Pharmacy technicians should also be able to read and manipulate **Roman numerals**. The Roman numeral system uses letters to represent numerical values, as shown in Table 8.4.

PHARMACY MATH

TABLE 8.4. Roman Numerals

Roman Numeral	Numeral Value
I	1
V	5
X	10
L	50
C	100
D	500
M	1000

Numerals are always arranged from greatest to least in value starting with the largest possible number. For example, the number 157 would be written as: 100 + 50 + 5 + 1 + 1 = CLVII.

Subtraction is used to avoid adding four of the same numerals in a row. If a numeral with a smaller value is placed before a numeral with a larger value, the smaller number is subtracted from the bigger number. For example, the number 9 is written as IX (10 − 1 = 9).

> **PRACTICE QUESTION**
>
> 4. Which of the following numbers is equivalent to the roman numeral CDVII?
>   - A) 407
>   - B) 107
>   - C) 602
>   - D) 452

Ratio, Proportions, and Percentage

A **ratio** describes how many of one thing exists in relation to the number of another thing. For example, if a bag contains 3 apples and 4 oranges, the ratio of apples to oranges is 3 to 4. Ratios can be written using words (3 to 4), fractions ($\frac{3}{4}$), or colons (3:4).

A **proportion** is an equation which states that 2 ratios are equal. Proportions are usually written as 2 fractions joined by an equal sign ($\frac{a}{b} = \frac{c}{d}$), but they can also be written using colons (a : b :: c : d). Note that in a proportion, the units must be the same in both numerators and in both denominators.

A missing value in a proportion can be found by **cross-multiplying**: multiply the numerator of each fraction by the denominator of the other to get an equation with no fractions, as shown below. You can then solve the equation using basic algebra:

$$\frac{a}{b} = \frac{c}{d} \rightarrow ad = bc$$

A **percent** describes a part of one hundred. For example, 25 percent means 25 out of 100. A percent is found by dividing the part by the whole:

$$\text{percent} = \frac{\text{part}}{\text{whole}}$$

$$\text{part} = \text{whole} \times \text{percent}$$

For example, if a person has read 5 pages (the part) of a 10-page article (the whole), they've read $\frac{5}{10} = 0.5$ or 50%. (The percent sign [%] is used once the decimal has been multiplied by 100.)

PRACTICE QUESTION

5. Grant needs to score 75% on an exam. If the exam has 48 questions, how many does he need to answer correctly?

   A) 14
   B) 34
   C) 36
   D) 38

Specific Gravity

Specific gravity is the ratio of the weight of the compound to the weight of the same amount of water (i.e., how heavy a substance is compared to water). For instance, the specific gravity of ethanol is 0.787 g/mL, meaning that ethanol is about 21 percent lighter than water.

When converting between weight and volume it is useful to know a particular compound's specific gravity. The equation for finding the specific gravity of a substance follows:

$$\text{specific gravity} = \frac{\text{weight (g)}}{\text{volume (mL)}}$$

PRACTICE QUESTION

6. In a compound, the weight of a solid is 45 grams and the volume of the solution used to dissolve it is 500 mL. What is the compound's specific gravity?

   A) 0.05 g/mL
   B) 0.09 g/mL
   C) 11.1 g/mL
   D) 12.5 g/mL

DID YOU KNOW?

The specific gravity of water is 1 g/mL, meaning 1 mL of water always weighs 1 gram.

Concentrations

Concentration refers to the amount of a particular substance in a given volume, or the substance's strength. The more of a substance that is in a given volume, the higher the concentration of the solution.

Concentrations can be expressed as a fraction (mg/mL), a ratio (1:1000), or a percentage (60%). When a pharmacy technician receives an order to prepare a solution, the following terms are used to determine what is required to compound:

- **final strength (FS)**: the strength of the final solution
- **final volume (FV)**: the volume of the final solution
- **initial strength (IS)**: the strength of the original product used to prepare the final solution
- **initial volume (IV)**: the volume of the original product used to prepare the final solution
- **final weight (FW)**: for solids, the strength of the final solution
- **initial weight (IW)**: for solids, the strength of the original product used to prepare the final solution

The following is the formula for compounding:

$$IV \text{ (or } IW) \times IS = FV \text{ (or } FW) \times FS$$

Three formulas are used to calculate concentrations by percentages. Percentages are changed to equivalent decimal fractions by dropping the percent sign (%) and dividing the expressed numerator by a fraction. The formulas are:

- **Weight/weight (w/w%)** is the number of grams of a mass solute dissolved in 100 grams of a total mass solution, or vehicle base. The weight—not the volume—of each chemical is determined:
  w/w% = (weight of solute/weight of solution) × 100

- **Volume/volume (v/v%)** is the number of milliliters of volume solute dissolved in 100 milliliters of volume solution, or vehicle base. The volume of each chemical—not the weight—is determined:
  v/v% = (volume of solute in mg/volume of solution in mL) × 100

- **Weight/volume (w/v%)** is the number of grams of mass solute dissolved in 100 milliliters of a volume solution, or vehicle base. This formula is used when a solid is dissolved into a liquid:
  w/v% = (weight of solute/volume of solution) × 100

> **HELPFUL HINT:**
>
> The substance dissolved in a solution is called the **solute**. The substance the solute is dissolved into is called the **solvent**.

PRACTICE QUESTIONS

7. What is the w/v% if 42 g of potassium is added to 1 L of sodium chloride?

    A) 0.42%

    B) 4.2%

    C) 42%

    D) 420%

8. If 15 g of hydrocortisone is added to 120 g of cold cream, what is the w/w% of hydrocortisone?

    A) 0.125%

    B) 1.25%

    C) 12.5%

    D) 125%

Ratio Strength

Many solutions require only a very tiny amount of a drug in order to be effective. When this happens, the **ratio strength** will be indicated on the product labeling; it is also known as **strength-to-weight ratio**. It is written using a slash (/) or colon (:). For example, ratio strength may be expressed in three concentrations: 1 mL/100 mL, 1 mL/1000 mL, and 1 mL/10,000 mL. Ratio strength may also be described as 1:100, 1:1000, and 1:10,000.

To calculate ratio strength in percentage, it is easiest to set up a proportion with the active ingredient on the top and the inactive ingredient on the bottom:

- In calculations, ratio strength is expressed as 1 in *x*, the corresponding fraction having a numerator of 1.
- In the ratio strength, the 1 in the ratio must correspond to the drug (active ingredient), not the solution.
- For w/v ratio strengths, volume is expressed in mL and weight in grams.

PRACTICE QUESTION

9. If 5 g of a product contains 250 mg of sodium chloride, what is the ratio strength?

    A) 1:25

    B) 1:20

    C) 1:10

    D) 1:5

Stock Solutions

HELPFUL HINT:

When solutions are **diluted**, the concentration of the drug decreases and the volume increases.

Stock solutions are solutions that have concentrations that are already known and are prepared for stock by the pharmacy staff for ease in dispensing. Rather than keeping large amounts of a solution in the pharmacy, concentrated amounts are kept. Then, the stock solutions can be **diluted** to the desired concentration needed for the preparation of the final product.

Stock solutions are prepared on a **weight-in-volume basis** so that other, weaker solutions can be made from them. Weight-in-volume is normally expressed as a percentage or ratio strength and is calculated with the following formula:

$$IV \text{ (or } IW\text{)} \times IS = FV \text{ (or } FW\text{)} \times FS$$

PRACTICE QUESTION

10. To what volume must 500 mL of a 10% w/v solution be diluted to produce a 2.5% solution?

    A) 1000 mL
    B) 1500 mL
    C) 2000 mL
    D) 2500 mL

Liquid Dilutions

Liquid solutions are normally diluted with water or saline solutions. These solvents are called **diluents**. **Dilutions** represent the parts of the concentrate in total mass or volume.

The formula for dilution is $C_1 V_1 = C_2 V_2$ where

- C_1 = concentration of stock solution,
- V_1 = volume of stock solution needed to make the new solution,
- C_2 = final concentration of new solution, and
- V_2 = final volume of new solution.

Note: This formula can apply to weight instead of volume.

PRACTICE QUESTIONS

11. Mary has 40 L of a 5 g/L solution. To this solution, she adds 10 L. What is the final concentration of the solution?

    A) 1 g/L
    B) 3 g/L
    C) 4 g/L
    D) 2.5 g/L

12. Mark has 5 L of a 10 g/L solution. He needs to add 15 L to this solution to make the needed concentration. What is the final concentration of the solution? (Hint: We are looking for C2.)

   A) 1.25 g/L
   B) 2.5 g/L
   C) 7.5 g/L
   D) 15 g/L

Solid Dilutions

Solids, such as ointments, creams, and lotions, can also be diluted with another solid. This is normally done with the **trituration method**. In trituration, a potent drug powder is diluted with an inert diluent powder (usually lactose). The dilution occurs proportionally by weight. A weighable portion, or **aliquot**, of the mixture contains the desired amount of substance.

The formula used for dilution of solids by trituration is:

$$\frac{\text{weight of drug in trituration}}{\text{weight of trituration}} = \frac{\text{weight of drug in aliquot}}{\text{weight of aliquot}}$$

PRACTICE QUESTION

13. To determine the weight of the diluent needed to prepare the trituration after solving the formula, a pharmacy technician must

   A) subtract the weight of the drug being used for trituration by the trituration weight.
   B) multiply the weight of the drug being used for trituration by the trituration weight.
   C) divide the weight of the drug being used for trituration by the trituration weight.
   D) add the weight of the drug being used for trituration by the trituration weight.

Alligations

Pharmacy alligation (also known as "tic-tac-toe" math) is a shortcut for solving algebra problems. It is mainly used as an alternative to standard algebra when calculating the volumes for a compound made from different strengths of a similar chemical.

The easiest way to learn how to use alligation is to work through a sample problem.

A prescription order has arrived for **500 mL of a 12% solution**. The pharmacy stocks the solution needed in **1 gallon of 30% solution** and **1 gallon of 10% solution**. You must mix the two solutions together to prepare a custom compound of the ordered volume. How much of the **30% solution** will you need?

Alligation Solution

Step 1: Draw a tic-tac-toe grid and put **higher % strength** in the top left square, **desired % strength** in the middle square, and **lower % strength** in the bottom left square:

Step 2: Calculate the difference between the bottom left number and the middle number going up diagonally as well as the difference from the top left and middle number going down diagonally (ignore any negatives). Then add up those two numbers to get 20. This sum becomes the "parts" needed to work with:

30		2
	12		2 + 18 = 20 parts
10		18

Step 3: Now, divide the needed volume by the total parts: 500 mL ÷ 20 parts = 25 mL per part.

Step 4: On the grid, multiply the numbers in the right column by the milliliters per part to find the final volume:

30		2 × 25 = 50 mL
	12	
10		18 × 25 = 450 mL

50 mL of the 30% solution is needed.

Alligation:

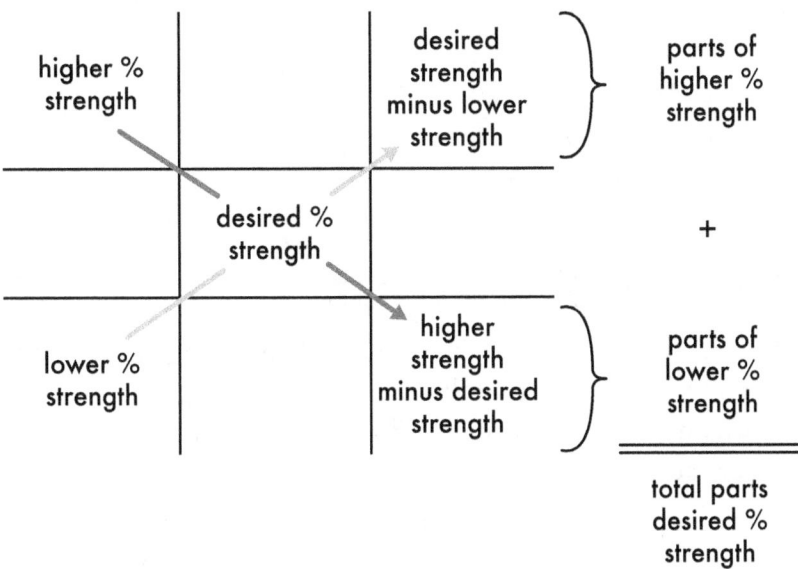

Figure 8.2. Alligations

Algebraic Solution

Let x = the amount of the 30% solution. Then $500 - x$ = the amount of the 10% solution, because they both must add up to 500 mL.

Now, fill out this chart:

	Amount	%	Total	
30% Strength	x	0.30	$0.3x$	**Multiply across**
10% Strength	$500 - x$	0.10	$0.10(500 - x)$	**Multiply across**
Total	500	0.12	60	**Multiply across**
(What we want)				
	Add Down		**Add Down:** $0.3x + 0.10(500 - x) = 60$; solve.

Next, solve for x, which is the amount of the 30% solution:

$0.3x + 0.10(500 - x) = 60$

$0.3x + 50 - 0.10x = 60$

$0.2x = 10$

x = 50 mL

> **PRACTICE QUESTION**
>
> 14. A prescription for a 30 g tube of 2% hydrocortisone needs to be made from a 1% solution and a 2.5% solution. Using alligation, how much of each available product is needed to prepare this prescription?
>
>   A) 1 g of 1% and 2.5 g of 2%
>   B) 10 g of 1% and 20 g of 2.5%
>   C) 15 g of 1% and 15 g of 2.5%
>   D) 20 g of 1% and 10 g of 2.5%

Pediatric Dosages

Pediatric refers to any patient eighteen years old or younger. Because infants and children cannot tolerate adult doses of drugs, drugs given to pediatric patients are dosed based on the child's age and weight. There are several methods for calculating pediatric dosages.

The most accurate way to calculate pediatric dosages is by weight (kilogram or pound), but they can also be calculated using age. There are three common formulas used for calculating pediatric dosages: Clark's rule, Young's rule, and Fried's rule. (Fried's rule is the least common calculation as it is only used for pediatric patients under twenty-four months of age.)

- Clark's rule: child's dose = $\frac{\text{weight of the child (lb.)}}{150} \times$ average adult dose

- Young's rule: child's dose = adult dose $\times \frac{\text{age}}{\text{age} + 12}$

- Fried's rule: child's dose = $\frac{\text{child's age in months}}{150} \times$ adult dose

Pediatric dosages can also be calculated by **body surface area (BSA)**. Charts called **nomograms** are used to estimate BSA using height and weight. A pediatric nomogram shows height on one side and weight on the other. When a line is drawn between a child's height and weight, it crosses another line that estimates BSA. The pediatric doses are then calculated by multiplying the BSA in square meters by the dose ordered.

The formula for calculation using a nomogram is:

$$\text{weight per dose} \times \text{BSA} = \text{desired dose}$$

It is important to stress how crucial it is to be accurate in calculating dosage strengths for children. A single mistake in the placement of a decimal point can cause injury or death in children. It is also important to emphasize that not all drugs can be given to children, even with changes in dosage strength. Because of severe side effects or because the drug has not been tested on children, certain drugs are not to be given to children at all.

HELPFUL HINT:

The most commonly used rule is Clark's rule. For Clark's rule, always use the weight of the child in pounds, not kilograms.

The Pediatric Dosage Handbook is one reference tool used in the pharmacy setting for resources on pediatric dosing; it includes manufacturer packaging, labeling information, and requirements. It is also important to state that if technicians have any questions, they should ask the pharmacist-in-charge or a supervisor for verification of correct dosing.

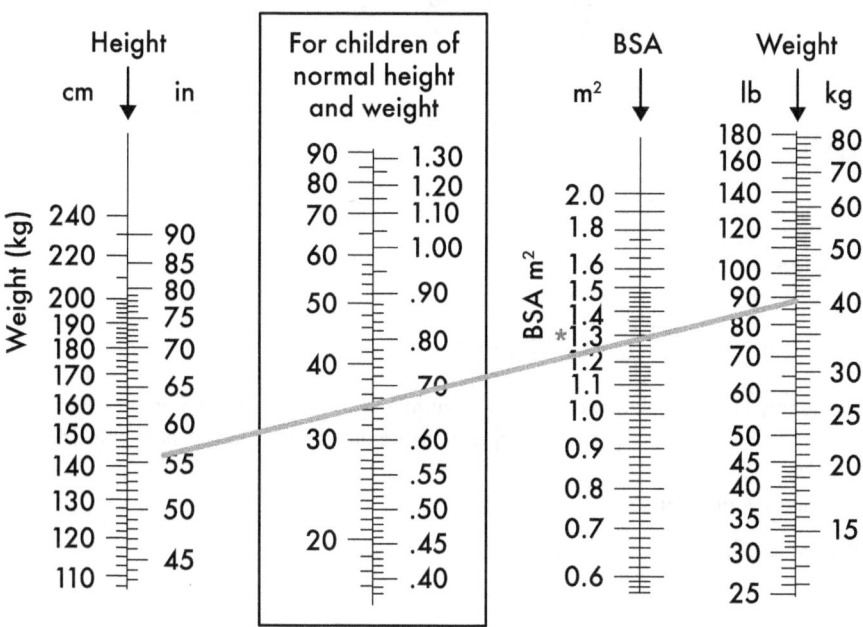

Figure 8.3. Pediatric Nomogram

PRACTICE QUESTIONS

15. If a physician orders Cefzil for a 38 lb child, what would be the pediatric dose given if the adult dose of Cefzil is 600 mg q 24 h? (Use Clark's rule.)

    A) 85.4 mg

    B) 150.2 mg

    C) 152 mg

    D) 250 mg

16. A physician orders Zyrtec 0.1 mg/kg daily for a child who weighs 70 lbs. What is the correct pediatric dose for the patient?

    A) 5.5 mg daily

    B) 3.18 mg daily

    C) 2.75 mg daily

    D) 1.25 mg daily

ANSWER KEY

1. **C)** $3 \text{ tbsp} \times \frac{15 \text{ mL}}{1 \text{ tbsp}} =$ **45 mL**

2. **C)** $4 \text{ oz} \times \frac{28 \text{ g}}{1 \text{ oz}} =$ **113 g**

3. **A)** $10 \text{ units} \times \frac{1 \text{ mL}}{100 \text{ units}} = 0.1 \text{ mL}$

4. **A)** C = 100, D = 500, V = 5, I = 1, I = 1
   Since C comes before D, 100 is subtracted from 500.
   500 − 100 + 5 + 1 + 1 = 407

5. **C)** part = whole × percent = 48 × 0.75 = 36

6. **B)** Identify the formula and variables:
   $$\text{specific gravity} = \frac{\text{weight (g)}}{\text{volume (mL)}}$$
   weight = 45 g
   volume = 500 mL
   Solve for specific gravity:
   $$\text{specific gravity} = \frac{45 \text{ g}}{500 \text{ mL}} = \mathbf{0.09 \text{ g/mL}}$$

7. **B)** Identify the variables and formula (weight must be in grams and volume in mL). Note that the solute is the potassium, and the vehicle base is the sodium chloride:
   weight of solute = 42 g
   volume of vehicle base (in mL) = 1 L = 1000 mL
   $$\frac{w}{v}\% = \frac{\text{weight of solute (g)}}{\text{volume of vehical base (mL)}} \times 100$$
   Solve for w/v %:
   $$\frac{w}{v}\% = \frac{42 \text{ g}}{1000 \text{ mL}} \times 100 = 0.042 \times 100 = \mathbf{4.2\%}$$

8. **C)** Identify variables and formula. Note that the solute is the hydrocortisone, and the vehicle base is the cold cream:
   volume of solute = 15 g
   volume of vehicle base = 120 g
   $$\frac{w}{w}\% = \frac{\text{volume of solute}}{\text{volume of vehicle base}} \times 100$$
   Solve for w/w %:
   $$\frac{w}{w}\% = \frac{15 \text{ g}}{120 \text{ g}} \times 100 = 0.125 \times 100 = \mathbf{12.5\%}$$

9. **B)** Convert the 250 mg of sodium chloride (the active ingredient) into grams, so the units will match:
   250 mg = 0.25 g
   Set up a proportion with the drug on the top and the sodium chloride solution on the bottom:
   $$\frac{0.25 \text{ g}}{5 \text{ g}} = \frac{1}{x}$$
   Cross multiply and solve for the ratio strength, which will be a number greater than 1. Then describe ratio strength in a ratio with 1 corresponding to the active ingredient amount:
   0.25x = 5
   x = 20
   1:20

10. **B)** Identify variables:
    x = volume of sterile water to be added
    C_1 = concentration of stock solution (actual drug) = 10%
    V_1 = volume of stock solution needed to make new solution = 500 L
    C_2 = final concentration of new solution = 2.5%
    V_2 = final volume of new solution = (500 + x) L
    Plug the values in the appropriate formula. Isolate x to get solution:
    $C_1V_1 = C_2V_2$
    0.10 × 500 = 0.025(500 + x)
    50 = 12.5 + 0.025x
    0.025x = 50 − 12.5 = 37.5
    $x = \frac{37.5}{0.025}$
    x = 1500 mL

11. **C)** Identify variables:
    x = final concentration of new solution
    C_1 = concentration of stock solution (actual drug) = 5 g/L
    V_1 = volume of stock solution needed to make new solution = 40 L
    C_2 = final concentration of new solution = x g/L
    V_2 = final volume of new solution = 40 L + 10 L = 50 L
    Plug the values into the appropriate formula. Isolate x to get the solution:
    $C_1V_1 = C_2V_2$
    5(40) = x(50)
    200 = x(50)
    200 = 50x
    x = 4 g/L

12. **B)** Identify variables:
    x = final concentration of new solution in g/L
    C_1 = concentration of stock solution (actual drug) = 10 g/L
    V_1 = volume of stock solution needed to make new solution = 5 L
    C_2 = final concentration of new solution = x
    V_2 = final volume of new solution = 5 L + 15 L = 20 L
    Plug the values into the appropriate formula. Isolate x to get the solution:
    $C_1V_1 = C_2V_2$
    10(5) = 20(x)
    50 = 20x
    $x = \frac{50}{20}$
    x = 2.5 g/L

13. **A)** Subtracting the weight of the drug being used for trituration by the trituration weight will determine the weight of the diluent.

14. B)
Alligation Solution:

Step 1: Draw a tic-tac-toe grid and put higher % strength in the top left square, desired % strength in the middle square, and lower % strength in the bottom left square:

1		
	2	
2.5		

Step 2: Calculate the difference between the bottom left number and the middle number going up diagonally, and the difference from the top left and middle numbers going down diagonally (ignore any negatives). Then add up those two numbers to get 1.5. This sum becomes the "parts":

1		0.5
	2	0.5 + 1 = 1.5 parts
2.5		1

Step 3: Now, divide the needed volume into the total parts: 30 g ÷ 1.5 parts = 20 g per part.

Step 4: On the grid, go back up to the parts and write the volume for each part:

1		0.5 × 20 = 10 g
	2	
2.5		1 × 20 = 20 g

sSo, 0.5 parts of the 1% solution × 20 g = 10 g, and 1 part of the 2.5% solution × 20 g = 20 g.

Algebraic Solution:
Let x = the amount of the 1% solution. Then $30 - x$ = the amount of the 2.5% solution because they both have to add up to 30 g.

Now fill out this chart:

	Amount	%	Total	
1% Strength	x	0.01	0.01x	Multiply across
2.5% Strength	30 − x	0.025	0.025(30 − x)	Multiply across
Total (desired quantity)	30	0.02	0.6	Multiply across
	Add Down		Add Down: 0.1x + 0.025 (30 − x) = 0.6; solve.	

Solve for x, which is the amount of the 1% solution:
0.01x + 0.75 − 0.025X = 0.6
−0.015x = −0.15
x = 10 g
Then, to get the 2.5% solution, subtract this from 30:
30 − x = 20 g

15. **C)** Identify the formula and variables; note that the child's weight is already in pounds:

child's dose = $\frac{\text{weight of the child}}{150}$ × adult dose

weight of the child = 38 lb

adult dose = 600 mg

Solve for child's dose.

child's dose = $\frac{38}{150}$ × 600 mg = 152 mg

16. **B)** Multiply by conversion ratios to cancel out units until arriving at the needed units; recall that that 1 kg ≈ 2.2 lb:

$\frac{0.1 \text{ mg}}{\text{kg}} \times \frac{1 \text{ kg}}{2.2 \text{ lb}} \times 70 \text{ lb}$ = **3.18 mg**

PART V

PRACTICE TESTS

PRACTICE TEST ONE

Read the question carefully and choose the most correct answer.

1. Salmeterol is used primarily to:
   A) prevent asthma attacks and bronchospasms.
   B) lower fevers and treat inflammation.
   C) treat autoimmune disorders.
   D) modulate estrogen levels.

2. The pharmacy receives the following prescription:

   > Spiriva Respimat, 1.25 mcg
   > Disp: one inhaler
   > Sig: 2 puffs BID

   How many days should the supply last if there are 60 metered doses in each inhaler?
   A) 15
   B) 30
   C) 45
   D) 60

3. DEA Form 106 is used for:
   A) ordering and returning Schedule II drugs.
   B) theft or loss.
   C) DEA registration.
   D) destroying controlled substances.

4. If a drug's expiration date is written as June 2021, the last day the drug may be used is:
   A) May 31, 2021.
   B) June 1, 2021.
   C) June 30, 2021.
   D) July 1, 2021.

5. Which of the following generic medications can be substituted for Vasotec?
   A) atenolol
   B) metoprolol
   C) metronidazole
   D) enalapril

6. A laminar flow hood in the pharmacy is designed to:
   A) provide filtered air directly over the work surface.
   B) be sterile on the inside.
   C) move air away from the work area.
   D) remove hazardous fumes from the work area.

7. All of the following information must be included on a Schedule II prescription hard copy EXCEPT:
   A) the manual signature of the physician.
   B) the patient's name and address.
   C) the prescriber's DEA number.
   D) the drug's NDC number.

8. A 2% dextrose stock solution and a 10% dextrose stock solution are being used to make 250 mL of a 5% dextrose solution. How many milliliters of the 10% solution should be used?
   A) 50 mL
   B) 31.25 mL
   C) 93.75 mL
   D) 145.8 mL

9. The generic name for Protonix is:
   A) omeprazole.
   B) esomeprazole.
   C) pantoprazole.
   D) lansoprazole.

10. Which auxiliary label should be affixed to a prescription bottle of metformin ER?
    A) Do not chew or crush. Swallow whole.
    B) Do not ingest any form of grapefruit.
    C) Take medication on an empty stomach.
    D) May cause drowsiness.

11. If 5 capsules of amoxicillin contain 2,500 mg of amoxicillin, how many capsules are required to fill a prescription for 50,000 mg?
    A) 25
    B) 50
    C) 75
    D) 100

12. Which of the following medications should be taken with food?
    A) meloxicam
    B) Fioricet
    C) ondansetron
    D) varenicline

13. The purpose of Tall Man lettering is to:
    A) differentiate among LASA drugs.
    B) ensure correct pronunciation of drug names.
    C) prevent spelling errors.
    D) speed up the prescription labeling process.

14. Which of the following medications is contraindicated for pregnant patients?
    A) Humalog
    B) chlorhexidine gluconate
    C) tizanidine
    D) warfarin

15. Which of the following is NOT a Schedule drug?
    A) pregabalin
    B) lorazepam
    C) metronidazole
    D) methylphenidate

16. Dr. Johnson became a physician in 1981. Which of the following could be her DEA number?
    A) AJ1673929
    B) BJ1673929
    C) JB1673929
    D) JA1673929

17. Which of the following is NOT a side effect of ciprofloxacin?
    A) vomiting
    B) diarrhea
    C) constipation
    D) headache

18. How long from the date it is written is a prescription for a noncontrolled substance valid?
    A) 2 years
    B) 1 year
    C) 6 months
    D) 30 days

19. Which health care professional does NOT have prescribing authority?
    A) nurse practitioners
    B) registered nurses
    C) physicians
    D) psychiatrists

20. A patient is taking hydrotussin, 2 teaspoons q 4 hrs as needed for cough. The doctor gave the patient 8 ounces of the hydrotussin. If the patient took the medication exactly as written, every 4 hours, how long would the 8-ounce bottle last?
    A) 7 days
    B) 6 days
    C) 5 days
    D) 4 days

21. A pharmacy technician should alert the pharmacist to counsel a patient who has presented a prescription for:
    A) doxycycline for a 4-year-old.
    B) omeprazole for a 70-year-old.
    C) famotidine for a 16-year-old.
    D) 81 mg aspirin for a 30-year-old.

22. Which of the following is used for weighing non-sterile compound ingredients?
    A) counterbalance
    B) compounding slab
    C) suppository mold
    D) mortar and pestle

23. Which of the following medications does NOT have edema as a potential side effect?
    A) sertraline
    B) lisinopril
    C) amlodipine
    D) sildenafil

24. Which of the following is a common side effect of ACE inhibitors?
    A) cough
    B) weight gain
    C) weight loss
    D) drowsiness

25. A pharmacy receives the following prescription:

    Norco 5/325
    Sig: 1 tab PO q 4–6 hours PRN × 10 days

    How many tablets will be needed to fill this prescription?
    A) 40
    B) 60
    C) 120
    D) 240

26. A prescription is written for amoxicillin 250-mg capsules × 2 BID × 10 days. If the pharmacy only has 500-mg amoxicillin capsules in stock, how many capsules should be dispensed?
    A) 10
    B) 20
    C) 40
    D) 80

27. Which of the following drugs does NOT have a warning for patients under 18 years old?
    A) paroxetine
    B) aspirin
    C) amoxicillin
    D) escitalopram

28. The pharmacy receives the following prescription:

    > Lortab 7.5 mg
    > Dispense: #12
    > Sig: ℥ PO q 4–6 ours PRN

    Which of the following drug forms will the pharmacy technician dispense?
    A) capsule
    B) syrup
    C) tablet
    D) lozenge

29. Orphan drugs are developed for:
    A) children with autoimmune conditions.
    B) management of chronic respiratory conditions.
    C) treatment of rare diseases.
    D) replacement of high-cost brand-name drugs.

30. A patient taking which of the following medications should be counseled to avoid taking the medication with grapefruit?
    A) lovastatin
    B) citalopram
    C) esomeprazole
    D) furosemide

31. The abbreviation *rep, rept* means:
    A) no refill.
    B) label.
    C) as needed.
    D) repeat.

32. A prescription is written for pravastatin 60 mg tab qhs × 30 days. Pravastatin is only dispensed in 20 mg, 40 mg, and 80 mg, and each tablet is scored so it can be split in half. How many tablets are needed to fill this prescription?
    A) 30
    B) 45
    C) 60
    D) 63

33. Ondansetron is prescribed for:
    A) pain.
    B) diabetes.
    C) stomach acid.
    D) nausea.

34. A prescription contains the code DAW-1. The pharmacy technician should:
    A) dispense a generic substitute.
    B) dispense the name-brand medication written on the prescription.
    C) call the prescriber to confirm which generic should be substituted.
    D) call the patient's insurance company before dispensing the medication.

35. NDC numbers include all of the following information EXCEPT the:
    A) manufacturer's name.
    B) drug's name.
    C) package size.
    D) drug's expiration date.

36. Which of the following symptoms is NOT a common potential side effect of prednisone?
    A) headache
    B) dizziness
    C) blurred vision
    D) weight loss

37. Which of the following could be the DEA number for a manufacturer of Schedule II controlled substances?
    A) E97548398
    B) X99384758
    C) A91627833
    D) R96059489

38. Which of the following is on a patient's compounding label?
    A) physician's DEA number
    B) patient's Social Security number
    C) patient's allergies
    D) quantity

39. A pharmacy technician is compounding a prescription and mistakenly over-dilutes the compound. What should the technician do next?
    A) properly dispose of the compound and start the compounding process from the beginning
    B) figure out how much of the solute is needed to prepare the proper concentration and add it to the compound
    C) adjust the patient's dose so they receive the correct amount of the drug
    D) alert the pharmacist and have them prepare the compound

40. What is a characteristic of a paste?
    A) use of a dry ingredient
    B) an oily texture
    C) use of gelatin
    D) a thin texture

41. Which controlled substance is classified as a Schedule II drug?
    A) tranquilizers
    B) anabolic steroids
    C) opioids
    D) heroin

42. If a patient has a history of drug abuse, pharmacists may do all of the following EXCEPT:
    A) monitor controlled medications.
    B) put restrictions on controlled medications.
    C) make sure the patient is complying with the directions.
    D) tell a family member to monitor the patient's use of the medication.

43. Of the following medication pairs, which two are considered therapeutic substitutions for each other?
    A) Lipitor and atorvastatin
    B) Aciphex and pantoprazole
    C) ciprofloxacin and amoxicillin
    D) Plavix and metoprolol

44. iPledge is an FDA program that regulates the sale of:
    A) isotretinoin.
    B) tretinoin.
    C) levotretinoin.
    D) dextrotretinoin.

45. How many days' supply can be prescribed with one Schedule II prescription?
    A) 7 days
    B) 30 days
    C) 60 days
    D) 90 days

46. A 6-year-old boy is 126 cm tall and weighs 34 kg. The adult dosage of his prescribed medication is 400 mg. Using Clark's rule, the dosage for the boy will be:
    A) 160 mg.
    B) 200 mg.
    C) 240 mg.
    D) 300 mg.

47. The DEA requires all of the following to be on the prescription for a controlled substance EXCEPT the:
    A) patient's date of birth.
    B) patient's address.
    C) prescriber's address.
    D) prescriber's registration number.

48. At what temperature should the influenza vaccine be stored?
    A) body temperature: 97.52–99.68°F (36.4–37.6°C)
    B) room temperature: 60–86°F (15–30°C)
    C) refrigerated: 36–46°F (2–8°C)
    D) frozen: −4–14°F (−20–10°C)

49. Which of the following medications should be counted on a tray not used for other drugs?
    A) methylphenidate
    B) sertraline
    C) penicillin
    D) methylprednisolone

50. A patient's insurance will only fill generics manufactured by a single company. The patient fills omeprazole 40 mg with an NDC of 79534-1357-40. Which of the following NDCs would also be filled by this patient's insurance?
    A) 52510-1357-40
    B) 79534-9708-20
    C) 95374-1357-30
    D) 97453-8563-40

51. Which of the following pieces of equipment can a pharmacy technician use to measure the diluent required to reconstitute an oral liquid?
    A) graduated cylinder
    B) measuring cup
    C) beaker
    D) syringe

52. Which of the following questions from a patient can a pharmacy technician answer?
    A) "Can I take Tylenol with this prescription?"
    B) "How does this medication work in my body?"
    C) "Does my insurance cover a ninety-day supply of this prescription?"
    D) "What are the side effects of this prescription?"

53. Which of the following medications should NOT be stored on the common pharmacy shelf?
    A) alprazolam
    B) penicillin
    C) chlorhexidine gluconate
    D) lisdexamfetamine

54. The abbreviation *QID* means:
    A) every day.
    B) every other day.
    C) four times daily.
    D) three times daily.

55. If 1 L of a solution contains 5 g of a drug, how much of the drug would be present in 750 mL?
    A) 1.5 g
    B) 3.75 g
    C) 2.75 g
    D) 4 g

56. NDC numbers were implemented under which act?
    A) Orphan Drug Act
    B) FDA Modernization Act
    C) Medicare Modernization Act
    D) Drug Listing Act of 1972

57. Succinylcholine is primarily used for:
    A) pain management.
    B) chemotherapy.
    C) anesthesia.
    D) treatment of autoimmune disease.

58. Which of the following drugs is a high-alert medication?

- A) metronidazole
- B) potassium chloride injections
- C) ketorolac
- D) lisinopril

59. Dispensing the LASA drug clonidine in place of Klonopin may result in:

- A) renal failure.
- B) seizures.
- C) hyperglycemia.
- D) neuropathic pain.

60. Deteriorated drug errors occur when:

- A) drugs that require specific laboratory values for dosing are not monitored properly.
- B) drugs are administered whose potency and integrity have been compromised.
- C) nurses fail to properly follow administration protocols.
- D) the prescribed dose is not administered at the correct time.

61. How many mL of a solution containing 150 mcg/mL of medication would be needed if a patient requires a dose of 1 mg?

- A) 5 mL
- B) 3.33 mL
- C) 6.67 mL
- D) 7.5 mL

62. Tall Man lettering should be used for:

- A) guanfacine and guaifenesin.
- B) Depakote and diltiazem.
- C) Avapro and Antivert.
- D) Zovirax and zolpidem.

63. Which of the following written quantities correctly follows procedures for preventing medication errors?

- A) 03 units
- B) .7 units
- C) 0.5 units
- D) 100.00 units

64. What can workers do in a clean room?

- A) garb
- B) generate labels
- C) prepare CSPs
- D) wash hands

65. A patient with a prescription for rivaroxaban should be referred to the pharmacist if they are also purchasing:

- A) aspirin.
- B) acetaminophen.
- C) diphenhydramine.
- D) omeprazole.

66. A doctor prescribes methylprednisolone 10 mg tablets with the following directions:

6 tabs po qd for 2 days;
5 tabs po qd for 2 days;
4 tabs po qd for 2 days;
3 tabs po qd for 2 days;
2 tabs po qd for 2 days;
Then 1 tab qd for 5 days

How many tablets should be dispensed to fill this medication?

- A) 25
- B) 45
- C) 50
- D) 100

67. Which of the following medications is labeled with a boxed warning?
- **A)** tamsulosin
- **B)** lisinopril
- **C)** allopurinol
- **D)** pioglitazone

68. Which FDA recall level is used when there is a probability that the use of the product could cause an adverse event?
- **A)** Class I
- **B)** Class II
- **C)** Class III
- **D)** Class IV

69. Hydralazine is primarily prescribed to treat:
- **A)** seizures.
- **B)** depression.
- **C)** hypertension.
- **D)** diabetes.

70. If a prescription is presented for 180 g of a 7.5% cream and the pharmacy only stocks 10% and 2% strengths, how much of each strength would be needed to compound this order?
- **A)** 123.75 g of the 10% and 56.25 g of the 2%
- **B)** 140.25 g of the 10% and 39.75 g of the 2%
- **C)** 125 g of the 10% and 55 g of the 2%
- **D)** 110.88 g of the 10% and 69.12 g of the 2%

71. The drug class suffix –pam is used for:
- **A)** benzodiazepines.
- **B)** beta blockers.
- **C)** antiviral medications.
- **D)** SSRIs.

72. Which of the following entities is NOT covered by the guidelines described in HIPAA?
- **A)** health care providers
- **B)** health insurance plans
- **C)** family members of the patient
- **D)** health care workers

73. Pharmacy technicians write a large X on drug containers to show others that the:
- **A)** drug is about to expire.
- **B)** container has been opened.
- **C)** medication is generic.
- **D)** medication is brand name.

74. Which federal law required that prescriptions be written by a physician for certain medications before they can be dispensed to a patient?
- **A)** Pure Food and Drug Act of 1906
- **B)** Food, Drug, and Cosmetic Act of 1938
- **C)** Durham-Humphrey Amendment of 1951
- **D)** Comprehensive Drug Abuse Prevention and Control Act of 1970

75. Which part of Medicare covers prescription drugs?
- **A)** Medicare Part A
- **B)** Medicare Part B
- **C)** Medicare Part C
- **D)** Medicare Part D

76. Which is NOT a law or requirement that was established under the Anabolic Steroids Control Act of 1990?
- **A)** Anabolic steroids are not allowed to be prescribed in the United States.
- **B)** Trainers and advisers cannot recommend anabolic steroid use to individuals.
- **C)** Anabolic steroids must be classified as a Schedule III controlled substance.
- **D)** Anabolic steroids are defined as a drug or hormonal substance that promotes muscle growth in a way similar to testosterone.

77. Which agency approves the use of investigational new drugs (INDs)?
- **A)** DEA
- **B)** CDC
- **C)** ASPCA
- **D)** FDA

78. Which two NDCs represent the same medication?
- **A)** 23096-1980-92 and 23096-1890-92
- **B)** 23096-1980-92 and 23096-1980-30
- **C)** 23096-8940-92 and 23096-9840-92
- **D)** 02934-9284-70 and 02934-9990-70

79. What is a decentralized pharmacy?
- **A)** a system that alerts the nurse when the medication should be administered
- **B)** the center of pharmacy operations in a hospital or health care facility
- **C)** nursing unit med rooms that contain an automated dispensing machine
- **D)** the sterile room

80. How many tablets are in a tapering methylprednisolone dose pack that starts with 6 tablets on day 1?
- **A)** 14
- **B)** 21
- **C)** 31
- **D)** 64

81. How many times can a patient refill a Schedule III or IV prescription?
- **A)** zero times
- **B)** two times
- **C)** five times
- **D)** six times

82. Which of the following substances should be used to clean counting trays?
- **A)** isopropyl alcohol 90%
- **B)** isopropyl alcohol 70%
- **C)** witch hazel
- **D)** hydrogen peroxide

83. Which of the following suffixes is used for histamine-2 blockers?
- **A)** –olol
- **B)** –pril
- **C)** –tidine
- **D)** –artan

84. Which reference book is a resource on drug pricing?
- **A)** the *Orange Book*
- **B)** *Drug Facts and Comparisons*
- **C)** the *Red Book*
- **D)** Martindale's *The Complete Drug Reference*

85. A physician orders sodium chloride 20 mEq. The pharmacy only has sodium chloride 40 mEq/20 mL available. How much is needed to make the solution?
- **A)** 2 mL
- **B)** 6 mL
- **C)** 10 mL
- **D)** 12 mL

86. Which auxiliary label should be affixed to a prescription bottle of metronidazole?
- **A)** Shake well before use.
- **B)** Do not drink milk or eat dairy products.
- **C)** May cause drowsiness.
- **D)** Do not drink alcoholic beverages when taking this medication.

87. Child doses are calculated by the child's:
- **A)** weight.
- **B)** height.
- **C)** age.
- **D)** grade.

88. Which of the following is NOT required on a prescription label?

   A) patient's name

   B) directions for use

   C) insurance information

   D) patient's order number

89. A patient taking which of the following medications should be counseled to avoid alcohol?

   A) gabapentin

   B) potassium chloride

   C) naproxen

   D) ranitidine

90. Which of the following drugs does NOT treat osteoporosis?

   A) raloxifene

   B) ibandronate

   C) zoledronic acid

   D) methotrexate

ANSWER KEY

1. **A)** Salmeterol prevents asthma attacks and bronchospasms.

2. **A)** The patient will need 2 puffs BID (twice daily), so they will require 4 puffs a day. If the inhaler contains 60 doses, the supply will last 15 days.

   $$\frac{60 \text{ doses} \div 4 \text{ doses}}{\text{day}} = \textbf{15 days}$$

3. **B)** DEA Form 106 is used for theft or loss.

4. **C)** If no day is given in the expiration date, the drug will expire on the last day of the listed month.

5. **D)** Enalapril is the generic equivalent of Vasotec.

6. **A)** Laminar flow hoods bring in and filter outside air to prevent contamination.

7. **D)** The drug's NDC number is not required.

8. **C)** Draw a tic-tac-toe grid and put the higher % strength in the top left square, the desired % strength in the middle square, and the lower % strength in the bottom left square. Then, subtract diagonally.

10		3
	5	
2		5

   Add to the numbers in the right column to find the number of parts: 3 + 5 = 8.

   Divide the needed volume by the total parts: 250 mL ÷ 8 parts = 31.25 mL per part.

   On the grid, multiply the numbers in the right column by the mL per part to find the final volume.

10		3 × 31.25 = 93.75 mL
	5	
2		5 × 31.25 = 156.25 mL

   The 5% dextrose solution will be made from **93.75 mL of the 10% solution** and 156.25 mL of the 2% solution.

9. **C)** Pantoprazole is the generic substitute for Protonix.

10. **A)** Extended-release medications should be swallowed whole, not chewed or crushed.

11. **D)** Set up a proportion with the number of capsules on top and the milligrams on the bottom. Five capsules of amoxicillin contain 2,500 mg of amoxicillin.

    $$\frac{5 \text{ capsules}}{2,500 \text{ mg}} = \frac{x \text{ capsules}}{50,000 \text{ mg}}$$

    Cross-multiply and solve for x.

    2,500x = 250,000

    x = 100 capsules

12. **A)** Meloxicam is an NSAID and should be taken with food or milk to minimize stomach irritation.

13. **A)** Tall Man lettering is used to differentiate among LASA drugs.

14. **D)** Warfarin is contraindicated during pregnancy because it affects fetal development and may lead to hemorrhage or spontaneous abortion.

15. **C)** Metronidazole is an antibiotic/antiprotozoal and is not a Schedule drug.

16. **A)** The letter A is used for providers who began practicing before 1985, and the second letter is the initial of the provider's last name. If Dr. Johnson began practicing in 1981, her DEA number would start with AJ.

17. **C)** Constipation is not a side effect of ciprofloxacin.

18. **B)** Noncontrolled prescriptions are good for 1 year from the date they are written.

19. **B)** Registered nurses do not have the authority to prescribe medications.

20. **D)** First set up a proportion with ounces on top and teaspoons on the bottom to determine how many teaspoons the patient must take to finish the 8 ounces.

    Use the fact that .

    $$\frac{1 \text{ fl.oz}}{6 \text{ tsp.}} = \frac{8 \text{ fl.oz}}{x \text{ tsp.}}$$

    x = 48 teaspoons

    So 48 teaspoons are needed, and the patient must take 2 teaspoons every 4 hours, day and night; thus the patient needs 12 teaspoons a day.

    Therefore, the 8-ounce bottle (48 teaspoons) will last 4 days.

    24 hours ÷ every 4 hours = 6 times a day

    6 times a day × 2 teaspoons = 12 teaspoons a day

    48 teaspooons total ÷ 12 teaspoons = **4 days**

21. **A)** Doxycycline may cause tissue hyperpigmentation or tooth enamel defects in children with developing teeth and so is used with caution in children younger than 8 years. The pharmacist should counsel the customer on the potential side effects.

22. **A)** A counterbalance is used for weighing non-sterile compound ingredients.

23. **B)** Edema is not a listed side effect of lisinopril.

24. **A)** Cough is a common side effect of ACE inhibitors.

25. **B)** The patient will take 1 tablet every 4–6 hours (up to 6 tablets a day) as needed for 10 days: 6 × 10 = **60 tablets**.

26. **B)** The two 250-mg capsules will be replaced with one 500-mg capsule. The patient will take 1 capsule twice a day for 10 days: 1 capsule × 2 capsules/day × 10 days = **20 capsules**.

27. **C)** Amoxicillin may be prescribed to patients under 18 years old. Paroxetine (Paxil) and escitalopram (Lexapro) are antidepressants, which may increase the risk of suicidal thinking and behaviors in children and adolescents. Aspirin may cause Reye syndrome in children with viral illnesses.

28. **C)** The abbreviation † means "tablet."

29. **C)** Orphan drugs are pharmaceuticals that are developed specifically for rare diseases.

30. **A)** Drinking grapefruit juice with lovastatin increases absorption and serum concentration of the drug.

31. **D)** The sig code for "repeat" is *rep, rept*.

32. **B)** The patient will take 1.5 tablets every day (40 mg × 1.5 = 60 mg).

    For a 30-day supply: 1.5 × 30 = **45 tablets**.

33. **D)** Ondansetron is used for nausea.

34. **B)** DAW-1 indicates that substitutions are not allowed by the prescriber. Doctors use this code when the brand medication is medically necessary, and substitution is not allowed.

35. **D)** The NDC number does not include the drug's expiration date.

36. **D)** Weight gain (not weight loss) is a common potential side effect of prednisone.

37. **A)** DEA numbers for manufacturers start with the letter *E*.

38. **D)** The quantity of the compounded medication would be on the medication label.

39. **A)** If a mistake is made during compounding, the technician should properly dispose of the incorrectly made compound and start the process again.

40. **A)** Pastes are thick, moist, and mixed with a dry ingredient.

41. **C)** Opioids are Schedule II drugs.

42. **D)** The pharmacist would be violating HIPAA by telling a family member to monitor the patient without the patient's permission.

43. **B)** Pantoprazole is a therapeutic substitution for Aciphex, a brand name of rabeprazole. Both medications are proton pump inhibitors.

44. **A)** iPledge is a Risk Evaluation and Mitigation Strategy for isotretinoin (Accutane).

45. **B)** A single Schedule II prescription can be filled for a 30-day supply.

46. **B)** Identify the formula and variables.

    Note that for Clark's rule, the child's weight needs to be in pounds, so you have to convert from kilograms (using dimensional analysis, a proportion may also be used).

    Recall that 1 kg ≈ 2.2 lb.

    child's dose = $\frac{\text{weight of the child}}{150}$ × adult dose

    weight of the child = 34 kg × $\frac{2.2 \text{ lb}}{1 \text{ kg}}$ = 74.8 lb

    adult dose = 400 mg

    Solve for child's dose.

    child's dose = $\frac{74.8}{150}$ × 400 mg = **200 mg**

47. **A)** The DEA does not require the patient's date of birth to be on the prescription for a controlled substance.

48. **C)** The influenza vaccine is refrigerated at a temperature of 36–46°F (2–8°C).

49. **C)** Penicillins are a common allergen and should be counted on their own tray to avoid cross-contamination.

50. **B)** The first five digits of the NDC (79534) identify the manufacturer and would have to be the same for all this patient's generic prescriptions.

51. **A)** A graduated cylinder is used to reconstitute an oral liquid.

52. **C)** The pharmacy technician may answer questions about insurance but not about pharmacology (e.g., side effects, drug interactions).

53. **D)** Lisdexamfetamine (Vyvanse) is an amphetamine, a controlled substance, and should be stored in a locked cabinet.

54. **C)** The abbreviation *QID* means "four times daily."

55. **B)** Set up a proportion with milliliters on top and grams on the bottom. You need to convert 1 L into 1,000 mL so that the units match.

    1 L = 100 mL

    $\frac{1{,}000 \text{ mL}}{5 \text{ g}} = \frac{750 \text{ mL}}{x \text{ g}}$

    Cross-multiply and solve for *x*.

    1,000*x* = 750 × 5

    x = 3.75 grams

    This can also be solved using dimensional analysis, multiplying by conversion ratios to cancel out units until the needed units are found:

    750 mL × $\frac{1 \text{ L}}{1{,}000 \text{ mL}}$ × $\frac{5 \text{ g}}{1 \text{ L}}$ = **3.75 g**

56. **D)** The Drug Listing Act of 1972 implemented NDC numbers.

57. **C)** Succinylcholine is a paralytic agent used in anesthesia.

58. **B)** Potassium chloride injections are considered high alert.

59. **B)** Clonazepam (Klonopin) is a benzodiazepine and antiseizure medication. Dispensing clonidine in its place may result in seizures.

60. **B)** Deteriorated drug errors are caused by using expired drugs or drugs whose chemical or physical potency and integrity have somehow been compromised.

61. **C)** Set up a proportion with milligrams (weight) on top and milliliters (volume) on the bottom.

    You need to convert 150 mcg to 0.150 mg so the units will match.

    150 mcg = 0.150 mg

    $$\frac{0.15 \text{ mg}}{1 \text{ mL}} = \frac{1 \text{ mg}}{x \text{ mL}}$$

    Cross-multiply and solve for x.

    0.15x = 1 mg

    x = 6.67 mL

    This can also be solved using dimensional analysis, multiplying by conversion ratios to cancel out units until the needed units are found:

    $$\frac{1 \text{ mL}}{150 \text{ mcg}} \times \frac{1{,}000 \text{ mcg}}{1 \text{ mg}} \times 1 \text{ mg} = \textbf{6.67 mL}$$

62. **A)** Guanfacine and guaifenesin are LASA drugs.

63. **C)** Leading zeroes should be used before decimal quantities, and trailing zeroes should not be used.

64. **C)** CSPs are prepared in a sterile room under a laminar airflow hood.

65. **A)** Aspirin is contraindicated with rivaroxaban because it increases the risk of bleeding.

66. **B)** The abbreviation *po* stands for "taken by mouth," and *qd* stands for "once a day" (for example, take 6 tablets orally once a day for 2 days).

    Compute the number of tablets for each part of the prescription. Then, add up the total number of tablets for all the days.

    6 tabs po qd for 2 days: 6 × 2 = 12
    5 tabs po qd for 2 days: 5 × 2 = 10
    4 tabs po qd for 2 days: 4 × 2 = 8
    3 tabs po qd for 2 days: 3 × 2 = 6
    2 tabs po qd for 2 days: 2 × 2 = 4
    1 tab po qd for 5 days: 1 × 5 = 5
    12 + 10 + 8 + 6 + 4 + 5 = **45**

67. **B)** Lisinopril has a boxed warning for potential fetal toxicity.

68. **A)** Recall Class I is used when there is a probability that use of or exposure to the product could cause an adverse event or health consequences, or death.

69. **C)** Hydralazine is a vasodilator taken to manage hypertension.

70. **A)** Step 1: Draw a tic-tac-toe grid and put the **higher % strength** in the top left square, the **desired % strength** in the middle square, and the **lower % strength** in the bottom left square:

10		
	7.5	
2		

    Step 2: Calculate the difference between the bottom left number and the middle number going up diagonally, and also the difference between the top left number and the middle number going down diagonally (ignore any negatives). Then add up those two numbers to get 8. This sum becomes the "parts" needed to work with.

10		5.5
	7.5	5.5 + 2.5 = 8 parts
2		2.5

    Step 3: Now, divide the needed volume into the total parts: 180 g ÷ 8 parts, resulting in 22.5 g per part.

    Step 4: On the grid, go back up to the parts and write the weight in g for each part.

10		5.5 × 22.5 = 123.75 g
	7.5	
2		2.5 × 22.5 = 56.25 g

    So 5.5 parts of the 10% solution × 22.5 g = **123.75 g**, and 2.5 parts of the 2% solution × 22.5 g = **56.25 g**.

71. **A)** The drug class suffix *–pam* refers to benzodiazepines.

72. **C)** Family members are not HIPAA-covered entities.

73. **B)** An *X* is written on a container to mark that it has been opened.

74. **C)** The Durham-Humphrey Amendment of 1951 required that prescriptions be written by a physician for certain medications before they can be dispensed to a patient.

75. **D)** Medicare Part D covers prescription drugs.

76. **A)** Anabolic steroids may still be prescribed in the United States.

77. **D)** The FDA (Food and Drug Administration) approves the use of INDs.

78. **B)** Two NDCs with the same four-digit product ID code (1980) represent the same medication.

79. **C)** The nursing unit med rooms with automated dispensing machines are the decentralized pharmacy.

80. **B)** Tapering methylprednisolone dose packs have one less tablet each day:

    $6 + 5 + 4 + 3 + 2 + 1 =$ **21 tablets**

81. **C)** A Schedule III or IV prescription can be refilled five times within six months from the original date.

82. **B)** Isopropyl alcohol 70% should be used to clean equipment such as counting trays and spatulas.

83. **C)** The suffix *–tidine* is used for histamine-2 blockers.

84. **C)** The *Red Book* is a resource on drug pricing.

85. **C)** Set up a proportion with mEq on top and milliliters on the bottom. Then, cross-multiply and solve for x.

    $$\frac{40 \text{ mEq}}{20 \text{ mL}} = \frac{20 \text{ mEq}}{x \text{ mL}}$$
    $$40x = 400$$
    $$x = 10 \text{ mL}$$

86. **D)** Patients taking metronidazole should be counseled to avoid alcohol.

87. **A)** Child doses are calculated by weight and BSA.

88. **C)** It is not necessary to include insurance information on the prescription label.

89. **A)** Both gabapentin and alcohol are CNS depressants; combining them may result in lethargy, dizziness, or impaired mental abilities.

90. **D)** Methotrexate is an immunosuppressant.

PRACTICE TEST TWO

1. The possibility of tooth discoloration is a side effect of which class of antibiotics?
   A) fluoroquinolones
   B) macrolides
   C) tetracyclines
   D) sulfonamides

2. A patient prescribed Diflucan would receive which generic?
   A) methotrexate
   B) adalimumab
   C) meclizine
   D) fluconazole

3. A pharmacy receives the following prescription:

   > Maalox 175mg/200mg oral suspension
   > Sig: 30 mL p.o. 30 min. p.c. and h.s.
   > Disp: 300 mL
   > Refills: 0

   How many doses of medication will the patient receive?
   A) 1
   B) 3
   C) 5
   D) 10

4. Using barcode technology to read NDCs can help prevent which type of error?
   A) incorrectly writing a medication's strength
   B) filling a vial with the incorrect tablets
   C) entering a prescription for the wrong patient
   D) dispensing a medication a patient is allergic to

5. A technician is filling a prescription for a buccal medication. Where should it be administered?
   A) under the skin
   B) into the muscle
   C) into the rectum
   D) in the cheek

6. Which medication requires close monitoring to prevent toxicity?
   A) Buspar
   B) Remeron
   C) Lithobid
   D) Aricept

7. The pharmacy receives the following prescription:

   > hydrocortisone 2% cream
   > Disp: 60 gm
   > Sig: app. daily prn

   What is the direction for use?
   - **A)** Apply cream daily as directed.
   - **B)** Apply ointment daily as needed.
   - **C)** Apply cream daily as needed.
   - **D)** Apply ointment daily as directed.

8. A 1-ounce prescription bottle holds how many milliliters of liquid?
   - **A)** 5
   - **B)** 10
   - **C)** 30
   - **D)** 60

9. Which medication is taken to prevent vomiting?
   - **A)** omeprazole
   - **B)** ondansetron
   - **C)** famotidine
   - **D)** docusate sodium

10. A customer asks the pharmacy technician to recommend an OTC medication for joint pain relief. The pharmacy technician should
    - **A)** suggest the anti-inflammatory ibuprofen.
    - **B)** recommend the supplement glucosamine.
    - **C)** tell the patient to look in the pain relief aisle.
    - **D)** refer the customer to the pharmacist.

11. Which medication can be used as a therapeutic substitute for Vasotec?
    - **A)** lisinopril
    - **B)** warfarin
    - **C)** zolpidem
    - **D)** valsartan

12. Which information does the pharmacy technician report to the Institute for Safe Medication Practices (ISMP)?
    - **A)** customer satisfaction survey data
    - **B)** prior authorization reports
    - **C)** controlled substance inventory
    - **D)** medication errors

13. The pharmacy technician should dispose of hazardous pharmaceutical waste in which color container?
    - **A)** red
    - **B)** black
    - **C)** blue
    - **D** green

14. Which over-the-counter medication can cause a patient to experience dark stools?
    - **A)** calcium
    - **B)** vitamin D
    - **C)** iron
    - **D)** vitamin B-12

15. A pharmacy receives the following prescription:

    > erythromycin 250 mg
    > Sig: 500 mg p.o. b.i.d
    > Disp: #20
    > Refills: 0

    How many tablets does the patient take each day?
    - **A)** 1
    - **B)** 2
    - **C)** 4
    - **D)** 6

16. Which of the following medications can be stored at room temperature?
    - **A)** Glucophage tablets
    - **B)** latanoprost drops
    - **C)** carmustine wafer
    - **D)** liraglutide

17. For a DEA number to be valid, the second letter must correspond to a practitioner's

  A) practice specialty.
  B) first name.
  C) state of licensure.
  D) last name.

18. Consider NDC 36457-345-01. A product with NDC 36457-346-01 has a different

  A) manufacturer.
  B) distributer.
  C) drug formulation.
  D) package size.

19. Which medication is indicated for the treatment of herpes zoster?

  A) gemfibrozil
  B) ramipril
  C) ciprofloxacin
  D) valacyclovir

20. Orthostatic hypotension is a common side effect of

  A) Cardura.
  B) Lipitor.
  C) Januvia.
  D) Tradjenta.

21. A pharmacy receives the following order:

  > Daytrana 10 mg/9 hours
  > Sig: use TOP daily u.d.
  > Disp: #30
  > Refills: 0

  What is the route of administration for the medication?

  A) orally
  B) subcutaneously
  C) topically
  D) rectally

22. A pharmacy is conducting an RCA to determine why a patient received the incorrect strength of lisinopril. Which step is NOT part of the procedure?

  A) collecting information about the event
  B) finding factors that increased the likelihood of the event occurring
  C) identifying which person was responsible for the error
  D) identifying changes that can be implemented to prevent future events

23. A patient takes Prilosec to manage which condition?

  A) arthritis
  B) hyperthyroidism
  C) heartburn
  D) anxiety

24. When dispensing medication, the pharmacy technician should refer the patient to the pharmacist to

  A) obtain the patient's first and last name.
  B) determine the type of medication the patient is picking up.
  C) ask the patient if they have questions about the medication.
  D) inform the patient about signs of an allergic reaction.

25. CII ordering requires a pharmacist to use which form?

  A) DEA Form 222
  B) DEA Form 41
  C) DEA Form 106
  D) DEA Form 224

26. Which is the correct temperature range for storing refrigerated medications in the pharmacy?

  A) between 30°F and 40°F
  B) between 36°F and 46°F
  C) between 40°F and 50°F
  D) between 50°F – 60°F

27. Which auxiliary label should be placed on a prescription bottle of metformin?
    A) Take with food.
    B) May cause drowsiness.
    C) Take on an empty stomach.
    D) Keep in refrigerator.

28. A pharmacy receives the following electronic prescription:

    prednisone 5 mg
    Sig: ½ daily × 4 d then 1 daily thereafter
    Disp: 30-day supply

    How many tablets should be dispensed?
    A) 14
    B) 15
    C) 28
    D) 30

29. Which pair of medications are considered therapeutic substitutions?
    A) Cardizem and furosemide
    B) Ativan and alprazolam
    C) Abilify and atenolol
    D) Benadryl and famotidine

30. What is the generic name of the insulin Lantus?
    A) insulin glargine
    B) insulin aspart
    C) insulin detemir
    D) insulin lispro

31. If a technician wishes to order drug NDC 12345-123-01 from a different manufacturer, which product should be chosen?
    A) 12345-234-01
    B) 12345-123-02
    C) 12345-234-02
    D) 45678-123-01

32. Which supplement should be avoided by a patient taking Losartan?
    A) calcium
    B) potassium
    C) iron
    D) fish oil

33. A pharmacy receives an electronic prescription with the following:

    Sig: 2 tablets tid a.c.

    Which instructions should the technician put on the label?
    A) Take 2 tablets 3 times daily as directed.
    B) Take 2 tablets 3 times daily as needed.
    C) Take 2 tablets 3 times daily before meals.
    D) Take 2 tablets 3 times daily after meals.

34. Which practice fails to adhere to OSHA health and safety practices?
    A) recapping contaminated needles
    B) using hemostats to remove contaminated blades
    C) placing contaminated materials in biohazard bags
    D) bandaging breaks in the skin before gloving

35. Warfarin is primarily used as an
    A) antihypertensive.
    B) anticoagulant.
    C) anticonvulsant.
    D) antidepressant.

36. The auxiliary label "Take on an empty stomach" would be attached to which of the following medications?
    A) metformin
    B) lovastatin
    C) NSAIDs
    D) levothyroxine

37. A pharmacy technician gives John Smith a prescription for John Brown at the point of sale. Which of the following multiple-check systems could have prevented the error?

- **A)** referring the patient to the pharmacist for a look-alike medication
- **B)** verifying the number of prescriptions for pickup
- **C)** using a second identifier, such as date f birth
- **D)** using the tall-man labeling system

38. Which asthma medication is most likely to cause neuropsychiatric symptoms?

- **A)** albuterol
- **B)** ipratropium
- **C)** tiotropium
- **D)** montelukast

39. The pharmacy receives the following prescription:

Nitrostat 0.4 mg/tablet
Sig: 1 tab SL u.d.

How should this medication be taken?

- **A)** subcutaneously
- **B)** under the tongue
- **C)** intranasally
- **D)** rectally

40. A pharmacy technician must refer a customer to the pharmacist

- **A)** for hearing aid replacement batteries.
- **B)** to obtain a blood glucose monitor copay amount.
- **C)** for verbal instructions on insulin pen use.
- **D)** when providing a medication guide.

41. Which of the following should be kept at a temperature range between −25° and −10°C?

- **A)** MMR vaccine
- **B)** Tdap
- **C)** rotavirus vaccine
- **D)** influenza vaccine

42. When is an FMEA performed?

- **A)** proactively, before an error can happen
- **B)** as a systemic review to improve workflow
- **C)** during a DUR
- **D)** as part of a root-cause analysis

43. In which pregnancy category is the medication methotrexate?

- **A)** category A
- **B)** category B
- **C)** category C
- **D)** category X

44. A pharmacy receives a prescription with the following sig:

Sig: inj. 10 units SC t.i.d. a.c.

How should the directions appear on the prescription label?

- **A)** Inject 10 units under the skin 3 times a week before meals.
- **B)** Inhale 10 units 3 times a day after meals.
- **C)** Inject 10 units under the skin 3 times a day before meals.
- **D)** Inject 10 units under the skin 3 times a day after meals.

45. Metformin is taken by patients with

- **A)** hypertension.
- **B)** high blood sugar.
- **C)** high cholesterol.
- **D)** hyperthyroidism.

46. A physician orders acetaminophen 10 mg/kg every 4 hours for a patient who weighs 35 kg. What is the correct dose?
    A) 3.5 mg
    B) 350 mg
    C) 35 mg
    D) 3500 mg

47. Which type of cleaning agent is appropriate for cleaning floors in the pharmacy?
    A) low-level disinfectants
    B) intermediate-level disinfectants
    C) high-level disinfectants
    D) sterilants

48. What is the brand name for the active ingredient atomoxetine?
    A) Strattera
    B) Adderall
    C) Vyvanse
    D) Actos

49. Tendon rupture is a side effect of which antibiotic?
    A) tetracycline
    B) azithromycin
    C) ciprofloxacin
    D) gentamicin

50. The following prescription is written for ADVAIR DISKUS 250/50:

    Sig: 1 inhalation twice daily
    Dispense 3 inhalers

    How long, in days, should the supply last if there are 60 doses in each inhaler?
    A) 30
    B) 60
    C) 90
    D) 120

51. Ciprofloxacin could be a therapeutic substitution for which medication?
    A) Augmentin
    B) Flagyl
    C) Bactrim
    D) Levaquin

52. What is the first segment of the complete NDC for OTC products?
    A) the labeler code
    B) the product code
    C) the package code
    D) the billing conversion code

53. Which of the following demonstrates the correct use of tall-man lettering?
    A) CeleBREX/CeleXA
    B) CeLeBrEx/CeLeXa
    C) CELEBREX/CELEXA
    D) CELEbrex/CELExa

54. Which medication is prescribed for the treatment of erectile dysfunction?
    A) Topamax
    B) Cialis
    C) Abilify
    D) Lyrica

55. Which of the following is a commonly used suffix for angiotensin II enzyme blockers?
    A) -azosin
    B) -mycin
    C) -artan
    D) -pril

56. Jantoven causes an increased risk of
    A) joint pain.
    B) drowsiness.
    C) dry mouth.
    D) bleeding.

57. A pharmacy receives the following order:

Calcijex 1 mcg/mL
Sig: 1.5 mcg IV t.i.w

How many doses of the medication should the patient receive each week?

- **A)** 1
- **B)** 3
- **C)** 4
- **D)** 21

58. A patient brings in a new prescription for Lipitor. Which of the following questions can the technician answer about the medication?

- **A)** Do I need to refill this medication?
- **B)** Do I take Lipitor with food?
- **C)** When should I test my cholesterol?
- **D)** How long does it take before Lipitor starts working?

59. What is the correct storage instruction for calcitonin nasal spray?

- **A)** Keep at room temperature.
- **B)** Store in the freezer.
- **C)** Keep refrigerated.
- **D)** Keep away from light.

60. Which abbreviation is included on The Joint Commission's "Do Not Use" list?

- **A)** PRN
- **B)** IU
- **C)** BID
- **D)** TID

61. Which medication can be used to dilate the airway of a patient with asthma?

- **A)** digoxin
- **B)** ezetimibe
- **C)** nitroglycerin
- **D)** albuterol

62. Which is an example of an oral antibiotic that comes prepackaged for dispensing?

- **A)** Spiriva
- **B)** Z-pak
- **C)** Augmentin
- **D)** Lantus Solostar

63. Nitrate use is contraindicated in patients taking

- **A)** sildenafil.
- **B)** finasteride.
- **C)** terazosin.
- **D)** tamsulosin.

64. The pharmacy receives the following prescription:

Altace 5.0 mg tablets
Sig: take 1 tablet daily for high blood pressure
Disp: #30
Refills: 3

Which part of the prescription is written incorrectly?

- **A)** drug strength
- **B)** drug indication
- **C)** quantity dispensed
- **D)** number of refills

65. A technician must wear PPE when performing which task in the pharmacy?

- **A)** reconstituting liquid antibiotics
- **B)** restocking controlled substances on pharmacy shelves
- **C)** compounding sterile products
- **D)** retrieving insulin from the refrigerator

66. Which medication could be used as a therapeutic substitution for Pamelor?

- **A)** carbamazepine
- **B)** bupropion
- **C)** terazosin
- **D)** amitriptyline

67. A patient who receives the generic equivalent of Lopid takes which medication?
    A) isosorbide
    B) fenofibrate
    C) rosuvastatin
    D) gemfibrozil

68. The NDCs for two naproxen products are: 49483-617-01 and 49483-617-50. What is the difference between the two products?
    A) distributer
    B) drug strength
    C) drug formulation
    D) package size

69. A technician fills a prescription with warfarin 5 mg instead of 2.5 mg, which was written on the hard copy. Which type of error is this?
    A) prescription error
    B) dispensing error
    C) compliance error
    D) abnormal dose error

70. Which medication is indicated for the treatment of osteoporosis?
    A) fluconazole
    B) tramadol
    C) hydralazine
    D) alendronate

71. The Controlled Substances Act classifies heroin in which schedule?
    A) CI
    B) CII
    C) CIII
    D) CIV

72. A patient should avoid exposure to the sun if taking which antibiotic?
    A) amoxicillin
    B) azithromycin
    C) tetracycline
    D) metronidazole

73. A physician prescribes the following medication:

    Keflex 0.5 g p.o. q. 6 h × 5 d

    How many milligrams of Keflex is the patient taking each day?
    A) 2
    B) 20
    C) 1000
    D) 2000

74. Which medication error might a technician make during the drug dispensing process?
    A) incorrectly recording a verbal medication order from a physician
    B) selecting the wrong drug formulation
    C) handing the patient the wrong bag through the drive-through window
    D) failing to enter the customer's phone number in their profile

75. Which medication is indicated for Parkinson's disease?
    A) Cozaar
    B) Singulair
    C) Strattera
    D) Sinemet

76. The quantity on a prescription is written with the Roman numeral notation XVIII. How many dosage units should the technician dispense?
    A) 8
    B) 18
    C) 58
    D) 158

77. Serotonergic drugs interact with which antiemetic medication?
    A) ondansetron
    B) prochlorperazine
    C) doxylamine
    D) pyridoxine

78. A pharmacy receives an order for:

    acetaminophen 120 mg
    Sig: use PR q. 6 h as directed
    Disp: #12

    What is the correct route of administration?
    A) topically
    B) subcutaneously
    C) orally
    D) rectally

79. Which type of hand hygiene is needed for sterile compounding?
    A) using soap and water
    B) aseptic handwashing
    C) applying antimicrobial gel
    D) utilizing an air blower when drying

80. Which inhaler can be therapeutically substituted for Proventil HFA?
    A) Ventolin HFA
    B) Combivent Respimat
    C) Advair HFA
    D) Spiriva

81. Which brand name medication could be dispensed for a prescription written for meloxicam?
    A) Celebrex
    B) Aleve
    C) Mobic
    D) Cambia

82. Which of the following medications has a narrow therapeutic index?
    A) metformin
    B) fluoxetine
    C) azithromycin
    D) digoxin

83. A patient taking Flagyl should be counseled to avoid drinking
    A) milk.
    B) grapefruit juice.
    C) coffee.
    D) alcohol.

84. A pharmacy receives an electronic prescription with the following:

    Sig: 1 tsp tid × 7 d

    What instructions should the technician put on the label?
    A) Take 1 teaspoonful 3 times a day for 7 days.
    B) Take 1 tablespoonful 3 times a day for 7 days.
    C) Take 3 teaspoonfuls daily for 7 days.
    D) Take 3 tablespoonfuls daily for 7 days.

85. How many numbers does an NDC for Lipitor contain?
    A) 4
    B) 7
    C) 10
    D) 13

86. When is it acceptable to use an abbreviation which appears on The Joint Commission's official "Do Not Use" list of abbreviations?
    A) on pre-printed forms only
    B) when handwriting a verbal order
    C) in electronic medication documentation
    D) never

87. Atorvastatin is given to patients with which condition?

   A) asthma
   B) diabetes
   C) high cholesterol
   D) seizures

88. A patient who is diagnosed with psoriasis has an autoimmune condition that primarily attacks the

   A) kidneys.
   B) lungs.
   C) nerve cells.
   D) skin.

89. Which supplement carries a black box warning for accidental overdose in children?

   A) calcium
   B) potassium
   C) ferrous sulfate
   D) folic acid

90. A pharmacy receives a prescription with the following sig:

   Sig: 1 tsp qhs prn cough

   How should the directions appear on the prescription label?

   A) Take 1 teaspoonful at bedtime as needed for cough.
   B) Take 1 tablespoonful at bedtime as needed for cough.
   C) Take 1 teaspoonful each morning as needed for cough.
   D) Take 1 tablespoonful each morning as needed for cough.

ANSWER KEY

1. **C)** An adverse effect of tetracyclines is tooth discoloration.

2. **D)** Fluconazole is the generic name for the antifungal medication Diflucan.

3. **D)** The patient is given 300 mL and is directed to take 30 mL per dose for 10 doses.

4. **B)** Barcode technology which reads National Drug Codes (NDCs) helps to ensure the correct stock medication is in the labeled prescription vial.

5. **D)** A buccal medication is inserted between the gum and the cheek.

6. **C)** Patients who are prescribed Lithobid (lithium), a medication for bipolar disorder, need close monitoring to prevent toxicity.

7. **C)** The prescription is for hydrocortisone cream, which is to be applied daily as needed (prn).

8. **C)** There are 30 milliliters of liquid in a 1-ounce prescription bottle.

9. **B)** Ondansetron is an antiemetic used to prevent nausea and vomiting.

10. **D)** Pharmacy technicians cannot advise customers on the purchase of over-the-counter (OTC) medications and should instead refer them to the pharmacist.

11. **A)** Vasotec (enalapril) and lisinopril are in the same class of medications called angiotensin-converting enzyme (ACE) inhibitors.

12. **D)** The Institute for Safe Medication Practices (ISMP) is a nonprofit organization that collects and reports medication errors.

13. **B)** Hazardous pharmaceutical waste is collected in appropriately labeled black waste containers.

14. **C)** Iron supplements can cause dark stools.

15. **C)** The patient takes 500 mg (2 × 250 mg tablets) twice daily (b.i.d.), or 4 tablets daily.

16. **A)** Glucophage (metformin) can be stored at room temperature like most by mouth (PO) tablets.

17. **D)** The second letter of a Drug Enforcement Administration (DEA) number is the first letter of the practitioner's last name.

18. **C)** The unmatching product code in segment 2 reflects a different drug formulation.

19. **D)** Valacyclovir is an antiviral medication indicated for herpes zoster infection.

20. **A)** The blood pressure-lowering effects of Cardura (doxazosin), a treatment for benign prostatic hyperplasia (BPH), can cause orthostatic hypotension.

21. **C)** Daytrana is a transdermal patch that administers the drug topically (TOP).

22. **C)** A root cause analysis (RCA) involves breaking down a process to determine why and how an error occurred; it does not involve assigning blame or individual responsibility for an error.

23. **C)** Prilosec (omeprazole) is a proton pump inhibitor used to treat heartburn.

24. **D)** Pharmacy technicians cannot advise customers on the side effects of prescription medications.

25. **A)** CII medications are controlled medications that require a Drug Enforcement Administration (DEA) Form 222 for ordering.

26. **B)** The correct temperature range for storing refrigerated medications is between 36°F and 46°F.

27. **A)** Metformin is an antihyperglycemic medication that should be taken with food.

28. **C)** A half a tablet daily for 4 days equals 2 tablets.

    One tablet daily thereafter equates to 26 days (30 days – 4 days).

    The number of tablets that should be dispensed is 28 (26 + 2 = 28).

29. **B)** Ativan (lorazepam) and alprazolam are in the class of medications called benzodiazepines.

30. **A)** Insulin glargine is the generic name for Lantus.

31. **D)** The unmatching code in segment 1 reflects a different manufacturer.

32. **B)** Since Losartan can raise levels of potassium in the body, potassium should not be taken as a supplement while taking this drug.

33. **C)** Take 2 tablets 3 times daily (tid) before meals (a.c.).

34. **A)** The pharmacy staff should not recap, bend, or break contaminated needles or sharps.

35. **B)** Warfarin is an anticoagulant prescribed for thrombus prevention.

36. **D)** Levothyroxine, a medication used to treat hypothyroidism, should be taken on an empty stomach.

37. **C)** Point-of-sale errors can be prevented by using a second identifier, such as address or date of birth, in addition to the name to correctly identify the patient.

38. **D)** Singulair (montelukast) has a black box warning for neuropsychiatric symptoms.

39. **B)** The medication is administered sublingually (SL), or under the tongue.

40. **C)** A technician must refer the patient to the pharmacist for verbal instructions on medication use.

41. **A)** The measles, mumps, and rubella (MMR) vaccine should be stored in the freezer at temperatures between −25° and −10°C.

42. **A)** A failure mode and effects analysis (FMEA) is a proactive process that determines steps that can be taken to avoid errors before the product or service is purchased.

43. **D)** Methotrexate causes fetal toxicity and is classified as category X.

44. **C)** The directions read: inject (inj.) 10 units under the skin (SC) 3 times a day (t.i.d.) before meals (a.c.).

45. **B)** Metformin is taken to control high blood sugar in patients with diabetes.

46. **B)** $\frac{10mg}{kg} \times 35 \text{ kg} = 350 \text{ mg}$

47. **A)** Low-level disinfectants kill most microorganisms and can be used to clean floors, walls, and surfaces not directly involved in clinical care.

48. **A)** Strattera is the brand name for the attention deficit hyperactivity disorder (ADHD) medication atomoxetine.

49. **C)** Ciprofloxacin, a fluoroquinolone antibiotic, causes an increased risk of tendon rupture.

50. **C)** If the patient takes 2 inhalations daily, each inhaler will last 30 days. Dispensing 3 inhalers will provide a 90-day supply.

51. **D)** Levaquin (levofloxacin) and ciprofloxacin are fluroquinolone antibiotics.

52. **A)** The first segment comprises the labeler code, which identifies the manufacturer or labeler.

53. **A)** With tall-man lettering, drugs are differentiated by capitalizing dissimilar letters.

54. **B)** Cialis (tadalafil) is indicated for the treatment of erectile dysfunction.

55. **C)** Medications with the suffix -artan, such as candesartan, block angiotensin II enzymes from specific receptor sites.

56. **D)** Jantoven (warfarin) causes an increased risk of bleeding.

57. **B)** The sig code *t.i.w.* (or *tiw*) means 3 times per week. The patient should receive 3 doses per week.

58. **A)** A pharmacy technician can provide patients with information regarding medication refills.

59. **C)** Calcitonin nasal spray needs to be stored in the refrigerator.

60. **B)** The abbreviation for international unit—IU—can be mistaken for IV (intravenous) and should not be used.

61. **D)** Albuterol is an inhaled bronchodilator used to reopen constricted airways of patients with asthma.

62. **B)** Z-pak (azithromycin) is an antibiotic that comes prepackaged for dispensing.

63. **A)** Nitrate use is contraindicated in patients taking sildenafil for erectile dysfunction.

64. **A)** To avoid a possible 10-fold medication error, trailing zeroes should never be used.

65. **C)** Personal protective equipment (PPE) is necessary to prevent microorganism transmission and should be worn when compounding sterile products.

66. **D)** Pamelor (nortriptyline) and amitriptyline are tricyclic antidepressants.

67. **D)** Gemfibrozil is the generic name for antihyperlipidemic Lopid.

68. **D)** The unmatching number in the final segment reflects a different package size.

69. **B)** A dispensing error occurs when the patient does not receive the medication as ordered in the prescription.

70. **D)** Alendronate is used to treat patients with low bone density, or osteoporosis.

71. **A)** Schedule I (CI) medications include Illegal drugs, such as heroin, that do not have any medical value, pose severe safety concerns, and have the most potential for misuse.

72. **C)** Tetracycline carries an increased risk of photosensitivity.

73. **D)** There is 1000 mg in each gram: 0.5 g = 500 mg per dose × 4 doses = 2000 mg each day.

74. **B)** Dispensing errors can happen if the technician incorrectly reads the label; one result might be to select the wrong drug formulation.

75. **D)** Sinemet (carbidopa and levodopa) is indicated for treating Parkinson's disease.

76. **B)** The number 18 is written as 10 + 5 + 1 + 1 + 1 = XVIII.

77. **A)** The antiemetic Zofran (ondansetron) interacts with serotonergic drugs.

78. **D)** The sig code *PR* means rectal administration.

79. **B)** Aseptic techniques, including proper handwashing, are used during sterile compounding to prevent contamination of medications.

80. **A)** Proventil hydrofluoroalkane (HFA) and Ventolin HFA are respiratory inhalers with albuterol as the active ingredient.

81. **C)** Mobic is the brand name for the non-steroidal anti-inflammatory drug (NSAID) meloxicam.

82. **D)** Digoxin has a narrow therapeutic index, as small changes in plasma levels can result in adverse effects or therapeutic failure.

83. **D)** Consuming alcohol is contraindicated when taking Flagyl (metronidazole).

84. **A)** Take 1 teaspoonful (1 tsp) 3 times a day (tid) for 7 days (× 7d).

85. **C)** A National Drug Code (NDC) is a 10-digit number that uniquely identifies a drug product.

86. **D)** The Joint Commission's official "Do Not Use" list applies to all orders and medication documentation.

87. **C)** Atorvastatin is an hydroxymethylglutaryl-coenzyme A (HMG-CoA) reductase inhibitor (statin) prescribed for high cholesterol.

88. **D)** Psoriasis is an autoimmune condition that attacks healthy skin tissue.

89. **C)** Ferrous sulfate (iron) carries a black box warning for accidental overdose in children.

90. **A)** The directions read: take 1 teaspoonful (1 tsp) at bedtime (qhs) as needed (prn) for cough.

To access two more PTCB practice tests, follow the link below:

www.ascenciatestprep.com/ptcb-online-resources

www.ingramcontent.com/pod-product-compliance
Lightning Source LLC
Chambersburg PA
CBHW080538300426
44111CB00017B/2781